Digital Photo Assignments

I0901209

Are you building a syllabus for your first photography class? Perhaps you have been teaching for many years and need to revitalize assignments for your students? Do you need to add DSLR video, workflow, or color correction to your class? This collection of more than 40 photo assignments begins with using the camera, and progresses through learning composition, aesthetics, and working in genres.

The systematic, assignment-based approach to learning photography is a wonderful working guide for teachers of introductory and intermediate photo courses at colleges and universities, or workshop and short-course formats. These lessons are designed to help all students—from beginning freshmen to experienced seniors—reach their full potential as photographers.

Even though the assignments have been designed for instructors to use in class, photographers at all levels can equally use them, beginner to advanced, to improve or reinvigorate their photography.

Steve Anchell has taught both digital and darkroom classes at Oregon State University. Internationally published, with his fine art work exhibited in galleries and private collections, Steve has conducted workshops since 1979, including workshops for the International Center for Photography in NYC, Santa Fe Photographic Workshops, Toscana Photographic Workshops (Italy), the Universities of California at Los Angeles, Santa Barbara, and Irvine, the University of Cincinnati, University of Denver.

Steve is a former contributing editor to *Outdoor Photographer*, *Camera & Darkroom*, and *PhotoWork* magazines, and has written for *Shutterbug*, *Rangefinder*, *photo technique*, *View Camera*, and *Camera Arts* magazines. He is the author of *The Variable Contrast Printing Manual*, *The Darkroom Cookbook*, and co-author of *The Film Developing Cookbook*, published by Focal Press.

Digital Photo Assignments

Projects for All Levels of Photography Classes

STEVE ANCHELL

Routledge
Taylor & Francis Group
LONDON AND NEW YORK

First published 2016 by Focal Press

Published 2019 by Routledge
52 Vanderbilt Avenue, New York, NY 10017
2 Park Square, Milton Park, Abingdon, Oxon OX14 4RN

Routledge is an imprint of the Taylor & Francis Group, an informa business

Notices
Knowledge and best practice in this field are constantly changing. As new research and experience broaden our understanding, changes in research methods, professional practices, or medical treatment may become necessary.

Practitioners and researchers must always rely on their own experience and knowledge in evaluating and using any information, methods, compounds, or experiments described herein. In using such information or methods they should be mindful of their own safety and the safety of others, including parties for whom they have a professional responsibility.

Library of Congress Cataloging in Publication Data
Anchell, Stephen G.

Digital photo assignments : projects for all levels of photography classes / authored by Steve Anchell.
pages cm
1. Photography—Study and teaching—Activity programs.
2. Photography—Digital techniques—Study and teaching—
Activity programs. 3. Photography—Digital techniques—Examinations, questions, etc. I. Title.
TR162.A53 2015
771.076—dc23 2014042864

ISBN: 978-1-138-79449-8 (pbk)
ISBN: 978-1-138-79448-1 (hbk)
ISBN: 978-1-315-75921-0 (ebk)

Typeset in Stone Serif and Frutiger
By Keystroke, Station Road, Codsall, Wolverhampton

Digital Photo Assignments is dedicated to Professor John Maul (1954–2012), a visionary artist and the former Oregon State University Director of the School of Arts and Communication.

Without John this book would never have been written.

Thank you, John.

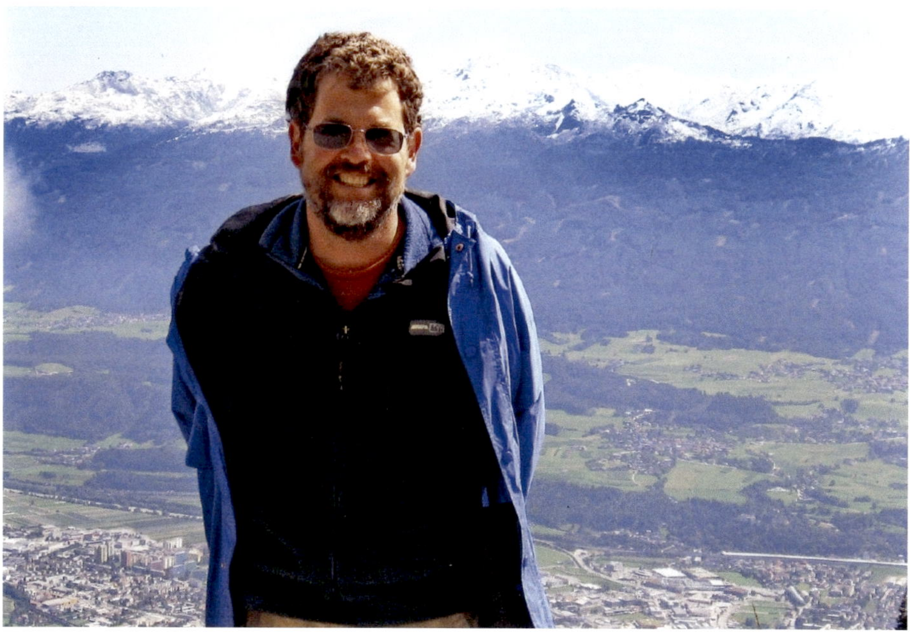

Table of Contents

Preface

When John Maul hired me to teach photography at Oregon State University, I admit to having been nervous. Even though I had been teaching adults since 1979 I had no training in conducting a semester-long course—one in which there was meant to be an orderly progression of learning from one class to the next.

I was confident that I would be able to go on amazon.com and find plenty of books with lots of ready-made assignments and inspirational ideas for teaching. Sure enough, there were about a dozen books that claimed to have photo projects and assignments. I ordered every one.

With almost no exception, these books proved to be worthless. Not that there weren't a few good ideas in each of them, but they were either so remedial as to be a joke, or so advanced you needed to be enrolled in a master of fine art program to use them. None could be effectively used to teach an undergraduate course in photography.

I asked other instructors for assignment ideas. I was disappointed to find that instructors at the university level, perhaps any level, were proprietary about their assignments. Not that they said "no" outright, they just weren't readily forthcoming. It soon became apparent they weren't intending to share anything substantial.

I know a great deal about photography, more than forty-four years' worth of knowledge. Much of it gained from working photographers who had enough self-confidence, that they didn't mind sharing. As a result, I tend to be inclusive, as can be seen in my first book, *The Darkroom Cookbook*. In that book I share as much as I know and then ask my peers to share their knowledge, so it will be there for everyone.

My theory is that no two people create alike, and that by sharing what each of us knows, another artist may be able to create something I couldn't or wouldn't, and thereby enrich the world.

After all, we're in this together.

Steve Anchell
April, 2015

Introduction

Digital Photo Assignments was originally written as a collection of teaching assignments to be used by instructors. In DPA instructors will find a series of assignments that can be used to teach a variety of digital techniques, from taking the first image to using DSLR video. The assignments can be used in a progressive order through a series of courses, or as needed.

The assignments are not intended as a complete course of study. Instructors are expected to use them to supplement their own assignments. Alternatively, they can be used as idea generators for an instructor's own version for a similar assignment more suited to their working style.

The assignments are divided into four sections based on my experience of when to introduce new skills. This is entirely subjective and the instructor will want to mix and match as needed for their program.

- Beginner (Freshman)—Assignments 1 to 12
- Intermediate (Sophomore)—13 to 21
- Advanced (Junior)—22 to 36
- Getting Noticed (Senior)—37 to 41

Even though the target audience for this book is instructors, I have tried to construct it so that anyone can use it to learn photography. If you are teaching yourself photography and don't have access to higher education, you can use this text as you would any course of study.

- If you are new to photography begin with Section 1: Beginner.
- If you are already comfortable with f/stops, shutter speeds, motion blur, stop action, and depth of field, begin with Section 2: Intermediate.
- Choose Section 3: Advanced if you have a grasp of all the elements and want to learn a specific area of photography, such as lighting. You will also want to augment the lessons with additional online reading and research.

- My recommendation for Section 4: Senior is to familiarize yourself with the online social media sites but do not post anything until you are comfortable with your work; this may require a peer review by an instructor, students, or a respected photographers. Were you to begin posting your first efforts immediately it would take more effort to overcome viewers' negative impressions than if you waited until your work stands up to what is out there already.

Looking ahead, I am collecting additional assignments. If you have an assignment that you would like to share, please forward it to me at steve@steveanchell.com and I will try to include it in future editions. You will be credited for the assignment, as the current contributors in this edition have been.

SECTION 1

Beginner

Freshman

ASSIGNMENT 1

Significant Photo

"To me, photography is an art of observation. It's about finding something interesting in an ordinary place . . . I've found it has little to do with the things you see and everything to do with the way you see them."

—Elliot Erwitt

PURPOSE: THIS ASSIGNMENT IS MEANT TO "KICK START" YOUR PHOTO CAREER.

You should begin your career in photography photographing things that interest you in a way that makes them interesting to other people. Once you are able to do this consistently, the next step is to find things that are inherently uninteresting to you and make them interesting to other people. For this assignment, find things that are interesting to you to photograph.

The inspiration for this assignment came from the example set by photographer Harry Callahan, who would walk his neighborhood every day returning with a photograph of something he had not previously photographed or something he had previously photographed but this time photographed in a new way.

This assignment is deceptively easy—but don't be fooled. This may be the single most important assignment you will ever do. I have used this assignment with students for more than twenty years and have found, even with experienced photographers, it changes their relationship towards their photography and image making.

Set your camera on "P" for Program (some cameras have two Program modes—for this assignment it doesn't matter which one you use). As you progress in your study of photography you will want to take your camera off Program and use one of the other settings that allow more control over the image—but for now use P.

Beginning today, make it your goal to make one photo every day that is *significant to you.* At the end of the day go through every photo you have taken, whether it is one or 500, and select the one that you want to remember that day by. Even if you have taken one hundred good photos that day, limit yourself to choosing the "one" (don't delete the others, though). Save your "one" photo in a file called Significant Photo.

Do this assignment for thirty days, one full month (a leap year doesn't count). Harry Callahan did it for at least thirty years—don't feel as if you need to stop at thirty days!

Make it a habit to always save the Original File Number as part of the image name. Regardless of what else you may name the image, if you preserve the original file number you will always be able to find and identify it—unless you delete it from your hard drive, in which case it no longer exits.

An example of how to name a file would be:

Original File Name and number: _DSC0134.NEF
Saved as: [Custom File Name]-0134.NEF

Aaron Davis made the following seven photos as part of his Significant Photo assignment.

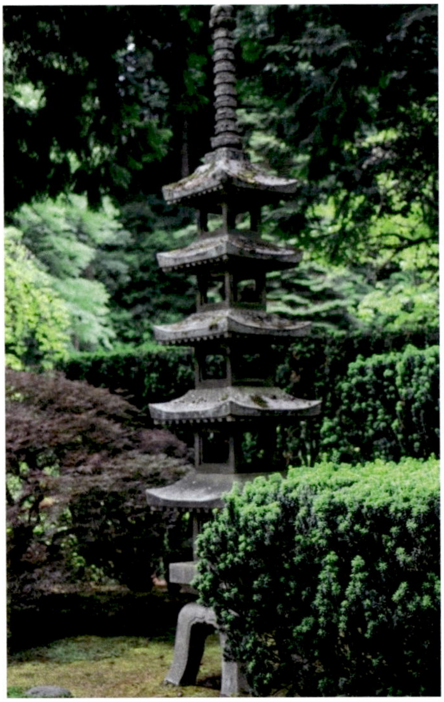

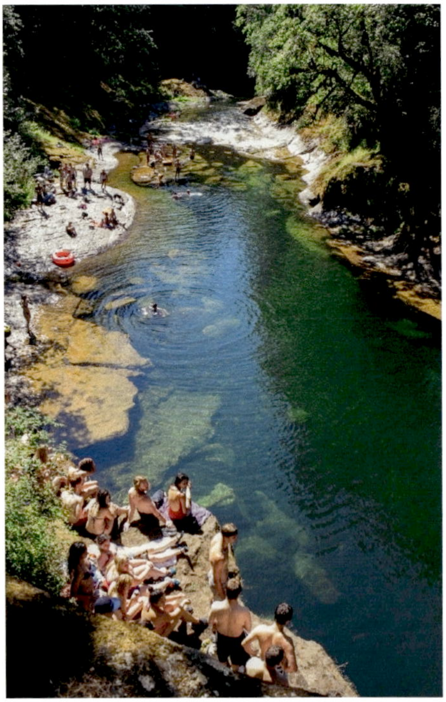

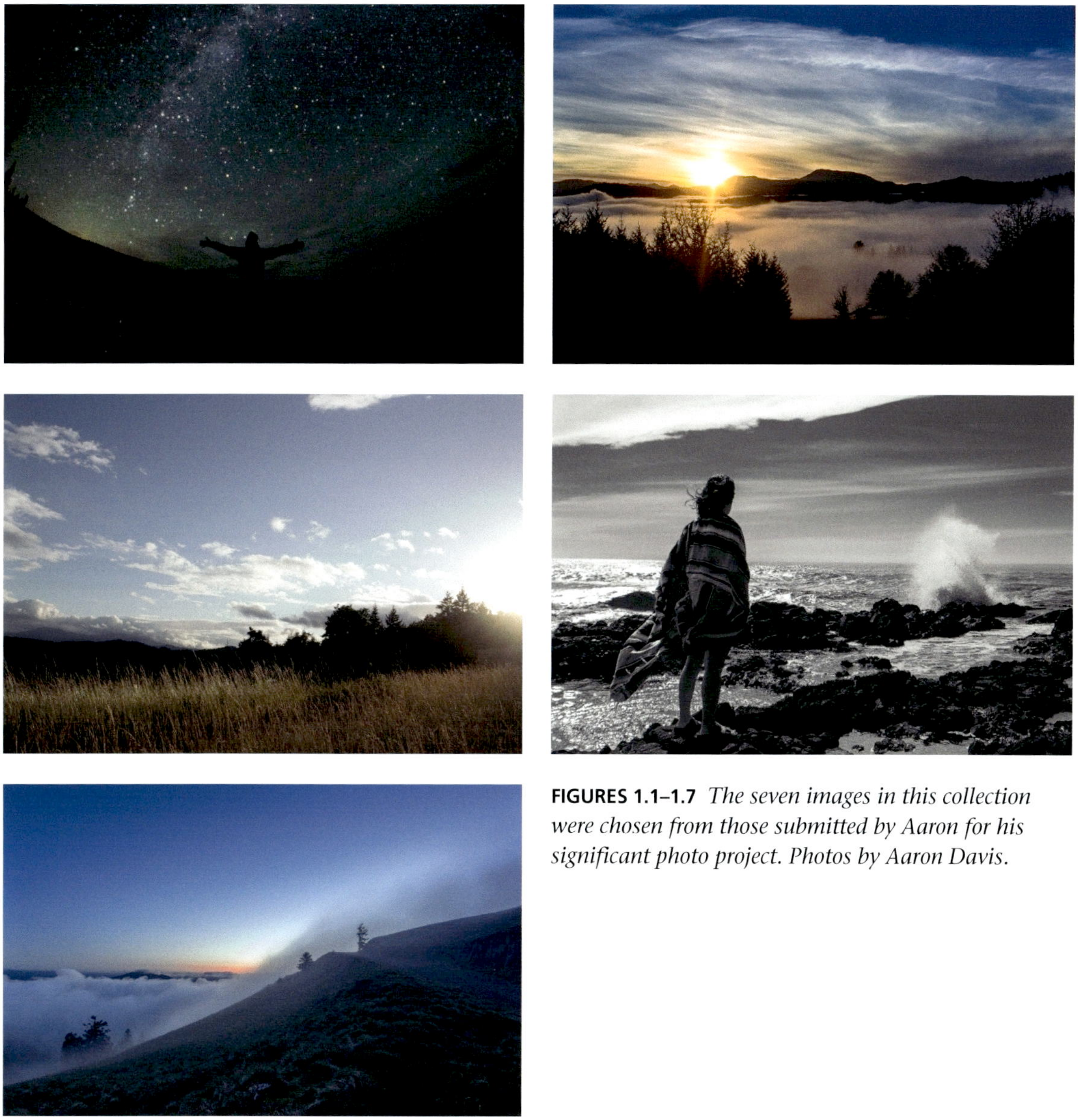

FIGURES 1.1–1.7 *The seven images in this collection were chosen from those submitted by Aaron for his significant photo project. Photos by Aaron Davis.*

ASSIGNMENT 2

Shutter Speed

"The whole point of taking pictures is so that you don't have to explain things with words."

—Elliott Erwitt

PURPOSE: TO PROVIDE A VISUAL UNDERSTANDING OF HOW TO USE SHUTTER SPEED TO EITHER FREEZE OR BLUR ACTION.

If possible, perform these exercises out-of-doors in open shade. If you live in a rainy area, such as the Pacific Northwest, and cannot go out-of-doors from September until August, see if you can perform these inside a well-lit gymnasium at your school.

- Use a normal to moderate telephoto focal length lens (50mm to 135mm with a full-frame sensor).
- Set your Shooting Mode to Shutter Priority (S), or Time value (Tv) for Canon.

SHUTTER SPEED

1. Focus on a friend's hands from about three feet away. Have them spin or shake their hands. Set the shutter speed to 1/8 and allow the in-camera meter to set the aperture for correct exposure. Make two exposures.

   NOTE: If the ambient light is too bright, try reducing your ISO as far as it will go (e.g., ISO 50, ISO 100). If the ambient light is too low, try increasing your ISO (e.g., ISO 400, ISO 800).

2. Double the shutter speed to 1/15 and repeat the exercise.
3. Double the shutter speed to 1/30.

4. Double the shutter speed to 1/60.
5. Double the shutter speed to 1/125.
6. Double the shutter speed to 1/250.

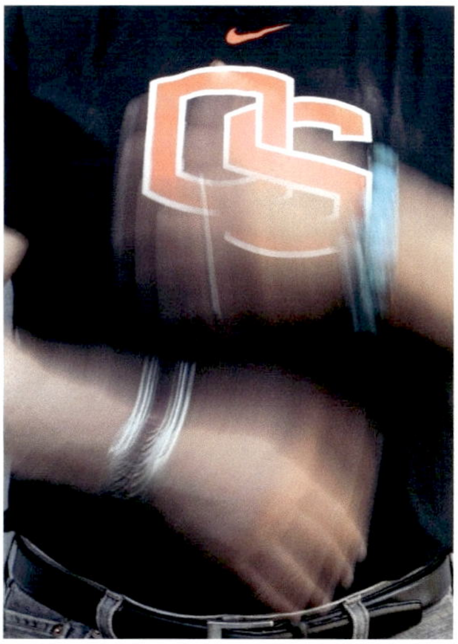

Shutter Speed: 1/8

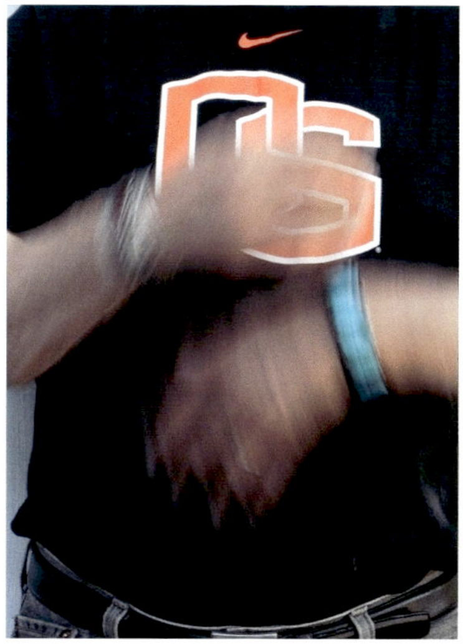

Shutter Speed: 1/15

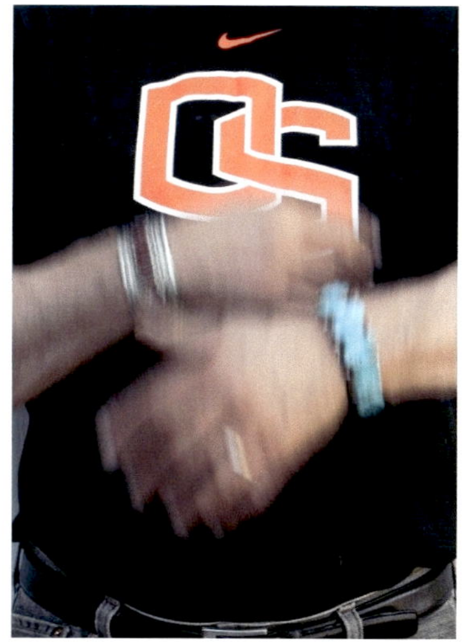

Shutter Speed: 1/30

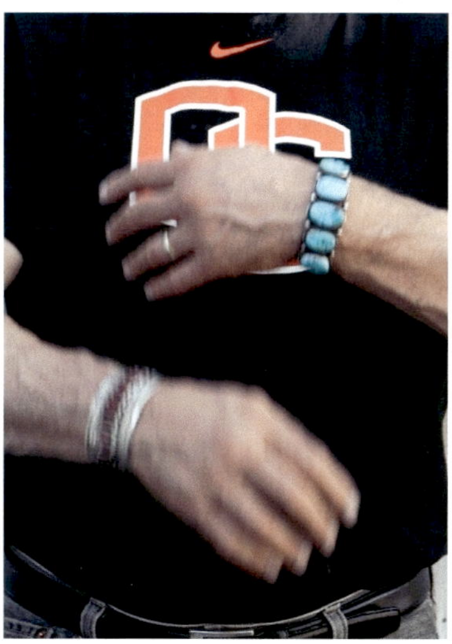

Shutter Speed: 1/60

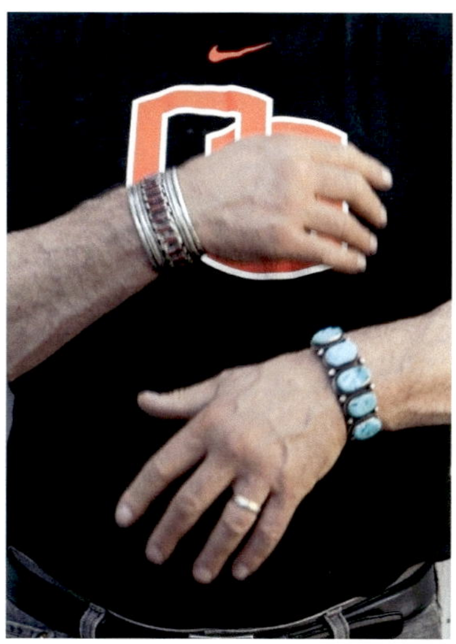

Shutter Speed: 1/125

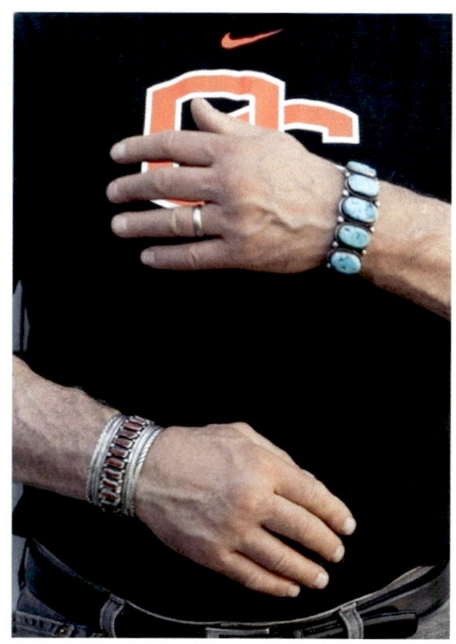

Shutter Speed: 1/250

FIGURES 2.1–2.6

REVIEW

1. What difference do you expect to see between the first two images and the second two images?
2. At which shutter speed do you first see any sign of stop action?
3. At which shutter speed do you see your friend's hands frozen?

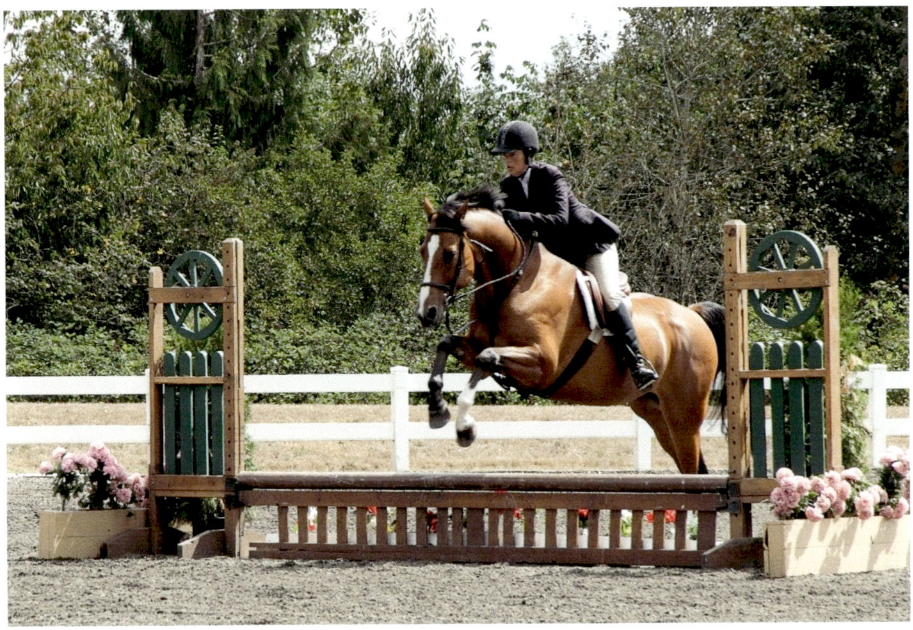

FIGURE 2.7 *Kimberley Anchell, Nikon D700, 120mm, f/10 at 1/400.*

ASSIGNMENT 3

Horizontal Motion

"Taking an image, freezing a moment, reveals how rich reality truly is."
—Anonymous

PURPOSE: TO DEMONSTRATE THE EFFECT OF SHUTTER SPEED ON MOVING SUBJECTS.

- Set the exposure mode to Shutter Priority (S), Nikon, or Time value (Tv), Canon.
- Do each of these as many times as necessary to get the hang of them.

1. Set your shutter at 1/30 and instruct your partner to run past you at a moderate speed. As they enter the frame, take a photo.

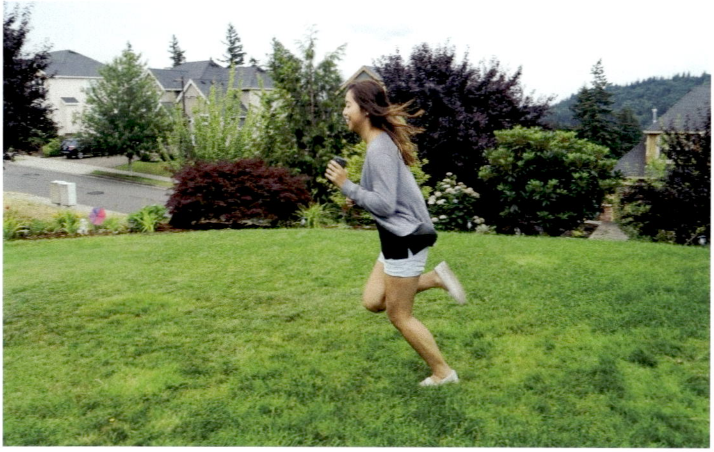

FIGURE 3.1 *The three photos demonstrate practical applications of fast and slow shutter speed. A fast shutter speed is able to freeze even the fastest runner. Model: Michelle Fok. 1/125 second at f/8. Photo by Tiffany Cha; 20mm lens; Sony ALT-A57.*

2. Repeat the previous exercise with the shutter speed set to 1/125 of a second.

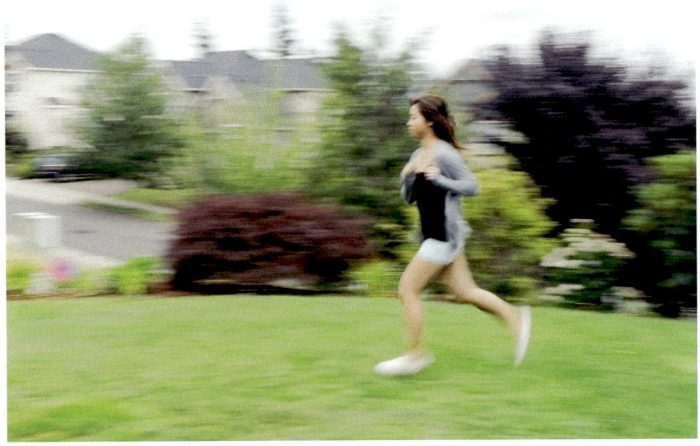

FIGURE 3.2 *A slower shutter speed blurs the runner, creating a sense of motion. Model: Michelle Fok. 1/15 second at f/16. Photo by Tiffany Cha; 30mm lens; Sony ALT-A57.*

3. Set the shutter speed to 1/30 and have your partner run directly towards you at a moderate speed. Photograph them at any point where they are still head to toe within the frame.

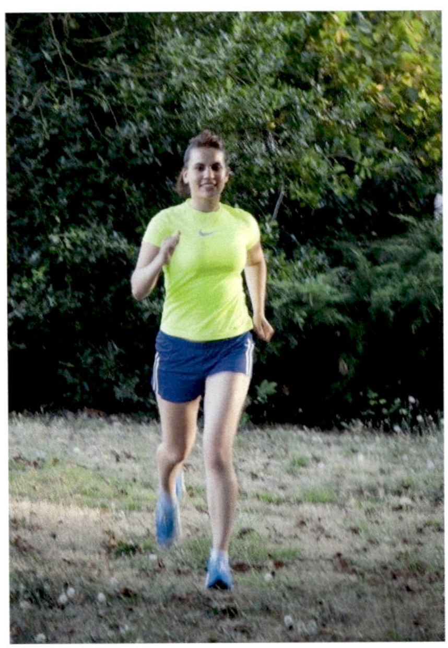

FIGURE 3.3 *When an object is moving towards you, a slower shutter speed can be used to freeze the action. 1/30 second at f/16. Model: Natasha Blair. Photo by Donna Conrad; 100mm lens; Nikon D700.*

Make as many additional photos as you can in which you try to:

- Freeze the action
- Blur the action

REVIEW

Even though they are only two stops apart, 1/30 is considered a slow shutter speed and 1/125 is considered a high shutter speed.

1. Which of the two shutter speeds, 1/30 or 1/125, blurred the action?
2. When photographing a subject moving towards you it is possible to use a slower shutter speed to freeze or blur the action?

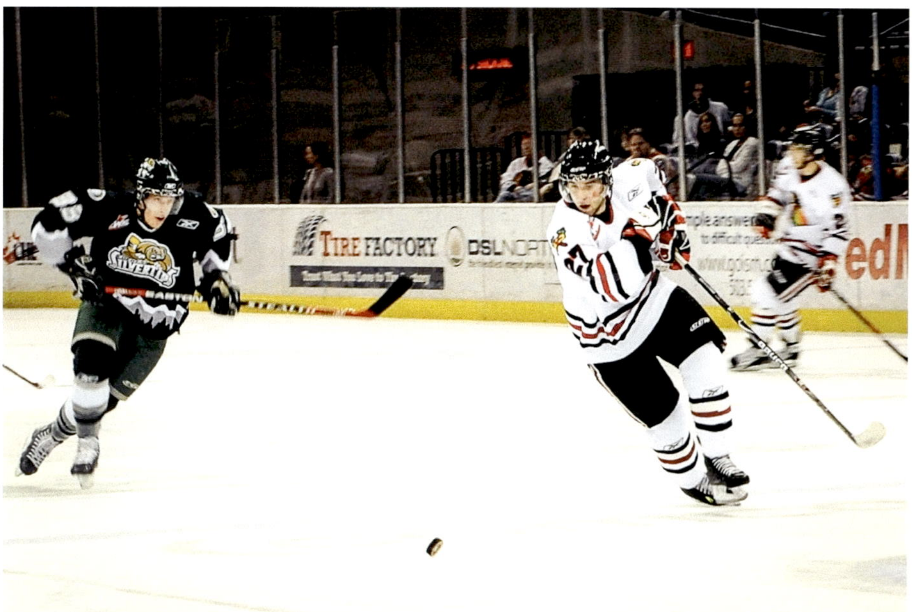

FIGURE 3.4 *Portland Winter Hawks, Nikon D3, 70mm lens, f/6.3 at 1/125.*

ASSIGNMENT 4

Panning

"I am not interested in shooting new things—I am interested to see things new."

—Ernst Haas

PURPOSE: TO FREEZE SUBJECT MOTION WHILE BLURRING THE BACKGROUND.

Panning allows you to keep your subject in focus while streaking the background, creating an illusion of subject movement. The best way to pan is to imagine where your subject will end up and point your feet 45 degrees in that direction so you can "unwind"—like a baseball or golf swing. Then rotate your upper body towards your subject (friend, automobile, bicycle), following with your camera until the subject passes the point where you want to release the shutter, and follow through with the camera.

Panning works well at 1/15 or 1/30 second, but can be done at both slower and faster speeds.

Choose a nondescript background directly across from you. Have your friend stand ten feet to the left or right of your composition, point your feet 45 degrees away from their line of motion, aim your camera at them and ask them to run across the background.

Watch them through the viewfinder and follow them with your camera (that means to keep them in the viewfinder, not that you should run after them). As they run in front of your pre-chosen background, release the shutter and continue to follow them with the camera.

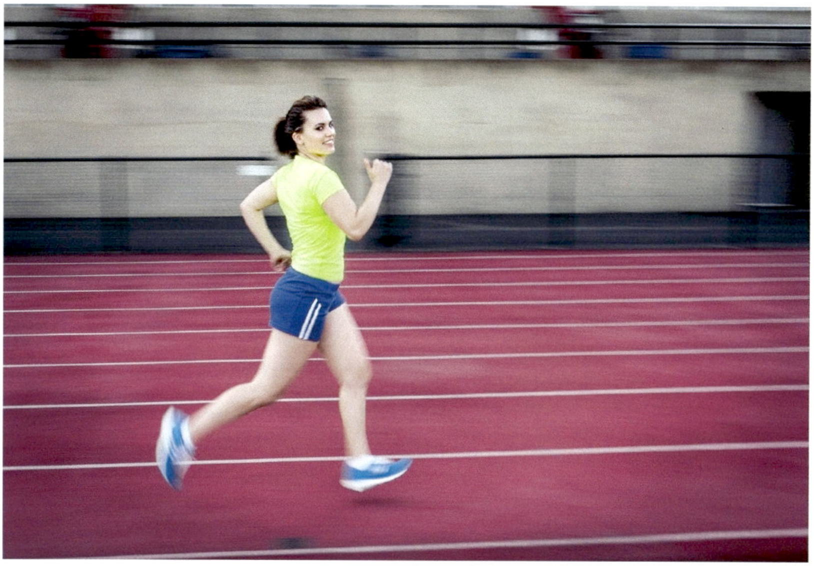

FIGURE 4.1 *1/30 second at f/11. Model: Natasha Blair. Photo by Donna Conrad.*

Do this exercise as many times as necessary to get good at it.

Once you have the hang of it, practice with a faster-moving object such as your friend on a bicycle. Do this with as many moving subjects as you can find.

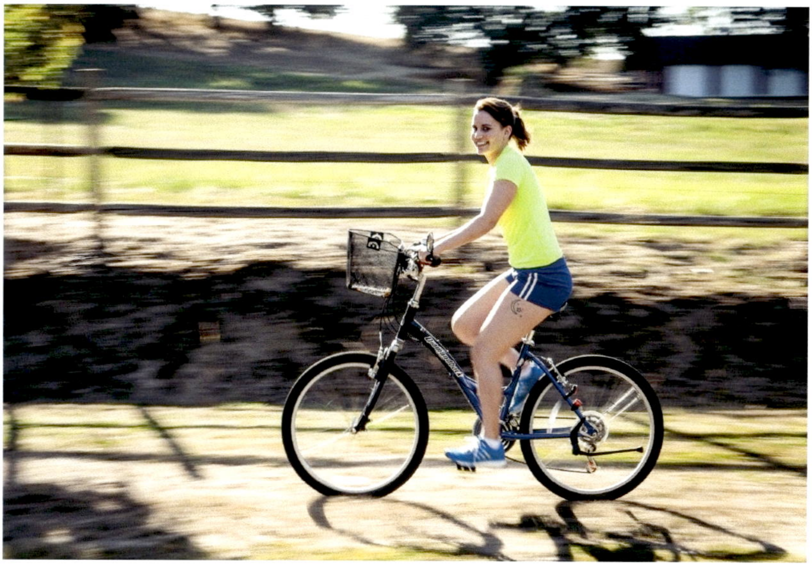

FIGURE 4.2 *1/30 second at f/8.5. Photo by Donna Conrad.*

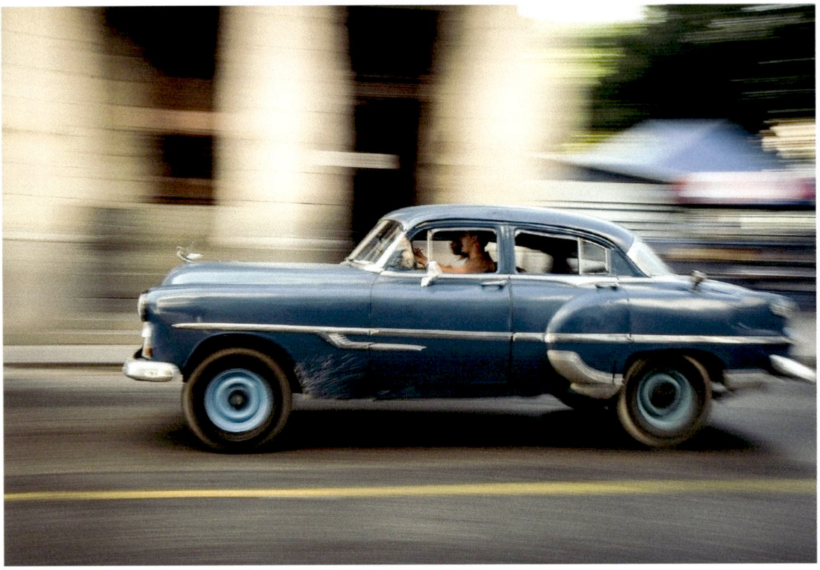

FIGURE 4.3 *Once you get tired of photographing your friends running or riding bikes, here is an example of panning made in Havana at 1/15 of a second. Photo by Donna Conrad.*

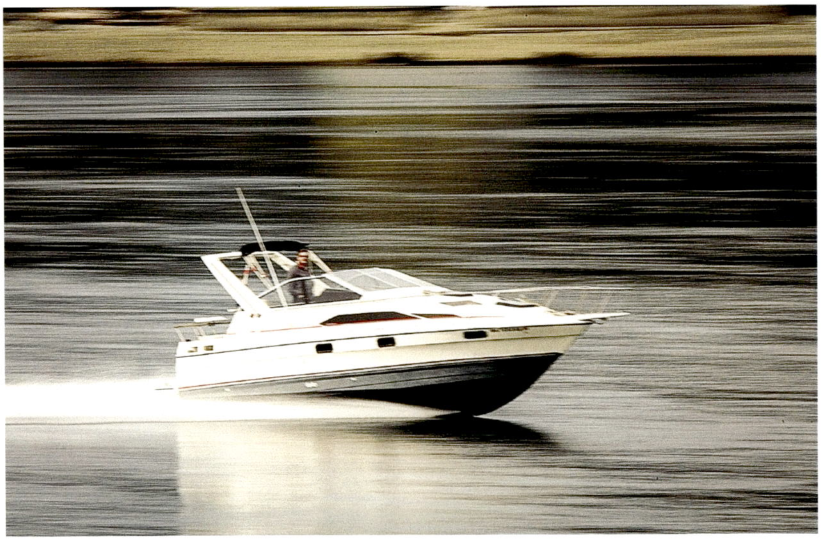

FIGURE 4.4 *Canon EOS 5D, 300mm lens, f/40 at 1/15.*

REVIEW

1. What is the purpose of panning?
2. What is the proper direction to "aim" your feet for panning?

ASSIGNMENT 5

Water in Motion

"I wish that all of nature's magnificence, the emotion of the land, the living energy of place could be photographed."

—Annie Leibovitz

PURPOSE: PRACTICE SHUTTER SPEED.

In a still photograph there are two kinds of action: frozen and blurred. While it is important to know how to freeze, or stop action, it is equally important to realize that blurred action is one way to depict motion in a still image. In fact, the crisp, sharp images you get when you use a fast shutter speed don't often create a sense of movement.

While it may be counter-intuitive to blur photographs of rushing water, it is often the most pleasing way of photographing it.

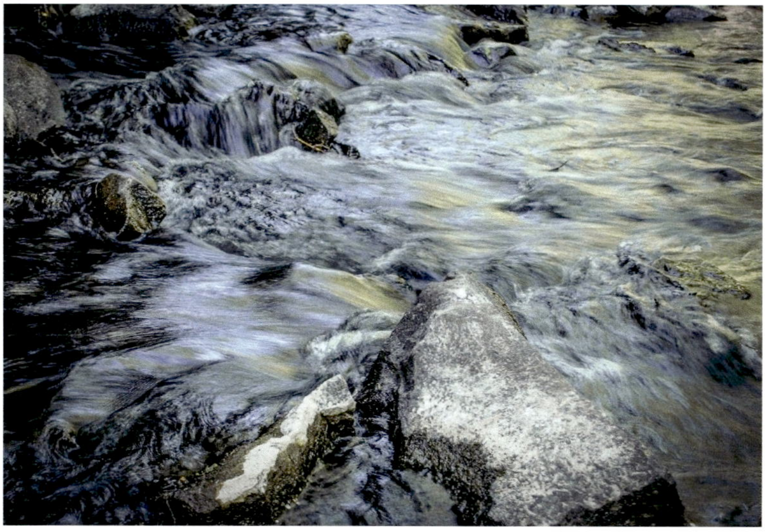

FIGURE 5.1

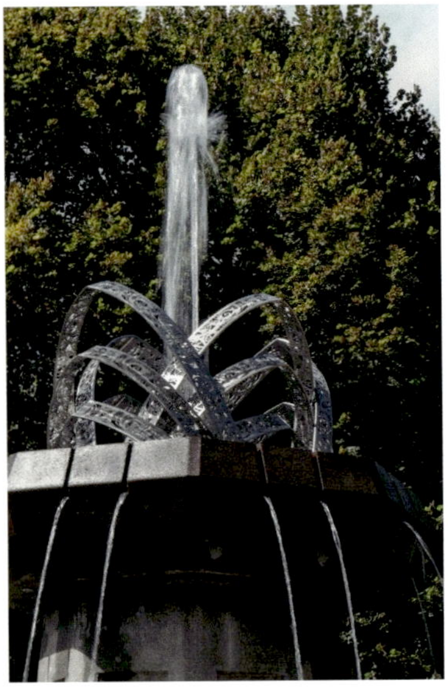

Shutter Speed: 1/15

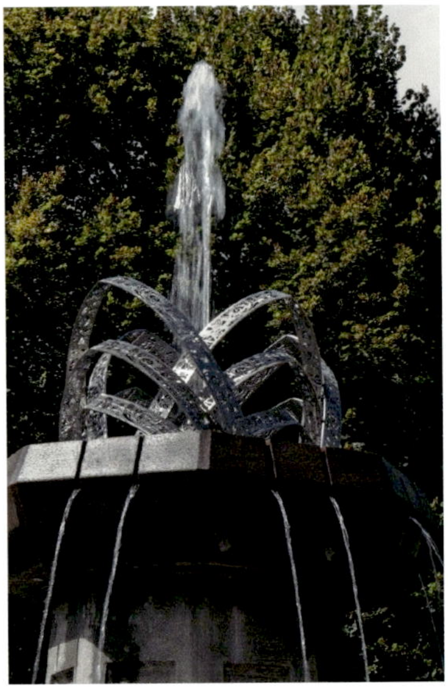

Shutter Speed: 1/30

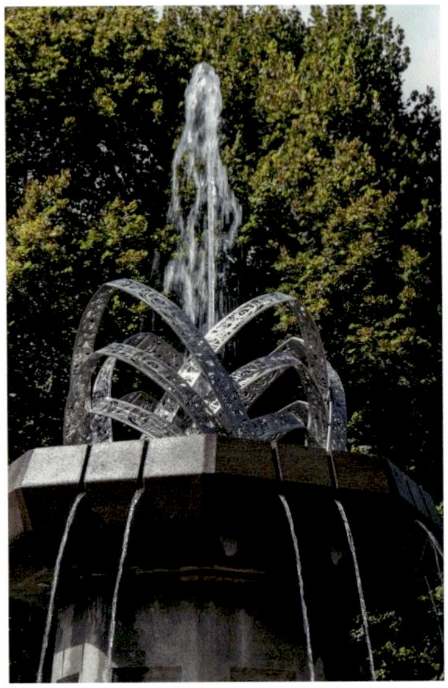

Shutter Speed: 1/60

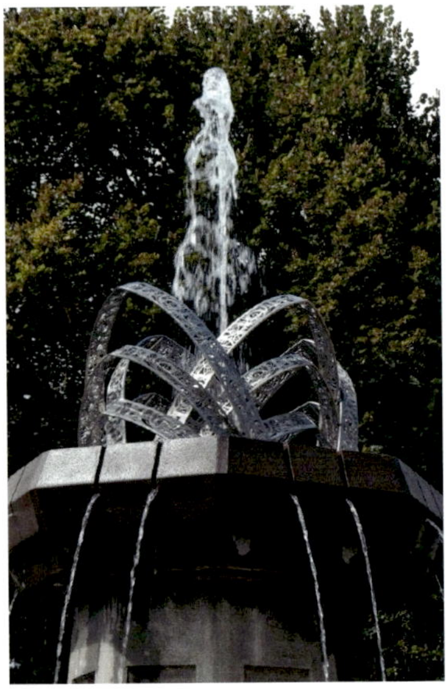

Shutter Speed: 1/125

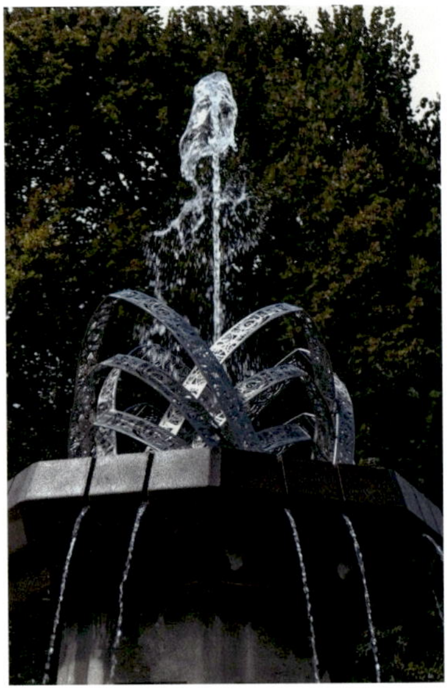

Shutter Speed: 1/250

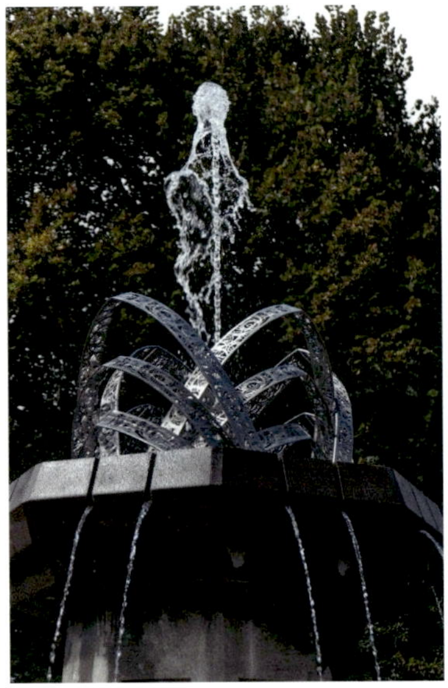

Shutter Speed: 1/500

FIGURES 5.2–5.7

For this assignment, you will need to locate fast water running. A creek or river is a great subject. But if you don't happen to live near one, you may have to be more resourceful, a public fountain perhaps (not a drinking fountain, but a large installation fountain where the water bubbles or runs out of an urn or an urchin's mouth).

One thing to consider. You will be photographing out-of-doors in the daylight. Unless the subject is in shade, the ambient light may be too bright to get a really slow shutter speed, even at a low ISO such as 50 or 100. Be prepared with either a polarizing filter, which will absorb 1 1/3 stops of light, or a 4X neutral density (ND) filter, which will absorb two stops of light.

Set your ISO so that you can make a correct exposure at one full second and make your first exposure. Change your shutter speed to 1/2 second, adjust your f/stop accordingly, and take your second exposure. Use the following shutter speed progression until you reach 1/500 second for a total of six images. You may have trouble obtaining a sharp image at 1/15 second. If so, you may need a tripod.

Shutter speed progression: 1/15 second, 1/30, 1/60, 1/125, 1/250, 1/500.

Start at 1/15 second to make certain you can make an exposure at that setting. If not, add the ND or polarizing filter.

In your editing program, compare the images two at a time side by side; start by placing 1/500 second next to 1/250 second. Keep the one you feel is the best on the screen and replace the other one with 1/125 second—there is no right or wrong choice. Do this for all the images until you have determined the one that is most aesthetically pleasing and gives a clear impression of motion.

REVIEW

1. Describe the effect of using a fast shutter speed.
2. Describe the effect of using a slow shutter speed.
3. Which of the six images is the most visually pleasing to you?

ASSIGNMENT 6

Depth of Field #1

"Great photography is about depth of feeling, not depth of field."
—Peter Adams

PURPOSE: TO PROVIDE A VISUAL UNDERSTANDING OF DOF AND HOW IT IS AFFECTED BY APERTURE.

- Use a normal to slight telephoto (70mm) focal length lens.
- Keep your camera in the same position for all of the images. A tripod is recommended but not required.
- Be absolutely certain your camera is set on Manual focus.
- Set the exposure mode on Aperture Priority (A), Nikon, or Aperture value (Av), Canon.

Arrange a still life using three objects with detail that can be seen and clearly identified—the best things to use are boxes and bottles with lettering (e.g., a large box of cereal; a bottle of shampoo; a quart-size bottle of water or soda pop; your little brother with a tattoo on his chest*).

- Set the first object as close as you can focus with your lens—with most normal focal length lenses, this would be approximately 1.5 feet away.
- Offset the next two objects so you can see all three at once.
- Set the second object two feet behind the front of the first object.
- Set the third object three feet behind the front of the *second* object.

*Just kidding about the little brother. They squirm too much and you won't be able to read the tattoo. Besides, you'd catch heck if you had his chest tattooed.

SET 1

- Focus on the nearest object.

1. Set the aperture at f/5.6.
2. Stop down two stops to f/11.
3. Stop down two stops to f/22 (if your lens only goes to f/16, use that).

- When you close or stop down a lens it means you're changing to a smaller aperture, for example from f/4 to f/5.6 or f/5.6 to f/16, etc.

SET 2

- Focus on the middle object.

1. Set the aperture at f/5.6.
2. Stop down two stops to f/11.
3. Stop down two stops to f/22 (if your lens only goes to f/16, use that).

- And you thought this was going to be hard.

SET 3

- Focus on the furthest object.

1. Set the aperture at f/5.6.
2. Stop down two stops to f/11.
3. Stop down two stops to f/22 (if your lens only goes to f/16, use that).

REVIEW

1. Study the images on your computer screen and describe what appears to be within the depth of field for each frame.
2. Select the two images from Sets 1, 2, or 3 that best demonstrate selective focus.
    1. Foreground object appears in focus, background out of focus.
    2. Background object appears in focus, foreground object out of focus.
    3. Identify one image from Sets 1, 2, or 3 that demonstrates maximum depth of field; that is, everything in the photo appears to be in focus.

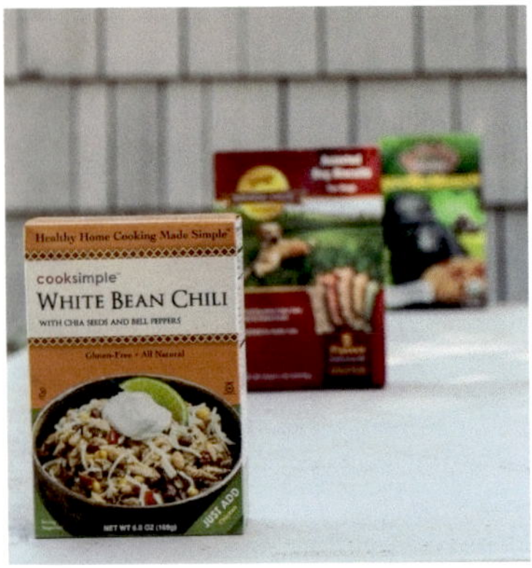

Focus is on the first box, White Bean Chili (yum); f/5.6.

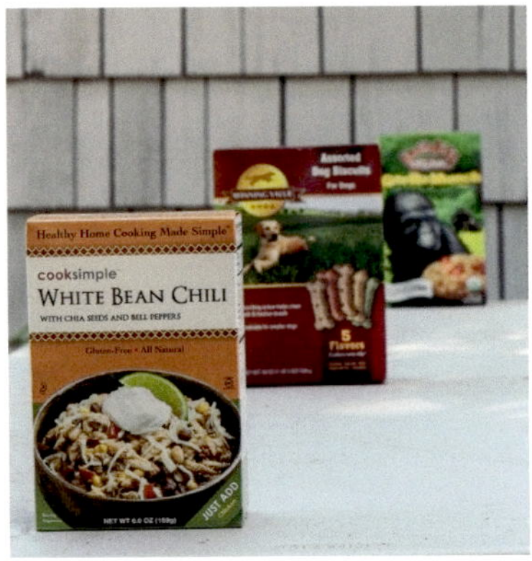

Focus is on the first box; f/11.

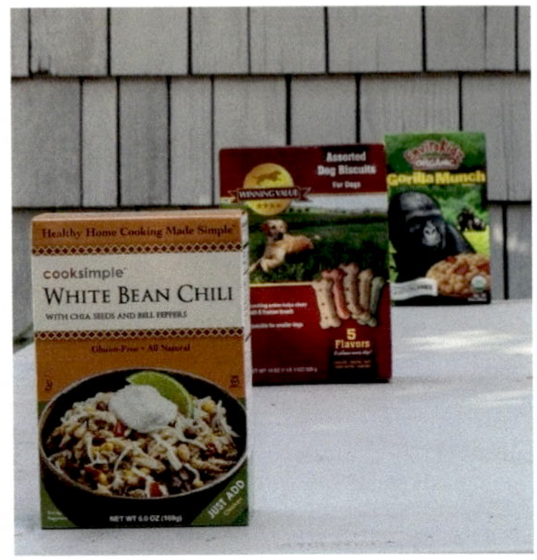

Focus is on the first box; f/22.

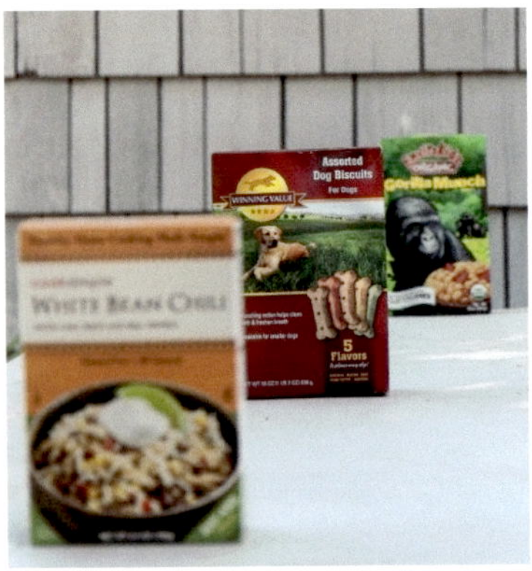

Focus is on the second box, Doggie Treats (yum—ask any dog); f/5.6.

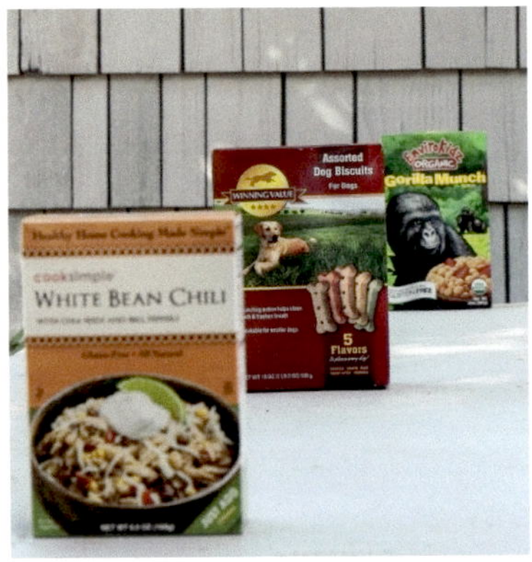

Focus is on the second box; f/11.

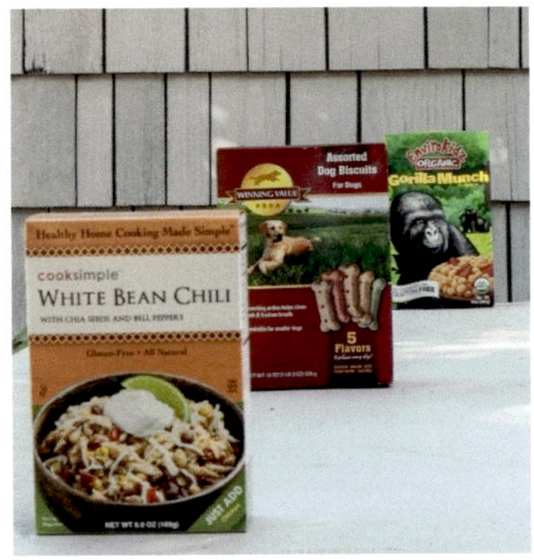

Focus is on the second box; f/22.

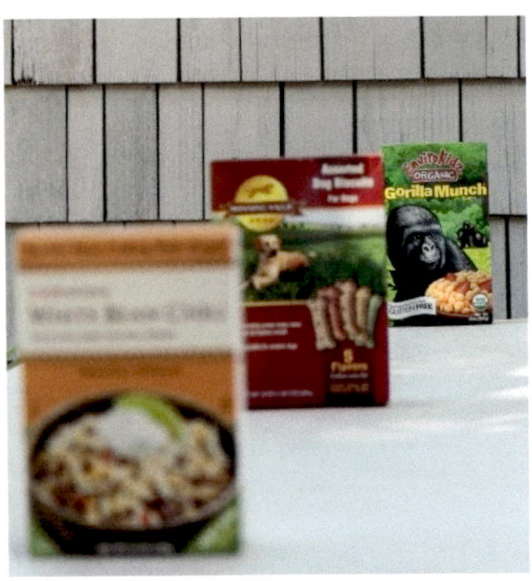

Focus is on the third box, Gorilla Munch (yum); f/5.6.

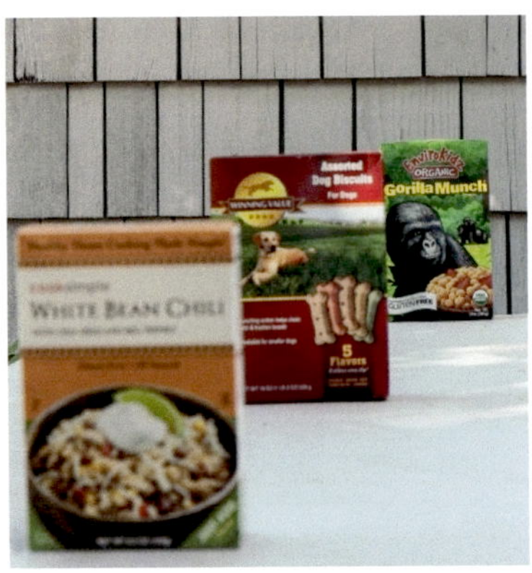

Focus is on the third box; f/11.

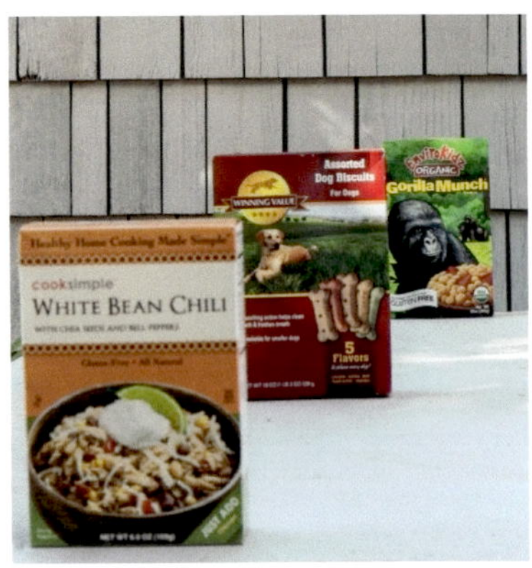

Focus is on the third box; f/22.

FIGURES 6.1–6.9

ASSIGNMENT 7

Depth of Field #2

"A camera is a tool for learning how to see without a camera."

—Dorothea Lange

PURPOSE: TO REINFORCE THE DOF LESSONS IN ASSIGNMENT 6.

PART 1

- Use the longest focal length you have up to and including 200mm—but no longer.
- Use a tripod if you have one. Be certain your shutter speed does not drop below 1/60 second—even with a tripod. If it does, increase your ISO by one or two stops (ISO 200 to 400 or 800).
- Set the exposure mode on Aperture Priority (A), or Aperture value (Av) for Canon.

You will need a partner for this part of the assignment.

Have your partner stand about six feet in front of a tree or other vertical object that is taller than they are. You should stand three to five feet in front of them. Compose the photo so there is background receding in the distance, not just a wall or building.

- The background should not be too bright.

1. Set your aperture wide open, focus on your friend's eyes and snap the photo.
2. Stop down two stops and repeat.
3. Stop down two more stops and repeat—watch your shutter speed.

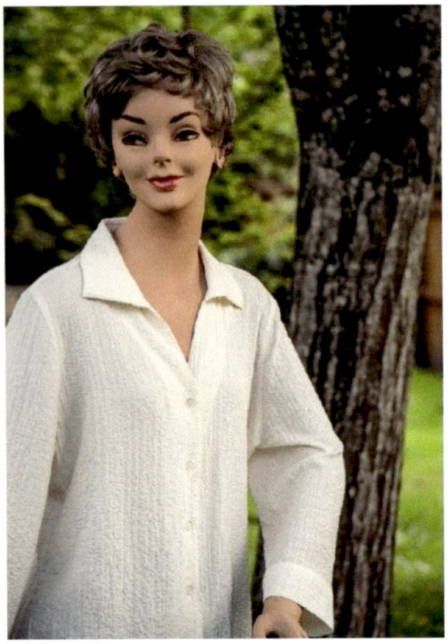

FIGURE 7.1 *This series of photos was made using a 105mm lens. The first photo was made at f/5.6.*

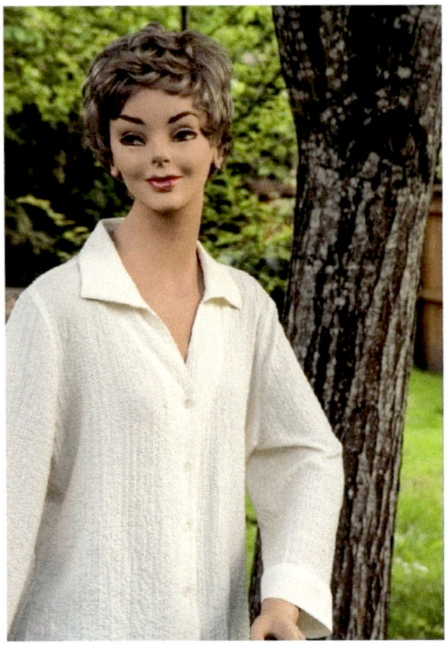

FIGURE 7.2 *f/11*

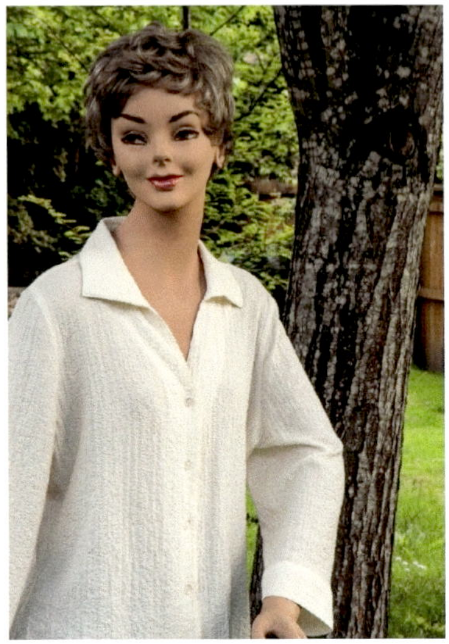

FIGURE 7.3 *f/22*

- Keep your friend in the same place, set your aperture wide open, but this time focus on the tree, and snap the photo.
- Stop down two stops and repeat.
- Stop down two stops and repeat—watch your shutter speed.

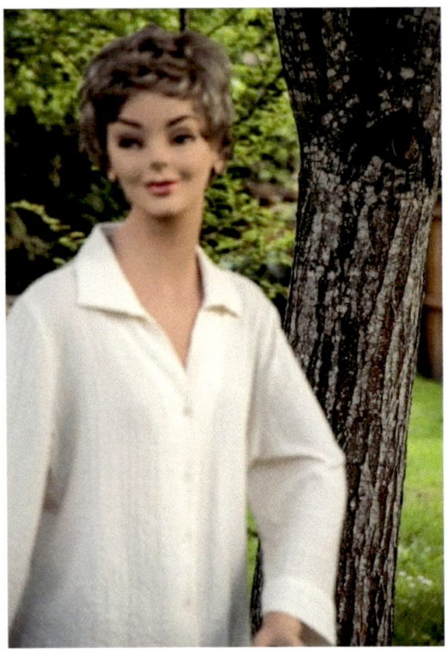

FIGURE 7.4 *f/5.6*

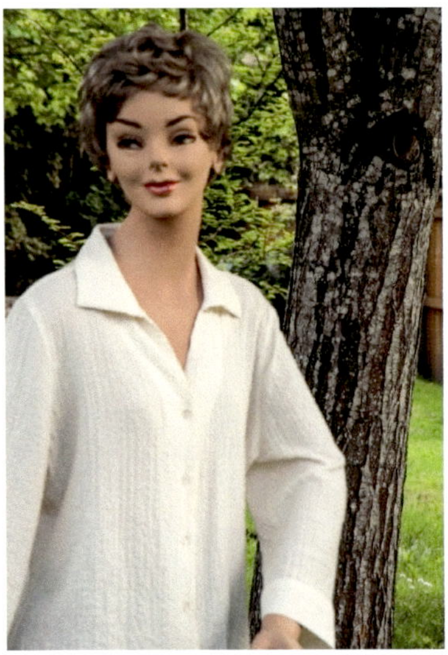

FIGURE 7.5 *f/11*

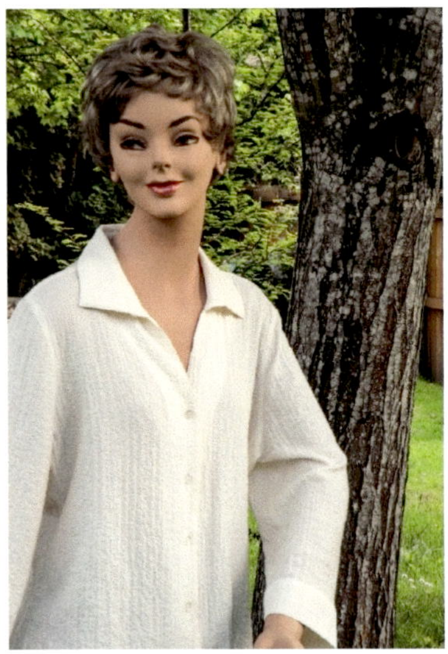

FIGURE 7.6 *f/22*

REVIEW

1. What appears to be in focus in the second photo that does not appear within the DOF of the first photo?
2. What appears to be in focus in the third photo that does not appear within the DOF of the first photo?
3. What is in clear focus in photo four?
4. Compare photo two with photo five. In photo five does DOF appear to extend further back or forward?
5. What appears to be in focus in photo 6?

PART 2

- Use a tripod and a medium-length telephoto lens, 70mm to 135mm.
- Use macro mode if it is available on your lens.

Locate a simple subject with a textured background, such as a flower in front of a wooden fence. Move in close and compose the subject straight on with your camera perpendicular to the background. Focus sharply on the subject and expose using the following progression of f/stops.

1. Wide open.
2. Stop down two stops.
3. Stop down two more stops.

Recompose the subject from a 45-degree angle so that the wall is "running away" in the background. Move in close but include some of the running wall in front and behind the subject.

Repeat the three-exposure sequence using the same aperture settings as in the first set.

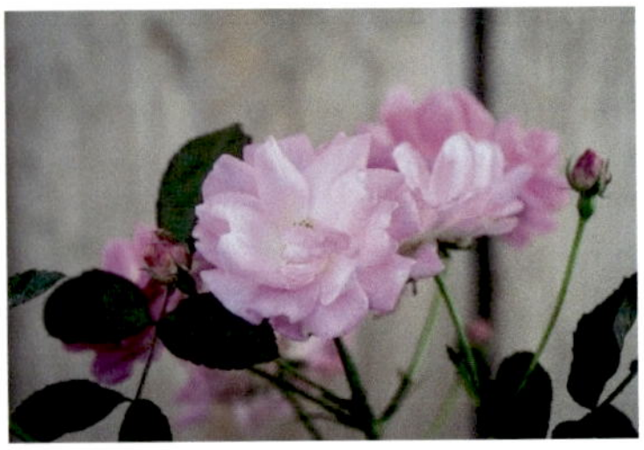

FIGURE 7.7 *f/5.6*

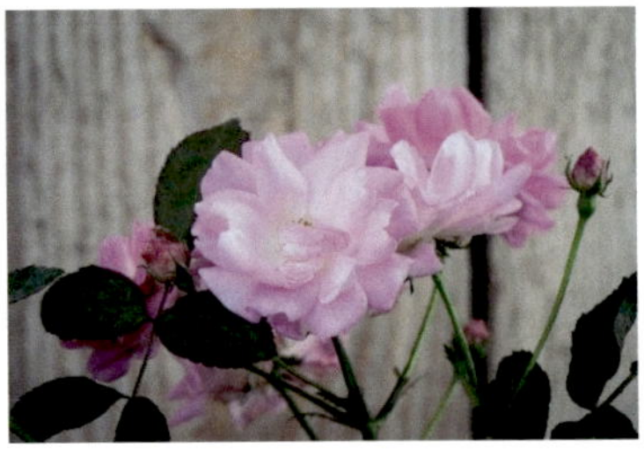

FIGURE 7.8 *f/11*

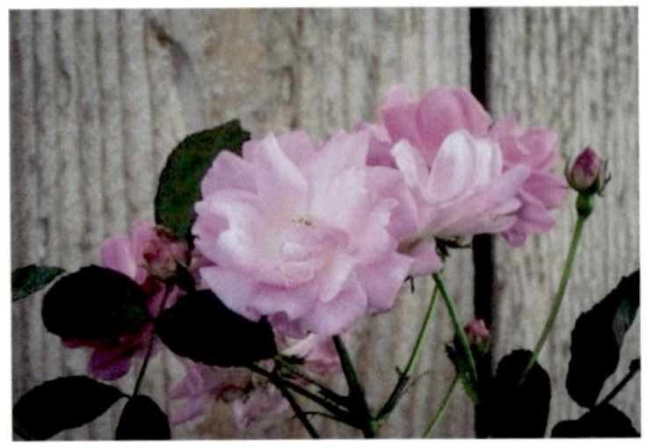

FIGURE 7.9 *f/22*

Figures 7.7 through 7.9 were taken with the fence parallel to the back of the camera. DOF decreases the closer you get to your subject, as in macro photography. The fence is approximately six inches behind the flowers.

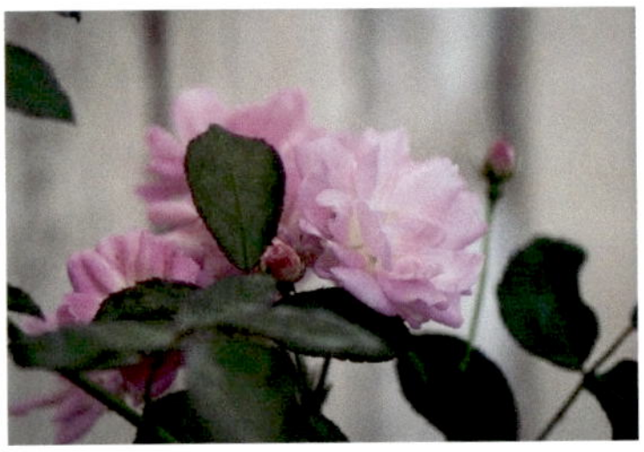

FIGURE 7.10 *f/5.6*

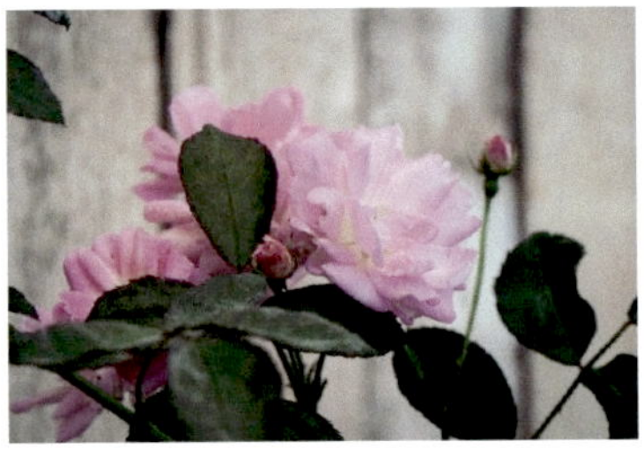

FIGURE 7.11 *f/11*

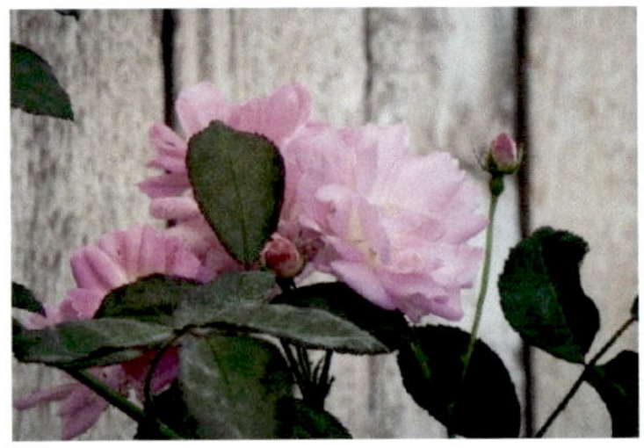

FIGURE 7.12 *f/22*

REVIEW

1. Compare each similar pair of f/stops from the two sets. What difference do you notice in DOF when the background is parallel to the subject and when it is receding?

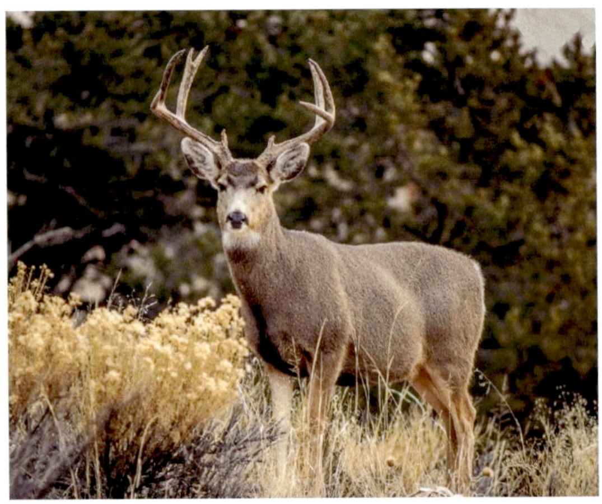

FIGURE 7.13 *A large aperture of f/4 limits the depth of field causing the deer to stand out against the background. Minolta Maxxum 7D, 450mm lens, f/4.0 at 1/20 second.*

ASSIGNMENT 8

Selective Focus vs. Maximum DOF

"Beauty can be seen in all things, seeing and composing the beauty is what separates the snapshot from the photograph."

—Matt Hardy

PURPOSE: TO LEARN HOW TO USE SELECTIVE FOCUS TO DRAW THE VIEWER'S ATTENTION TO A PARTICULAR SUBJECT. TO USE MAXIMUM DOF WHEN NO SINGLE OBJECT IS THE CENTER OF ATTENTION.

SELECTIVE FOCUS

PART 1

A good photograph draws the viewer's attention to what you want them to see. Selective focus is used to draw the viewer's attention to a particular subject, such as a single person in a crowd, a specific cactus in the desert, or an object you want them to notice.

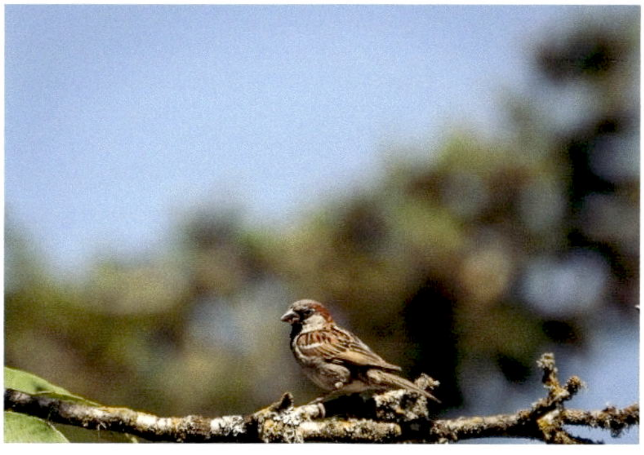

FIGURE 8.1 *By using f/8 and a long lens the photographer was able to blur the background and selectively focus on the sparrow. Photo by Donna Conrad; Minolta Maxxum 7D, 300mm lens, f/5.6 at 1/2000.*

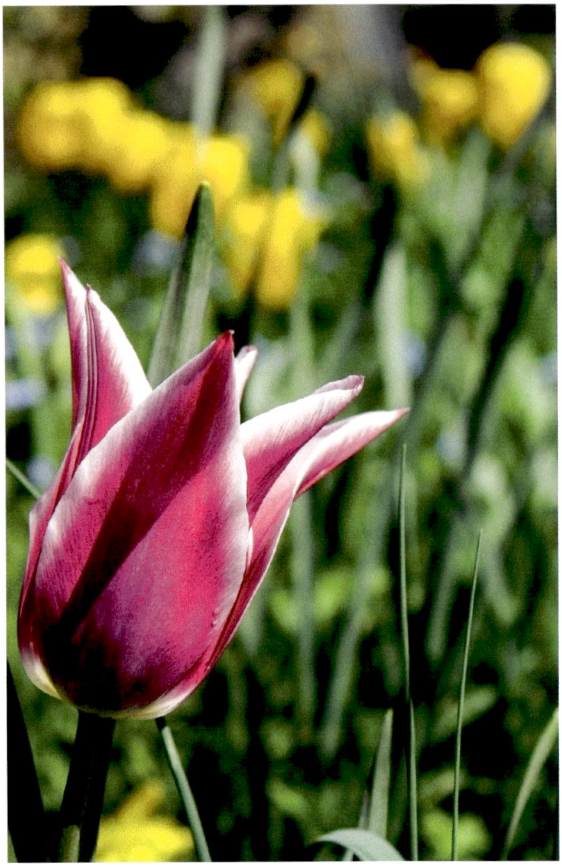

FIGURE 8.2 *Selective Focus. Photo by Dianni Freeman; 55mm lens, Canon EOS Digital Rebel XS.*

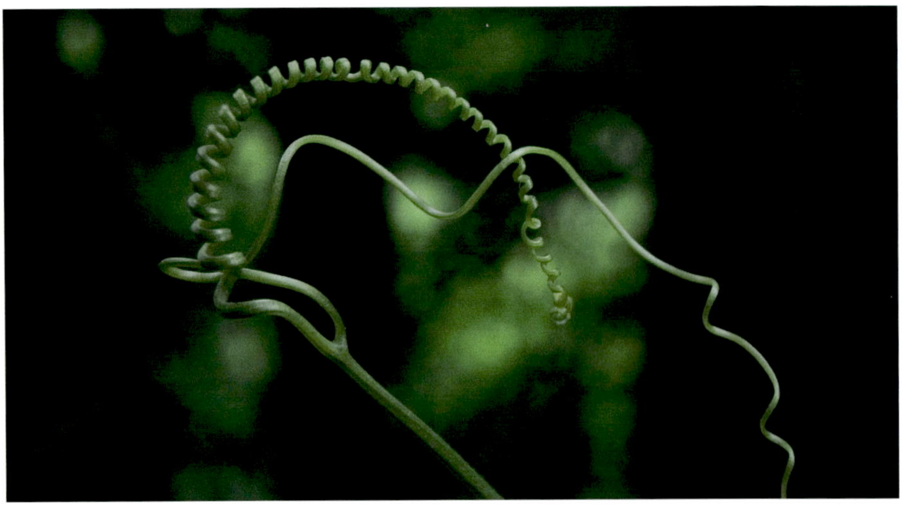

FIGURE 8.3 *Selective Focus. Photo by Jeff Hume; 55mm, Canon EOS Digital Rebel XTi.*

In order to achieve selective focus you need to focus carefully on the subject you intend to emphasize, and use a wide aperture setting. When photographing people, that means focusing on their eyes.

- Find a location where there are lots of people. This could be a dining hall on campus; a busy downtown street or mall.
  - You need a crowd so that you can focus on one person in particular and see how selective focus makes them stand out from the crowd.
  - Butt shots of your main subject (photos taken of people walking away) are absolutely forbidden on this assignment. Anyone can take a photo of someone's butt—as a photographer you must learn to photograph their face.
  - If you are not comfortable photographing strangers, then take a friend with you. Have them walk in and out of the scene and photograph them at the predetermined distance. You should still photograph this in a busy area so you can gauge the effect of the selective focus technique. And no butt shots!
- Find a vantage point with a good background and settle in.
  - In photography, the background is nearly as important as the subject. Unless the subject is unusually intense or simply unusual, the choice of background can make or break an image.
- Use a focal length between 50mm and 85mm.

PART 2

Pre-focus the camera on an area approximately eight to ten feet away.

1. Use Aperture Priority. Set your aperture to f/11 or f/16. Set your ISO so that the shutter speed is 1/30 or faster. When your subject walks into the zone of focus snap the photo. To get the eyes in focus takes speed and practice.
2. Set your aperture to f/4 or 5.6 and repeat number one.

Do one and two as many times as needed to get your subject in focus and without motion blur.

- Change your zone of focus to twelve to fifteen feet and repeat.
- Change your zone to fifteen to twenty feet and repeat.

REVIEW

Select the best images from each of the three zones and compare them against one another in an editing program.

1. What difference do you see between the photos of each set using a small aperture and the photos using a large aperture?
2. In which of the three zones does the subject stand out the most from other people?

MAXIMUM DEPTH OF FIELD

Maximum depth of field is used to make everything in the image appear in focus. You would use maximum DOF when the scene is more important than any single subject. For example, a landscape, an anonymous crowd scene, or a field of flowers.

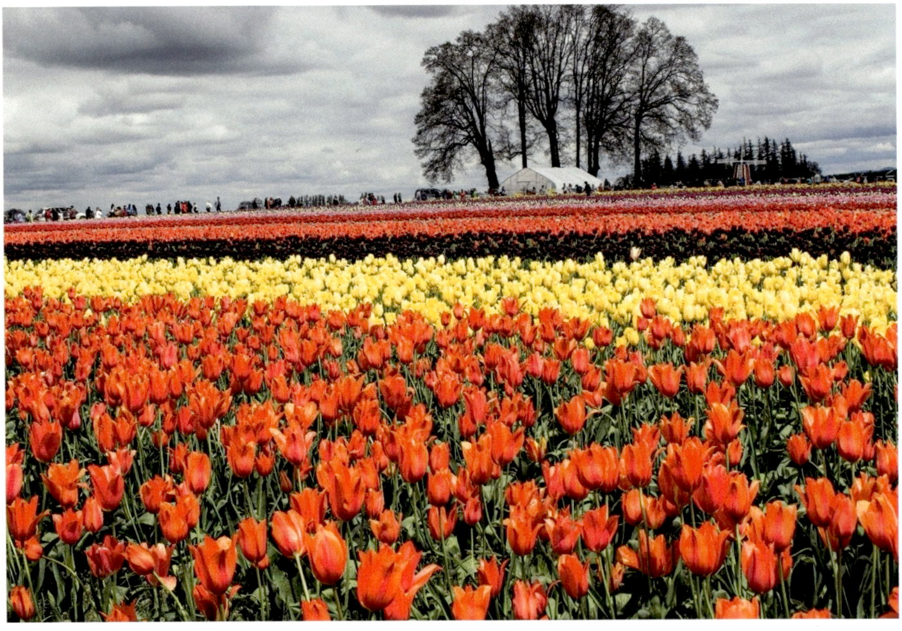

FIGURE 8.4 *Everything from the flowers in front to the tree in the background appears to be in focus. Photo by Leslie Mason; 35mm lens, Canon EOS Rebel T3i.*

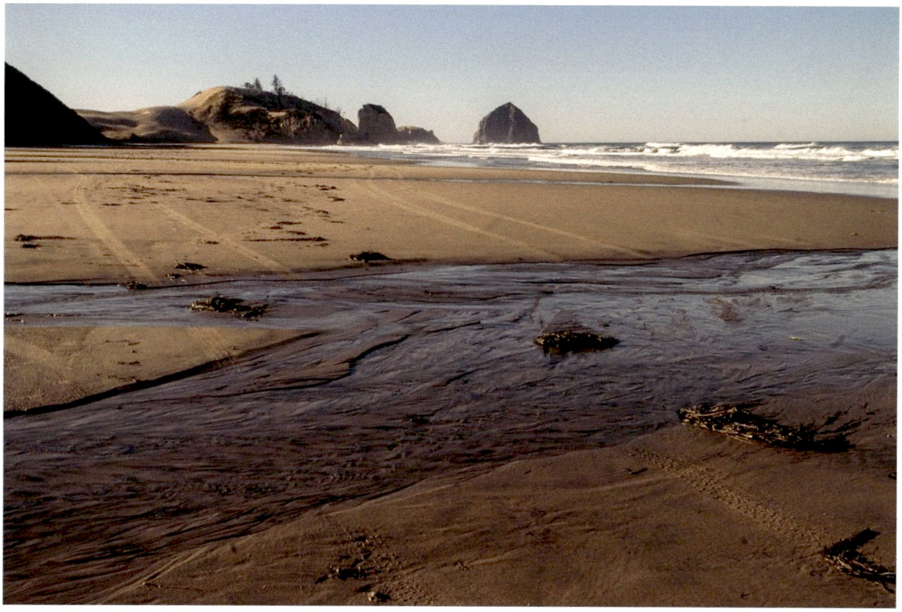

FIGURE 8.5 *Maximum DOF. f/25, Minolta Maxxum 7D, 20mm lens, f/25 at 1/30.*

In order to achieve maximum depth of field you should focus approximately one third into the composition and stop down one f/stop less than the smallest f/stop on the lens. For example, if the smallest aperture is f/22, use f/16. This will prevent diffraction at the smallest aperture that can cause an in-focus image to appear unsharp.

- For this assignment, you need a landscape, vista, or other scenic area. You also need to locate a composition in that area with a prominent foreground subject. This could be anything from a bench, large rock, cactus, patch of flowers, etc.
- Alternatively, you could have a friend sit on the grass with a building or tree approximately thirty feet behind. Stand far enough away so the foreground subject or friend is approximately 1/3 of the way into the composition.
- Use a normal to short telephoto focal-length lens—no wide-angle lenses.
- Set your camera on a tripod or a stationary object—the roof of your car, a park bench, a sleeping tortoise.
- Stop down to one f/stop larger than the smallest f/stop on the lens and take the photo (e.g., f/11, f/16, or f/22). The shutter speed is not important except for camera vibration, see Box 1.

1. Without moving the camera or changing focus, expose the second image at f/5.6.

Locate two more subjects to practice maximum depth of field for a total of three subjects and six images.

REVIEW

Based on what you have learned so far, what do you expect to see in the first image? In the second?

DSLR cameras have mirrors that cause vibration when they flip out of the way to allow light to reach the sensor. While this vibration may seem minimal, it is enough to cause camera shake when the camera is handheld at shutter speeds slower than the reciprocal of the lens focal length.

For example, a 135mm lens should not be used at less than about 1/100 or 1/125 of a second or blur will appear from mirror vibration and normal body tremors. This rule can be mitigated somewhat by using anti-shake technology now found on many DSLR cameras and lenses, but usually not by more than one stop (e.g., a 135mm lens can be handheld at 1/60 second using anti-shake technology).

However, tripods are another matter. Surprisingly, mirror vibration can cause vibration blur with tripods, especially but not limited to aluminum, because the tripod transmits rather than absorbs the vibration. This will almost always occur at shutter speeds between 1/2 second and 1/30 second. Slower than 1/2 second and the overall exposure is long enough that the vibration doesn't usually appear; and 1/60 or faster is too fast for the vibration to record on the image.

More than one photographer has discovered this the hard way.

Finally, there are two kinds of anti-shake technology—in the lens and in the camera body.

Anti-shake in the lens should always be switched off when the camera is tripod mounted. This is because in-lens anti-shake systems create a small oscillation of their own, meant to counter handheld shake that blurs the image if there is none.

Anti-shake systems in the camera body don't usually do this. When in doubt, switch off the anti-shake system when the camera is tripod mounted.

ASSIGNMENT 9

Foreshortening

"Photography is a love affair with life."

—Burk Uzzle

PURPOSE: TO DEMONSTRATE HOW THE LENS-TO-SUBJECT DISTANCE AFFECTS PERSPECTIVE.

You will need a willing subject—preferably one who does not mind if you make them look bad.

1. Start with a normal focal length, approximately 50mm, and frame your subject's face square to the camera in what is referred to as a "head and shoulders" photo. Focus on the subject's eyes and stop down to f/5.6 or f/8.
2. Next, use the widest focal length you have, and move closer until you have reframed the photo as closely as you can to the first image. Use the same f/stop as in exposure 1.
3. Finally, use a focal length no longer than 200mm. Move back until the image is framed as closely to the first image as possible. Use the same f/stop.

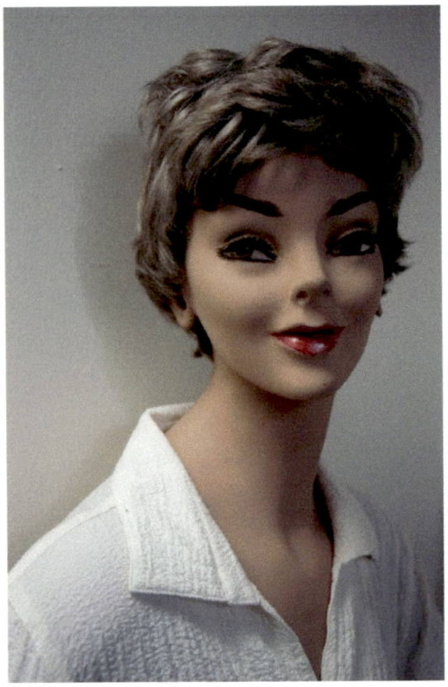

FIGURE 9.1 *This image made with a normal lens at a distance of about six feet creates an image that appears normal to the eye.*

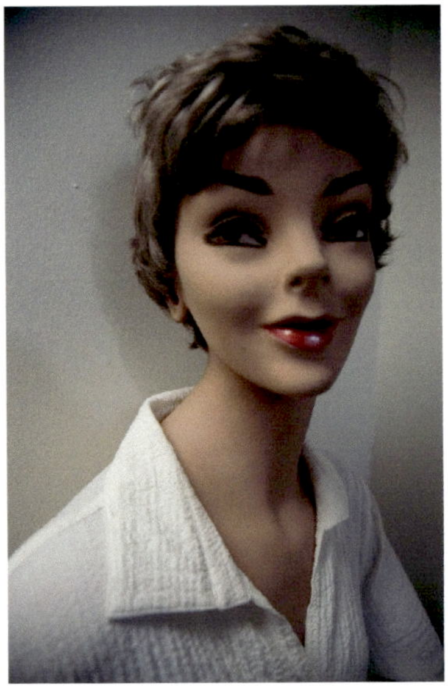

FIGURE 9.2 *Moving to three feet with a 24mm lens shows the effect of foreshortening. All the lines in the image appear to converge towards the center. The nose, which is the closest point to the lens, appears to be unnaturally large.*

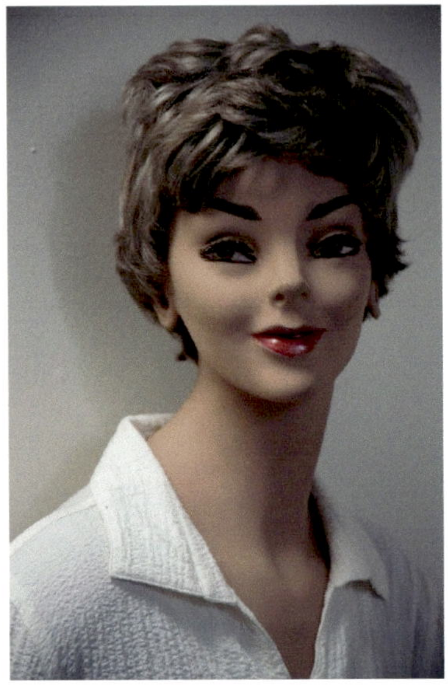

FIGURE 9.3 *The final image was made with a 120mm at about ten feet. Mollie's face appears more rounded than with the normal lens. The overall result is generally more pleasing.*

REVIEW

When reviewing the three images on your screen you will notice that the wide lens distorts the face in an unflattering way. Elements on the face that are closest to the lens appear larger than they are in proportion to the rest of the face. You can use this effect if you want your subject to appear maniacal, deranged, or you just don't like them very much.

The normal lens places everything into a normal spatial relationship. Even though there is no evidence of foreshortening, the face is flattened and lacks dimension. This is perhaps the least interesting and/or useful of the three.

The long lens creates the most pleasing image. It avoids any evidence of foreshortening and causes the features to appear more rounded and three-dimensional.

The lesson here is that the choice of lens can alter your visual statement. If you want to create monsters, move close with a wide-angle lens. If you want to flatter your subject, step back and use a moderate telephoto, between 85mm to 200mm. It all depends on the message you wish to convey.

ASSIGNMENT 10

Keystoning

"When people ask me what equipment I use—I tell them my eyes."

—Anonymous

PURPOSE: TO DEMONSTRATE HOW POINT OF VIEW AFFECTS THE CONVERGENCE OF LINES.

Keystoning is what happens when you tilt your camera up to include the top of a building and it appears to be falling backwards (Figure 10.1). This is due to a low point of view, resulting in converging parallel lines moving away from your vantage point.

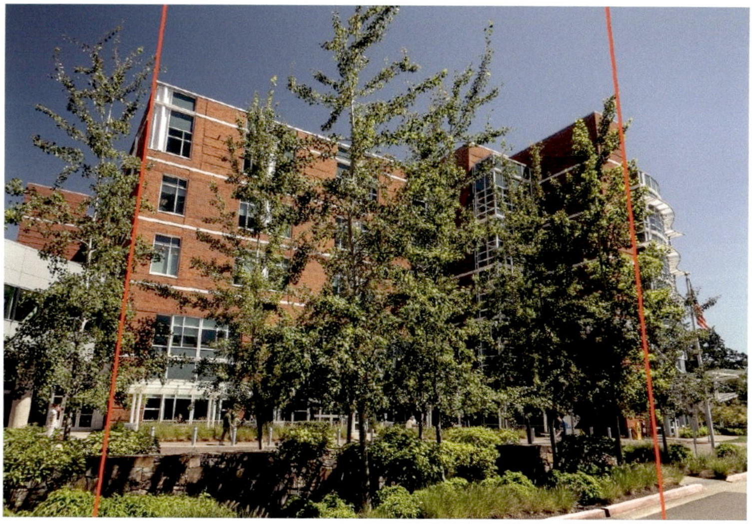

FIGURE 10.1 *A 24mm lens was used at street level to create the keystone effect in this image. The red lines were added in Photoshop to emphasize the effect; they were not in the original image.*

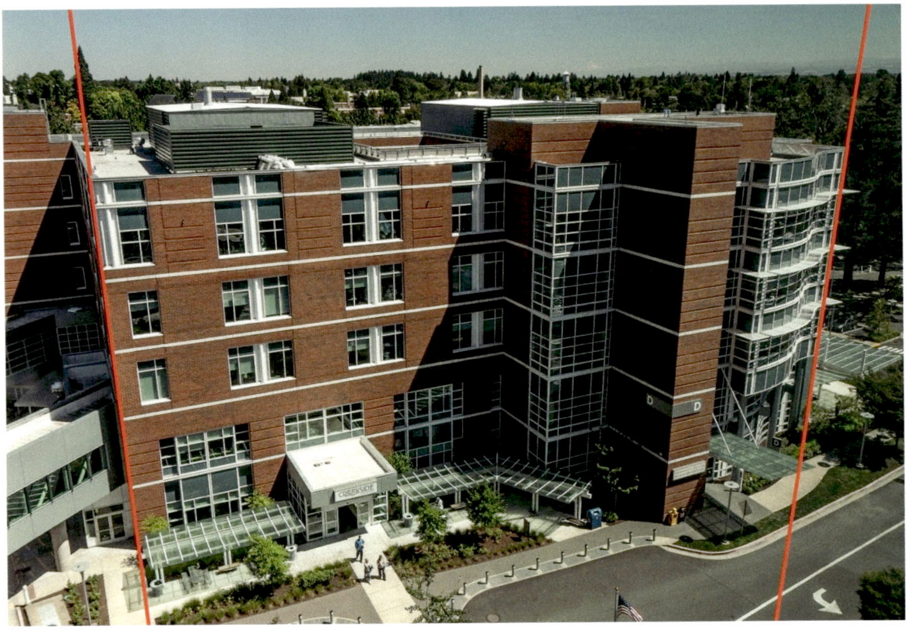

FIGURE 10.2 *A 24mm lens was used from the seventh floor of the building across the street to record this view.*

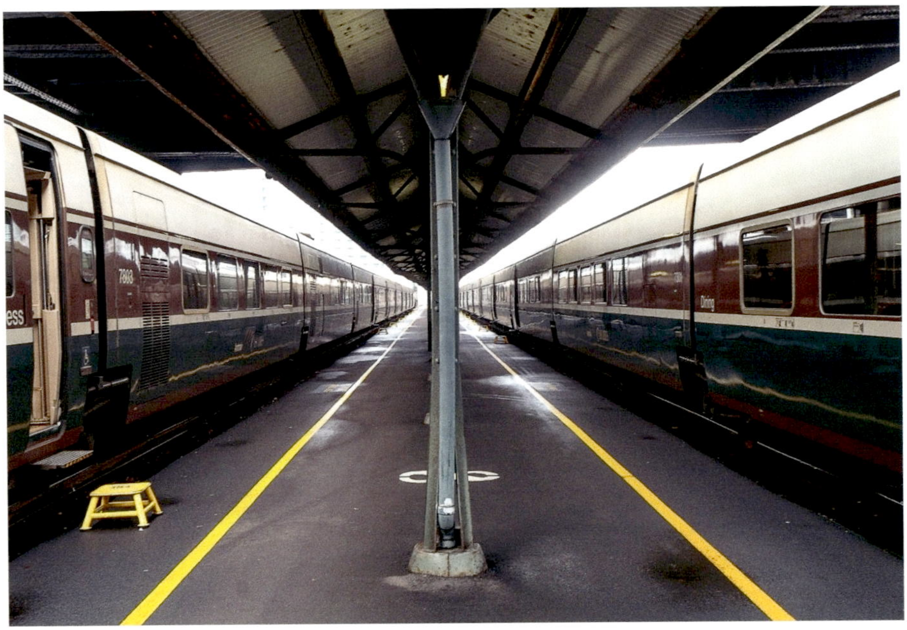

FIGURE 10.3 *When the convergence appears with horizontal lines, we call it vanishing perspective, convergence of line, etc.*

Keystoning works in reverse should you take a high point of view (Figure 10.2).

The same effect occurs with receding horizontal lines, such as a row of buildings on a street, railroad tracks, etc. However, we don't consider it keystoning because we expect railroad tracks to converge, and buildings to become smaller as they recede. When this occurs we call it vanishing perspective (Figure 10.3).

Keystoning can be minimized by standing farther away from the building or with the use of perspective-correcting software, such as DxO Optics (Appendix).

- Find a tall building to photograph, at least three stories.
- Use a wide-angle lens.
- Find a vantage point at street level and across the street.

1. Aim the camera towards the top of the building, taking in as much as you can include of some sky.
2. Locate a second building that allows you to access one of the top floors with a window. Photograph looking down on a building across the street.

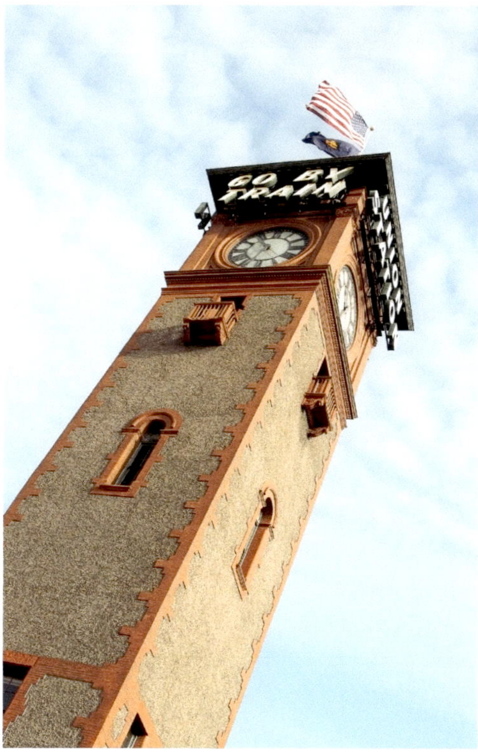

FIGURE 10.4 *Union Pacific Station, Portland, Ore. Minolta Maxxum 7D, 40mm lens, f/8 at 1/250.*

ASSIGNMENT 11

Compressing Perspective

"I don't think there's any such thing as teaching people photography, other than influencing them a little. People have to be their own learners."

—Imogen Cunningham

PURPOSE: TO DEMONSTRATE HOW INCREASING FOCAL LENGTH COMPRESSES THE SCALE BETWEEN FOREGROUND AND BACKGROUND OBJECTS.

PART 1—USING A FOOT ZOOM

Foot zooming is when you walk closer or further from the subject without changing focal lengths. Doing so causes a change in both vantage point and point of view. This is the way photos and movies were made before zoom lenses came of age.

When you use a foot zoom, foreground and background elements maintain the same relative size and spatial relationship to one another.

- Use a normal lens for all three photos.
- Stand approximately ten feet from the foreground subject and compose a horizontal image with foreground and background elements.
- Position your camera approximately ten to twelve feet from your subject (Figure 11.1).
- Maintain a normal focal length and position the camera at half the distance (Figure 11.2).
- Move half again closer (Figure 11.3).

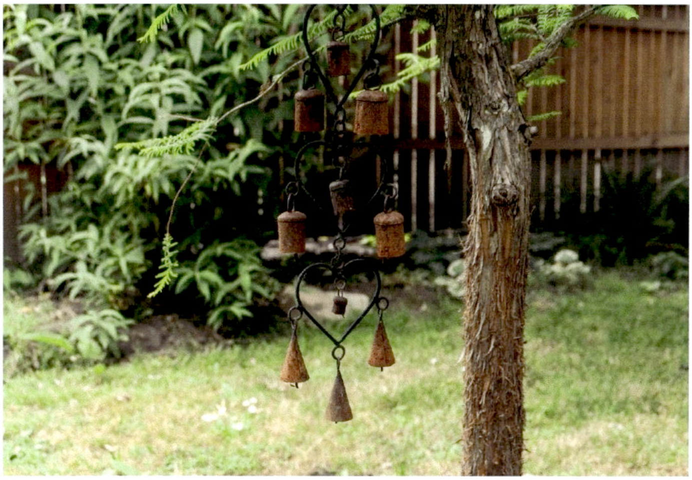

FIGURE 11.1 *Use a normal focal length lens for these three images. For the first photo stand about twelve feet from the foreground subject.*

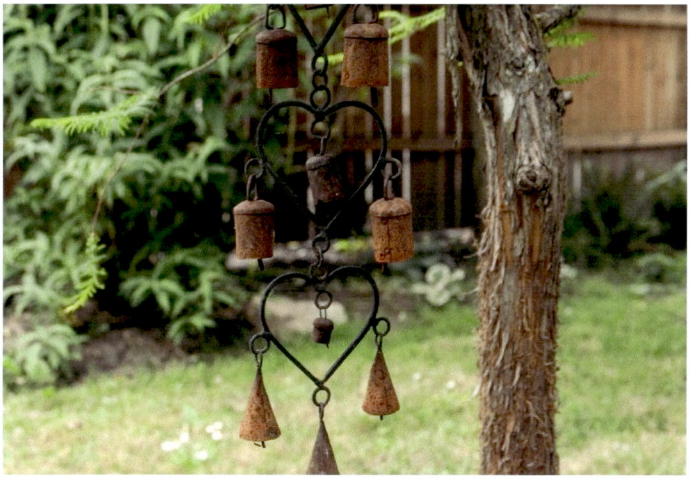

FIGURE 11.2 *Move to about six feet. Keep the near/far objects as closely aligned to the original image as possible.*

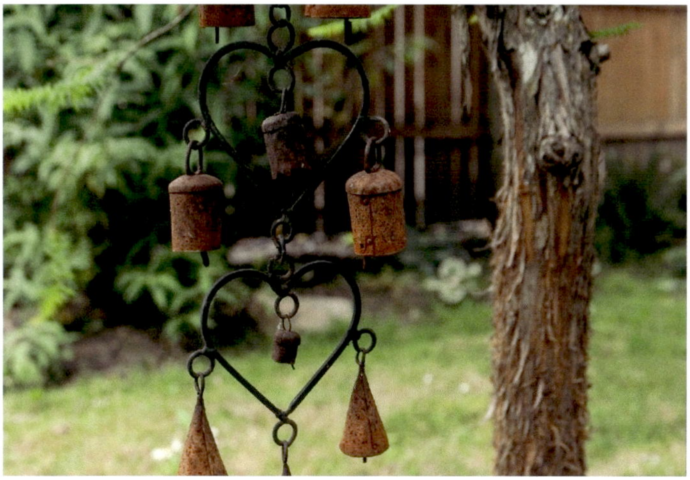

FIGURE 11.3 *Move to about three feet.*

REVIEW

Observe how the foreground and background maintain the same relative size and spatial relationship in all three photos. Even as you get closer, the background appears to remain at the same distance from the camel bells.

PART 2—ZOOM LENS

Standing in one spot and zooming the lens in or out crops the photo in the camera. Doing this magnifies everything in the image equally, so the foreground and background objects enlarge proportionately. This results in what is known as compressing, or flattening, perspective.

- Use the same starting position as for Part 1.
- Make the first photo with a 50mm focal length, Figure 11.4.
- Remain in the same position and zoom out to 75mm to 90mm, Figure 11.5.
- Remain in the same position and zoom out to 120mm to 135mm, Figure 11.6.

REVIEW

Observe how as you zoom out to enlarge the foreground object the background objects enlarge proportionately.

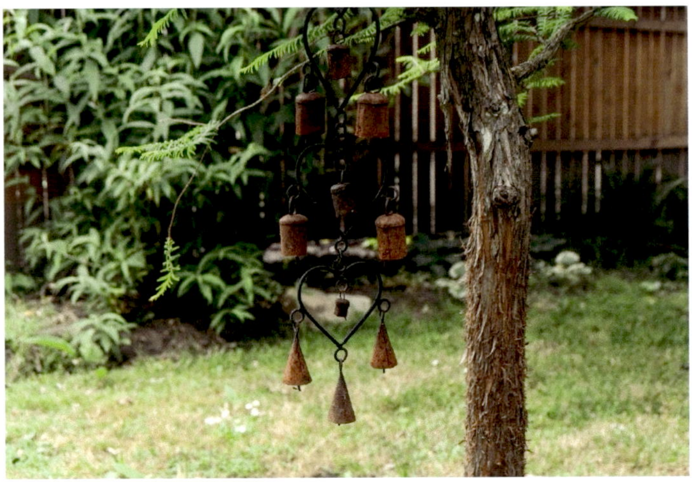

FIGURE 11.4 *With a 50mm lens stand about twelve feet from the foreground object.*

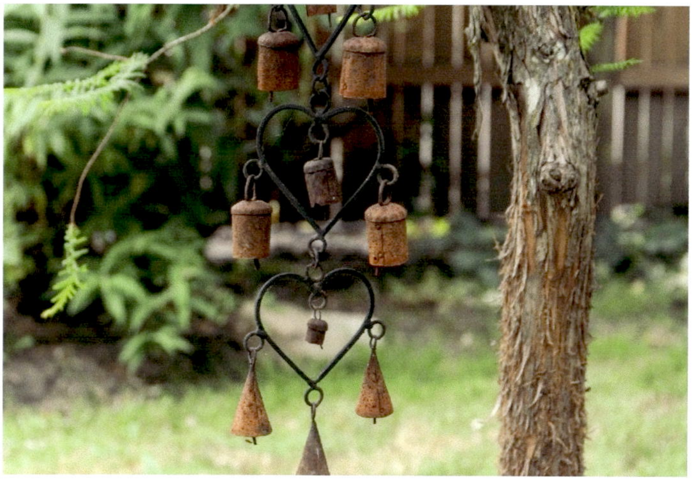

FIGURE 11.5 *Without moving your camera position, zoom in to 75mm to 90mm. This image was made using a 80mm lens.*

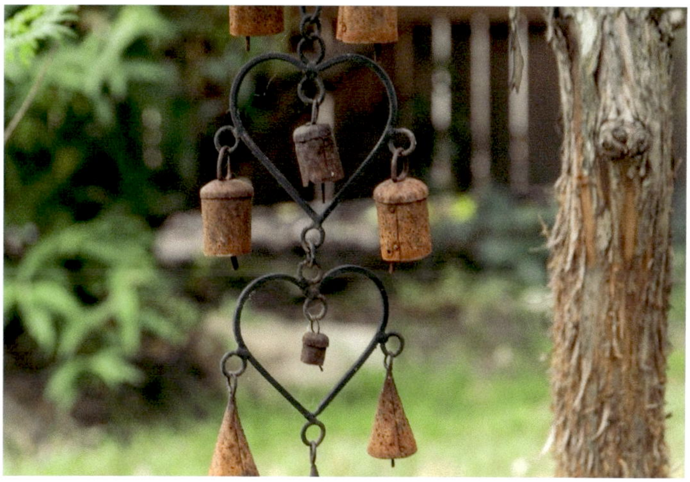

FIGURE 11.6 *Without moving your camera position, zoom in to 120mm to 135mm. This image was made using a 120mm lens.*

PART 3—ZOOM LENS AND A FOOT ZOOM COMBINED

Combining a zoom lens with a foot zoom will allow you to maintain the same combination while expanding or compressing the background.

Find a location with a large background object and a smaller foreground object. The background object should be at least fifty feet behind. A friend standing, or a parked car, makes a good subject.

- It is important that your foreground object doesn't move. If you are using a friend, have them lean or sit against something, or have them professionally stuffed.
- Use a zoom lens with wide to medium focal-length range.

1. Carefully compose the image using your widest-angle lens. Take note of where the foreground object begins and ends in the frame, top, bottom, and sides (Figure 11.7).
2. Zoom out to a normal focal length then use your foot zoom to physically move away from the foreground subject. Use the LCD preview on the

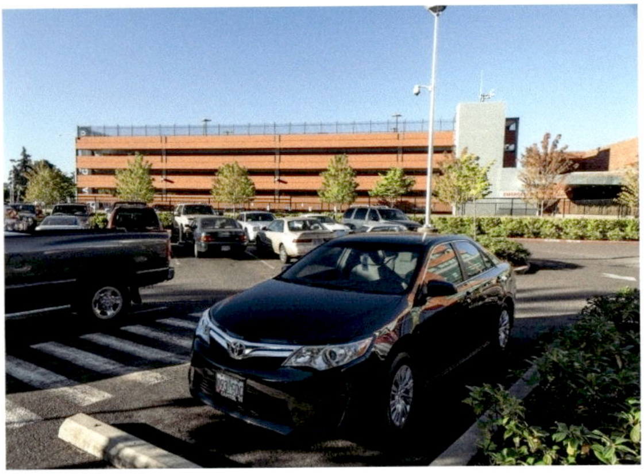

FIGURE 11.7 *The 24mm wide-angle distorts the image through the convergence of lines. Observe the size of the parking structure and the cars in the second row relative to the main subject.*

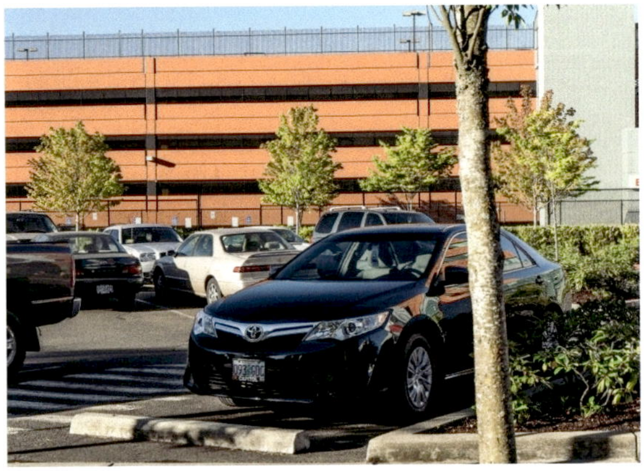

FIGURE 11.8 *Zooming the lens to 50mm and using the foot zoom to move further away enables you to maintain the same composition while compressing the background. Notice that at 50mm the cars in the second row and the parking structure appear larger. Also observe that the distortion caused by converging lines has disappeared.*

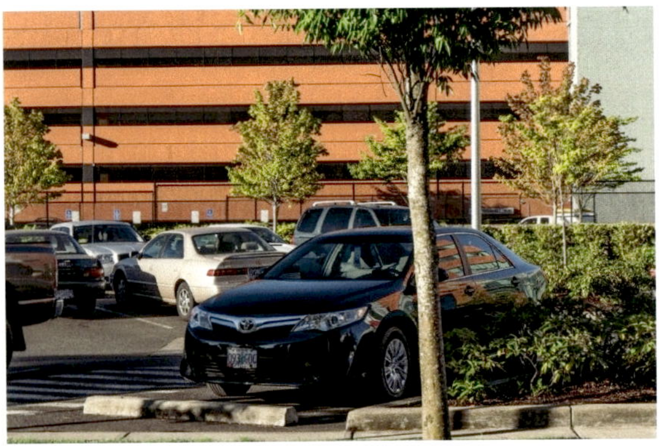

FIGURE 11.9 *Here the lens has been zoomed out to 75mm and the foot zoom employed to maintain the same composition.*

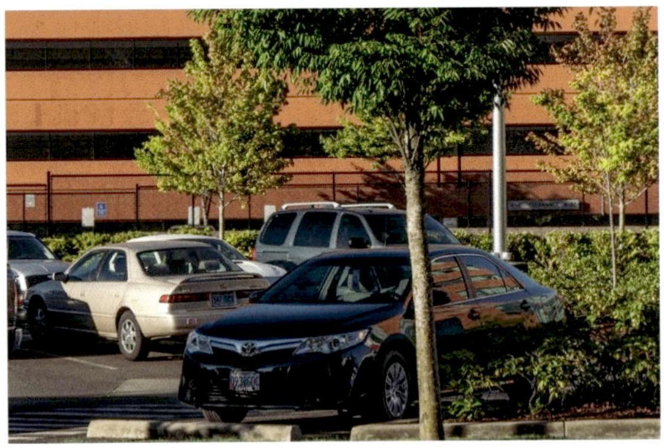

FIGURE 11.10 *Here the lens has been zoomed out to 120mm. Notice throughout that the car has been kept at approximately the same size and position by using the foot zoom, but the background objects have been magnified by the zoom lens.*

back of your camera to place the foreground subject as closely as you can to the first frame (Figure 11.8).

3. Zoom out to 75mm to 90mm. Use your foot zoom to physically move away from the foreground subject (Figure 11.9).
4. Finally, zoom out to your longest focal length and repeat (Figure 11.10).

REVIEW

Compare the images in your editing program. Describe the difference in scale (size in relation to one another) between the foreground and background

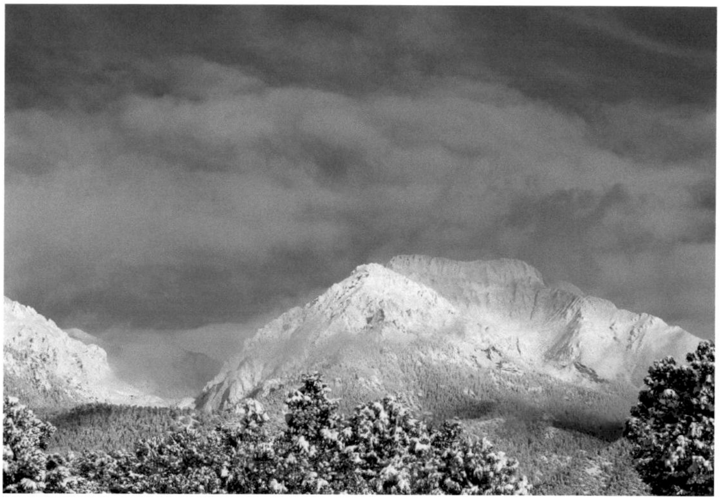

FIGURE 11.11 *A wide-angle focal length expands the vista of Crestone Peak in winter. Minolta Maxxum, 300mm lens, f/16 at 1/250.*

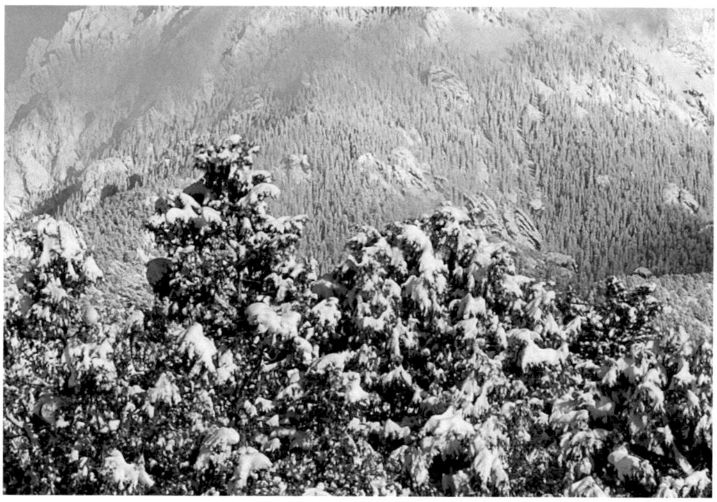

FIGURE 11.12 *A telephoto from the same vantage point compresses the perspective. Minolta Maxxum, 600mm lens, f/11 at 1/500.*

elements. Notice that the widest angle appears to be distorted due to the convergence of lines. Notice, too, how background objects at all distances appear larger, creating the illusion of compression.

Were you trying to depict a landscape, the best choice would be to use a wide lens to expand the vista.[1] On the other hand, if you were trying to isolate a specific subject in the landscape—a waterfall, trees on the side of a distant mountain—a long lens would be a better choice.[2]

NOTES

1 For an example of using wide lenses for landscape photography, see Ansel Adams' photographs of Yosemite and the Sierra Nevada mountains.

2 For examples of using a telephoto lens for isolating elements in the landscape, see the work of Galen Rowell.

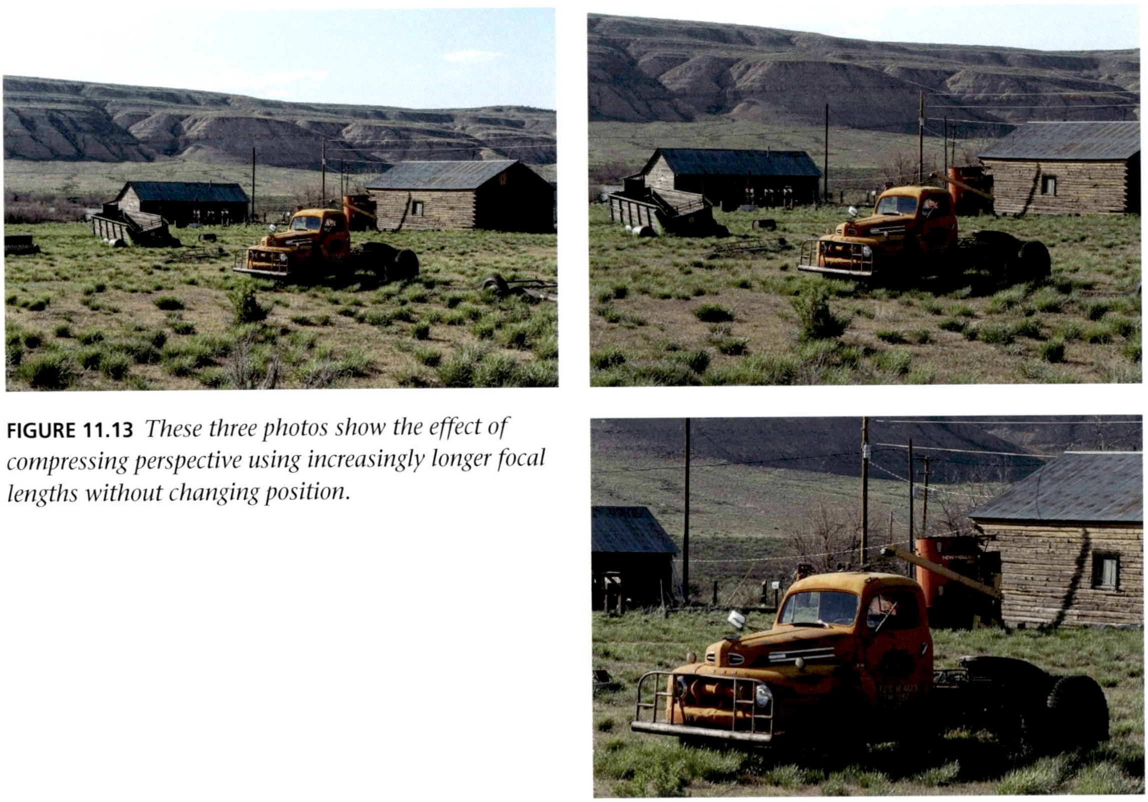

FIGURE 11.13 *These three photos show the effect of compressing perspective using increasingly longer focal lengths without changing position.*

ASSIGNMENT 12

Scale

"In photography there are no shadows that cannot be illuminated."

—August Sander

PURPOSE: TO CREATE THE ILLUSION OF DEPTH USING OBJECTS TO DEFINE THE SIZE AND DISTANCE OF OTHER OBJECTS IN THE IMAGE.

NEAR/FAR RELATIONSHIP

Using a focal length between 24mm and 35mm, create a composition using a subject of known size, or a size the viewer will assume to know, in the foreground. The background should be completely visible in the picture.

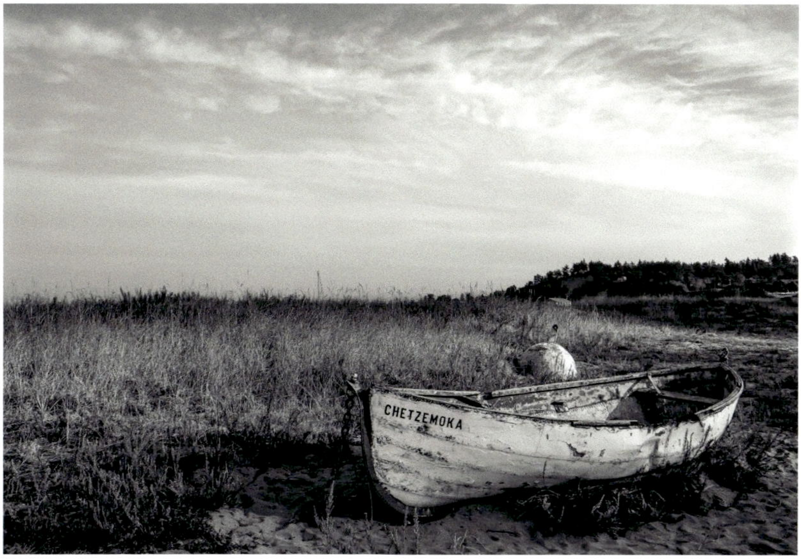

FIGURE 12.1 *Knowing the size of the boat allows the viewer to intuit the distance to the trees. This creates the illusion of three dimensions in this two-dimensional image. Photo by Austin Hodaie.*

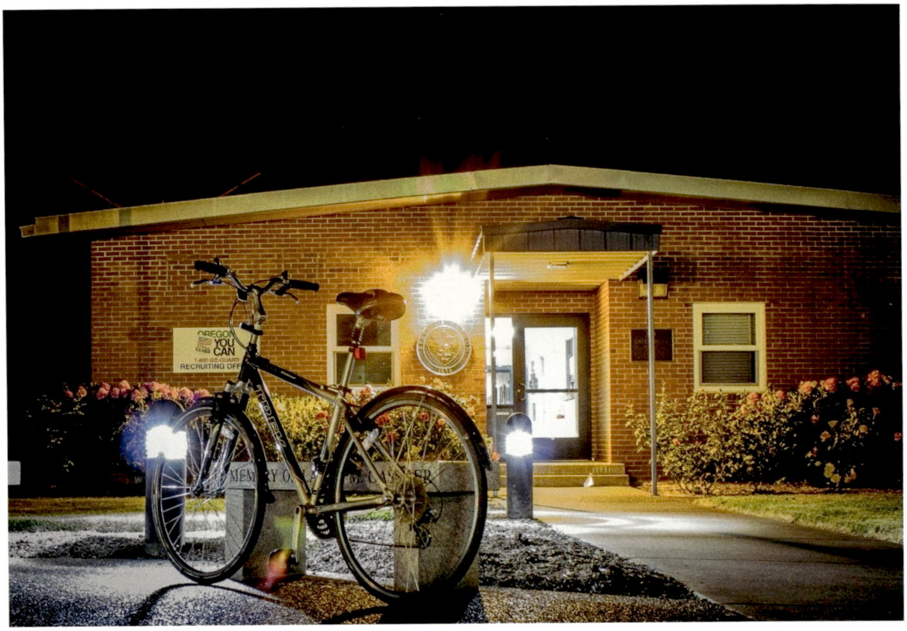

FIGURE 12.2 *The bicycle provides a visual clue as to the size of the structure and the distance to it. As with image #1, this creates the illusion of depth. Photo by Leslie Mason; 21mm lens; Canon Rebel EOS T3i.*

Locate and photograph at least four more near/far image combinations.

REVIEW

By using the wide-angle lens and placing the main subject close to the lower edge of the frame, it is possible for the viewer to get a sense of the size and distance of the landscape and other objects within it.

SECTION 2

Intermediate

Sophomore

ASSIGNMENT 13

Subject Placement

"It is impossible to give you rules that will enable you to compose. If it were possible to compose pictures by rule, Titian and Veronese would be ordinary men."
—John Ruskin

PURPOSE: PRACTICE FOR PLACING THE SUBJECT IN AN OPTIMAL AREA OF THE IMAGE.

PART 1—RULE OF THIRDS #1

Using the rule of thirds, choose a subject and place it at the intersection of each of the four lines.

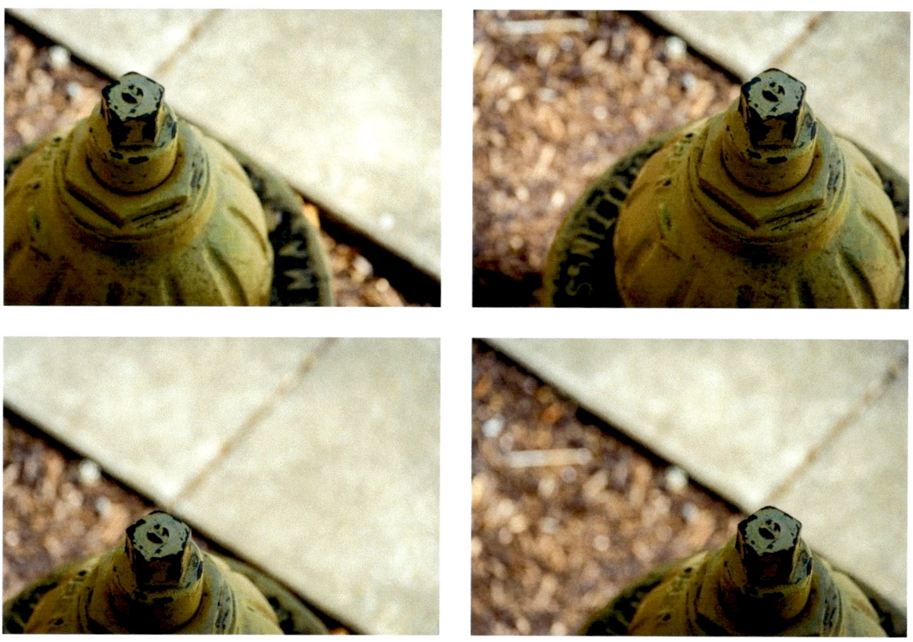

FIGURE 13.1–13.4 *In Figures 13.1 thorough 13.4 the subject has been placed on the four intersecting lines according to the rule of thirds.*

PART 2—HORIZON LINES

Locate a subject that contains a horizon line.

1. Place the horizon in the lower third of the image.
2. Place the horizon on the upper third of the image.
3. Place the horizon in the center.
4. "Disappear" the horizon at the top edge of the image.

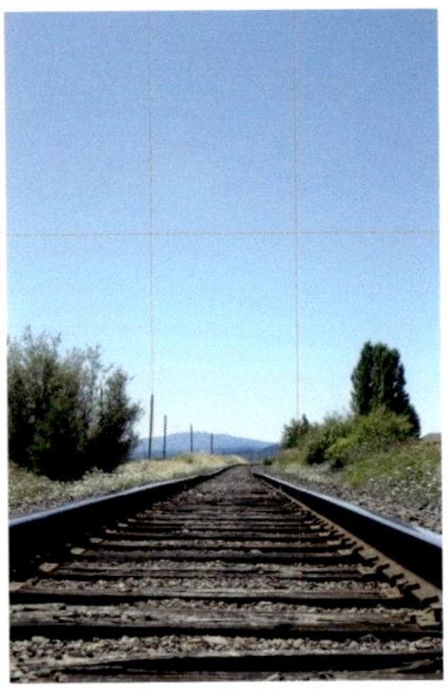

FIGURE 13.5 *Low horizon placement. Photo by Megan Jaeger; 28mm lens; Canon EOS Rebel T3i.*

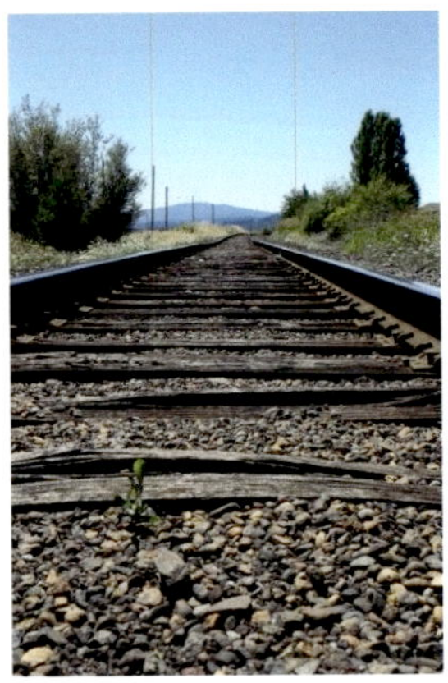

FIGURE 13.6 *High horizon placement. Photo by Megan Jaeger; 28mm lens; Canon EOS Rebel T3i.*

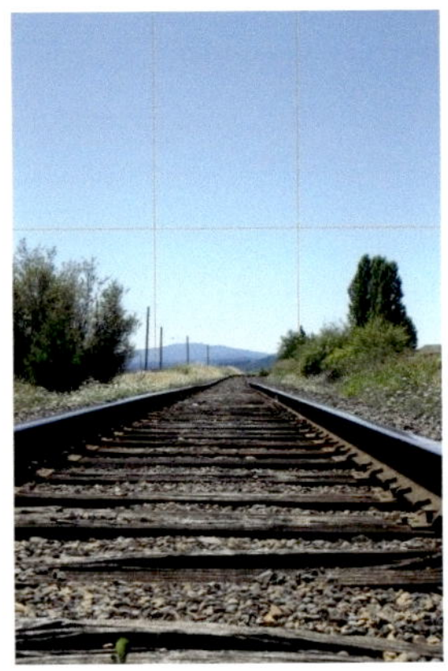

FIGURE 13.7 *Center horizon placement. Photo by Megan Jaeger; 28mm lens; Canon EOS Rebel T3i.*

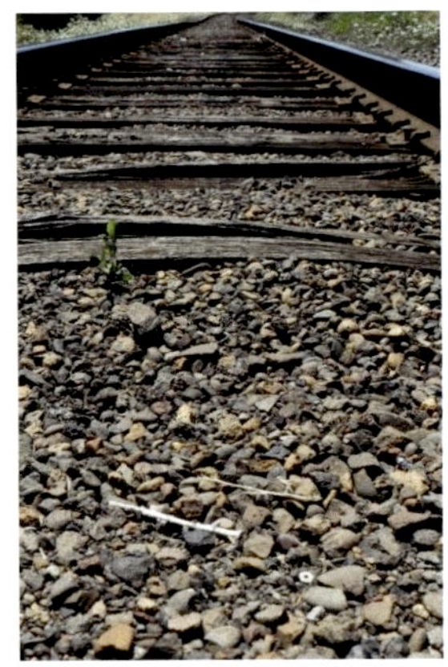

FIGURE 13.8 *No horizon. Photo by Megan Jaeger; 28mm lens; Canon EOS Rebel T3i.*

PART 3—VERTICAL LINES

- Locate a building that interests you.
- Turn the camera to a vertical orientation and level it front to back and side to side; use a level if necessary.

1. Choose one edge of the building and place it in the left third of the image.
2. Place the same edge of the building in the right third.
3. Place the same edge in the center.

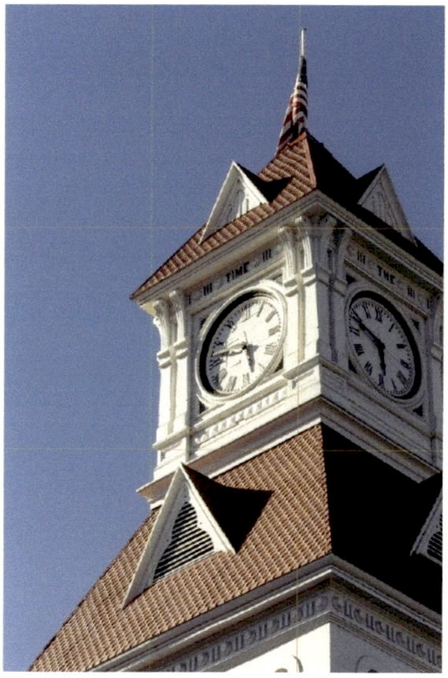

FIGURE 13.9 *The edge of the structure has been placed on the left line according to the rule of thirds. Photo by Megan Jaeger; 50mm lens; Canon EOS Rebel T3i.*

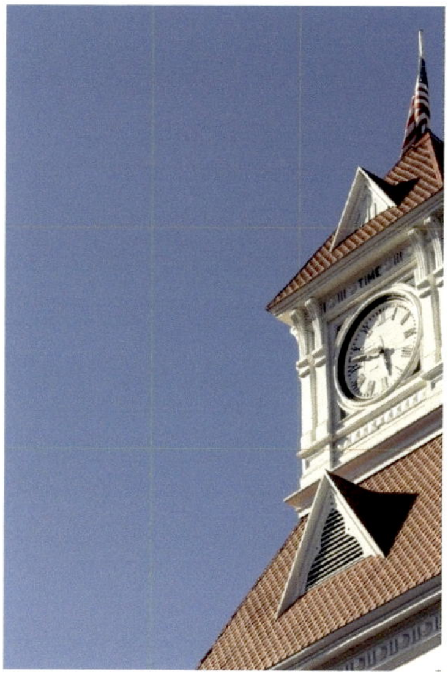

FIGURE 13.10 *The structure has been placed on the right line according to the rule of thirds. Photo by Megan Jaeger; 50mm lens; Canon EOS Rebel T3i.*

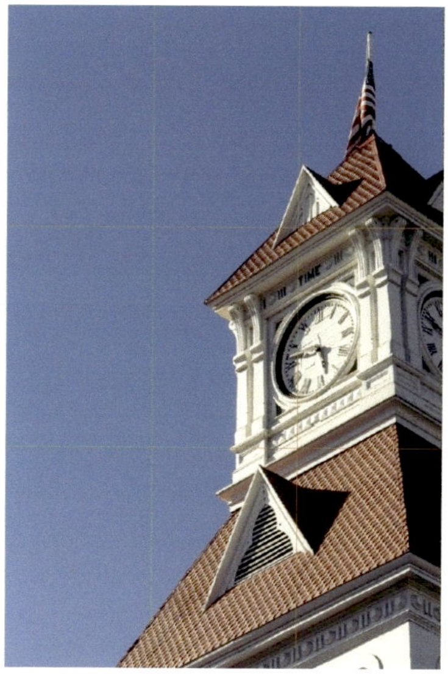

FIGURE 13.11 *The structure has been placed in the center. Photo by Megan Jaeger; 50mm lens; Canon EOS Rebel T3i.*

PART 4—RULE OF THIRDS #2

Identify a unique object and photograph it in the following three ways:

1. Centered on one of the four line intersections according to the rule of thirds.
2. Placed within one of the eight sectors surrounding the center.
3. Placed within the center sector of the image.

REVIEW

Compare the images in each of the four parts of this assignment to one another in an image-editing program. Try to analyze what effect the different placements of the subject have upon your relationship to the image.

ASSIGNMENT 14

Vantage Point and Point of View

"A good photograph is knowing where to stand."

—Ansel Adams

PURPOSE: TO SHOW THE DIFFERENCE BETWEEN VANTAGE POINT AND POINT OF VIEW.

PART 1

- Use a slightly wide-angle lens, approximately 28mm to 35mm.
- Find a friend—if you don't have a friend, buy somebody lunch. After lunch have them sit on the ground.

1. Lie on your back in front or slightly to one side of them and get as close as you can. Focus on your subject's eyes and photograph them from a worm's-eye view.
2. Kneel in front of them so that your camera is level with their eyes. Have them look directly into the lens. Focus on their eyes and photograph them from their eye level.
3. Remain kneeling and repeat #2, only this time have them look anywhere except into the lens—up, down, to the side.
4. Stand up and photograph them from a bird's-eye view.

REVIEW

When you change your point of view, you change your relationship to your subject—and the viewer's relationship to the subject. Point of view is one of the ways we show how we feel about a person.

1. What do you, as the viewer, feel when you look up at the subject?
2. What do you, as the viewer, feel when you look down on the subject?
3. What do you feel when you look at your subject from their eye level?
4. What difference does it make if they are looking away or towards you?

PART 2

Locate a building that you can photograph from the roof or upper floor of a facing building. If you are on campus you may find buildings that meet this requirement facing each other across a quad.

1. Stand as close as you can—without blocking foot traffic—in front of the entrance of the building facing the target building—that's your vantage point. Your point of view is eye level.

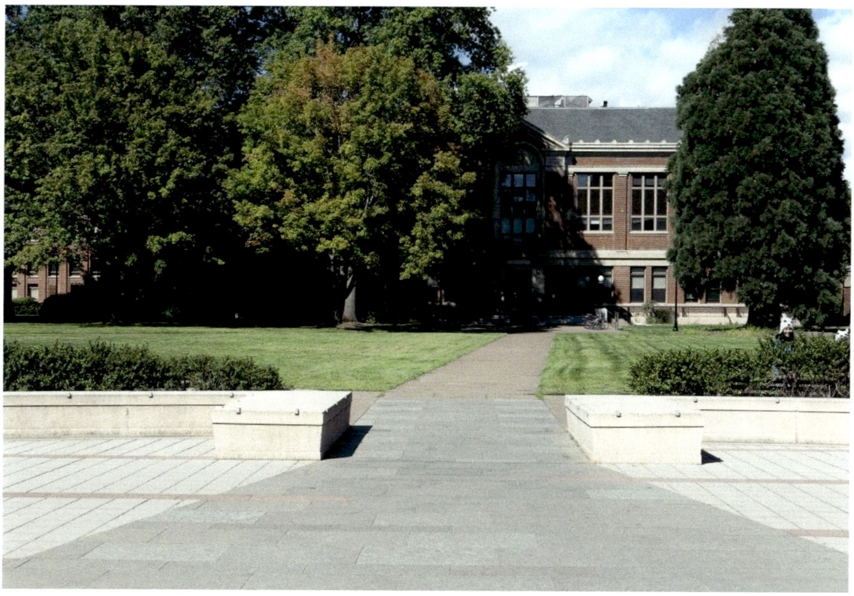

FIGURE 14.1 *The first photo was taken from ground level using a normal focal-length lens.*

2. Enter the building behind you and photograph the target building from the roof or the highest floor possible. Your vantage point is approximately the same as in #1 but your point of view has changed.

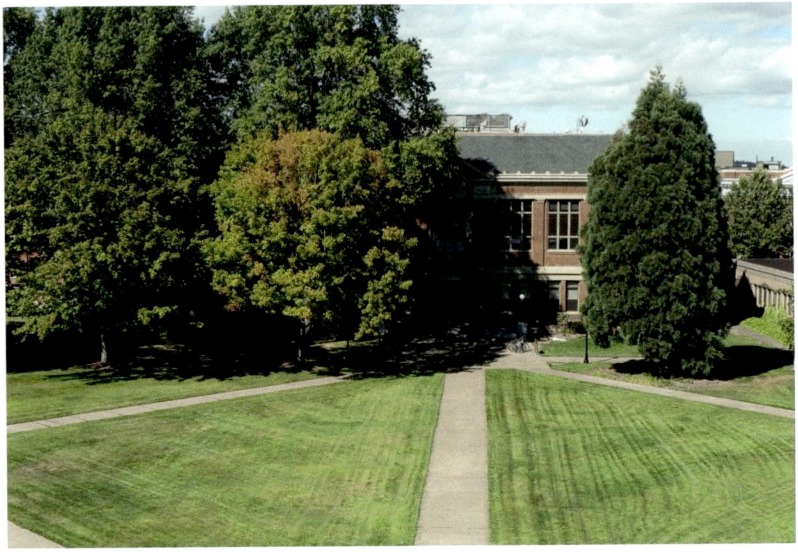

FIGURE 14.2 *The second image was taken from the sixth floor of the building across the quad from the target building. The vantage point has hardly changed but the point of view has changed significantly.*

3. Return to ground level and walk approximately half the distance towards the target building and photograph it from eye level. Where you are standing is your vantage point; your point of view is eye level.

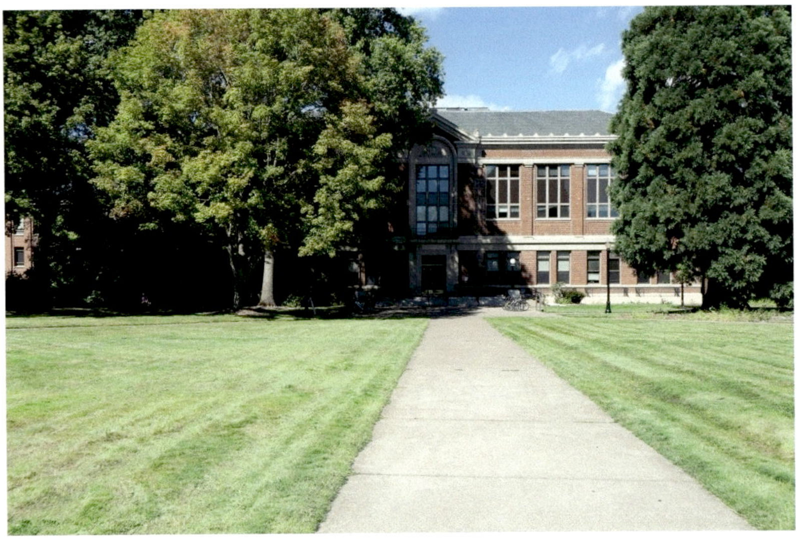

FIGURE 14.3 *The third image was made approximately halfway to the target building. The point of view is eye level. The result is boring.*

4. Sit or lie on the ground and photograph the building from the same vantage point. Your point of view is now worm's eye.

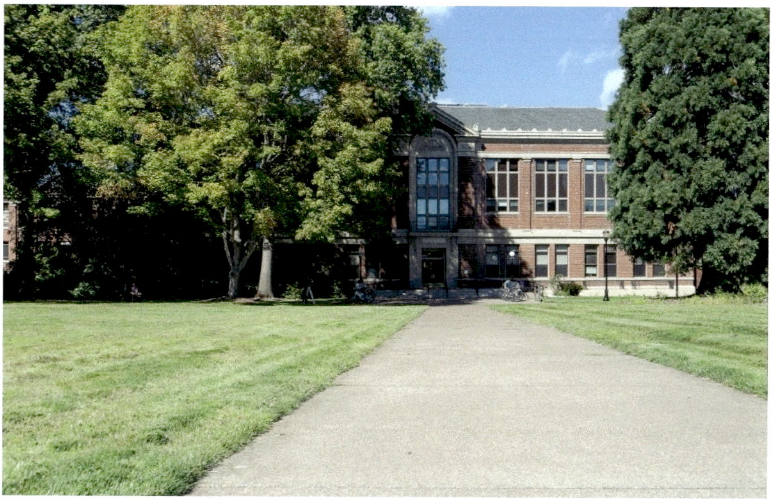

FIGURE 14.4 *Sitting on the ground at the same distance has little effect on the image. However, due to the sidewalk being wider, the diagonal lines converge more dramatically, causing this image to appear more dynamic.*

5. Walk close up to the building and photograph straight ahead. Your point of view is eye level.

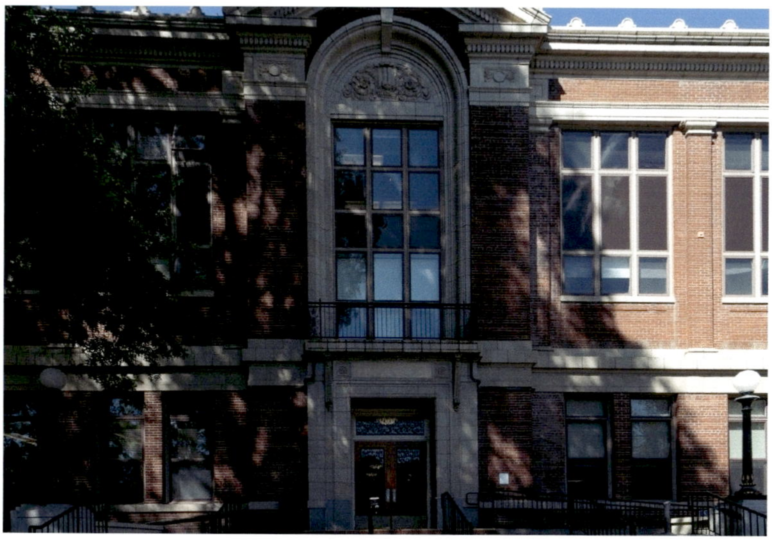

FIGURE 14.5 *This photo is from a vantage point directly in front of the building with an eye-level point of view.*

6. Aim the camera up; try to capture some sky if possible. Your vantage point has remained the same but your point of view is now worm's eye.

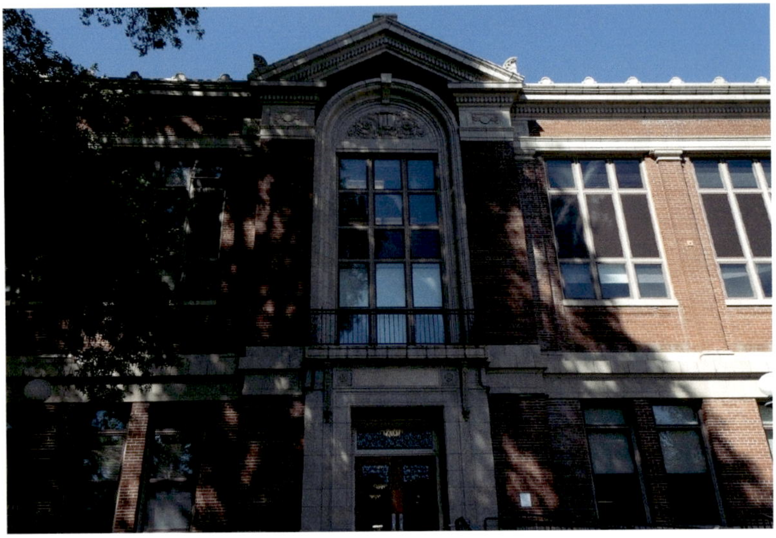

FIGURE 14.6 *From this close to the subject, looking up changes the point of view without changing the vantage point.*

7. For the last image move to either corner of the building at approximately the same distance as image #6. Aim up to include some sky.

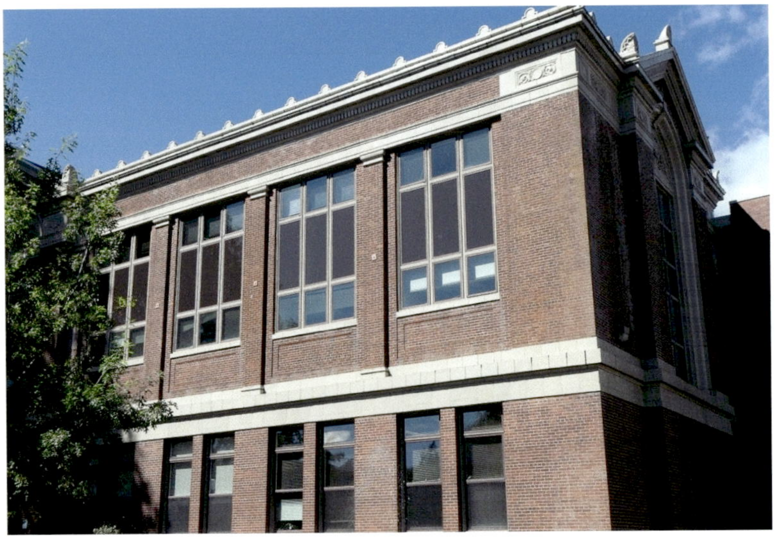

FIGURE 14.7 *In this image the vantage point has changed but the point of view is the same as in image #6.*

REVIEW

Notice the farther away you are from any subject, the more you need to change your elevation in order to change your point of view. When you are at a distance you have to physically relocate to a higher elevation to make an obvious difference in point of view.

In the second set of images, halfway to the target, standing or sitting makes only a minor difference in point of view. However, due to the sidewalk being wider, the diagonal lines converge more dramatically, causing this image to appear more dynamic.

When you move close to the target building all you have to do to change your point of view is look up.

In the last image, made from the building corner, even though you are photographing the exact same building, you have made a major change in the vantage point while maintaining the worm's-eye view of image #6.

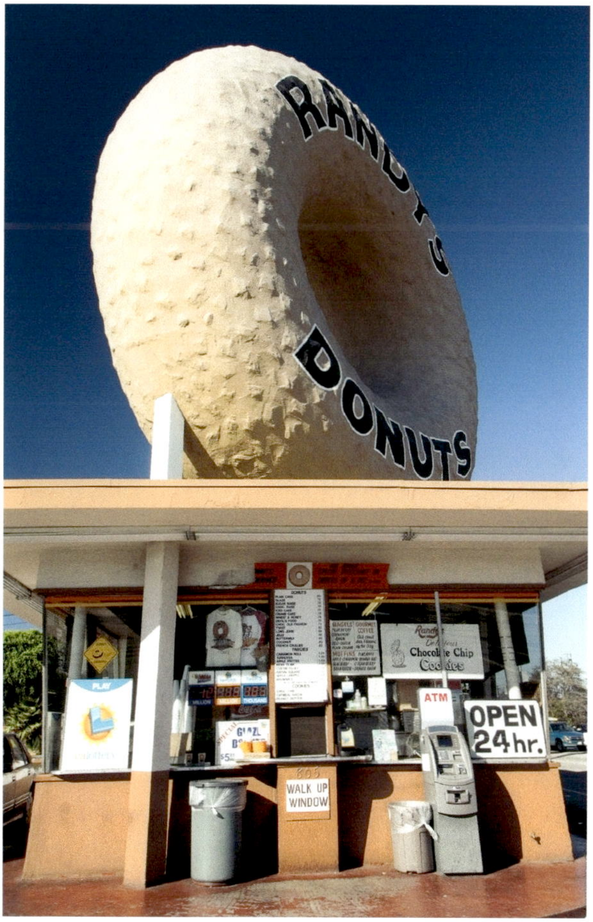

FIGURE 14.8 *Randy's Donuts, Los Angeles. Nikon D700, 24mm lens, f/22 at 1/160.*

ASSIGNMENT 15

The Art of Seeing

Contributed by Mary Ellen Wortham
Photography Instructor, Fillmore High School

> *"I really believe there are things nobody would see if I didn't photograph them."*
> —Diane Arbus

PURPOSE: TO PRACTICE THE ART OF SEEING.

Photography is a visual, non-verbal art form, a medium of observation. Photographers are skilled in observing what is before them, finding meaningful connections, and dismissing muddle. Iconic American documentary photographer Dorothea Lange saw the camera as an instructional device for teaching people how to *see* without a camera. *Photography* for Lange was a product of total attention.

Through mindful and habitual practice, you can cultivate the discerning eye of a skilled photographer, and affect a shift in how you engage with the world.

EQUIPMENT

For this assignment use a normal focal-length lens—no zoom, wide-angle or telephoto lens is to be employed in this assignment.

SELECT A LOCATION

Scout a location you find interesting, one that draws you in for whatever the reason. The location can be indoors or outdoors: an alley, a bustling city street, a public courtyard, private garden, bedroom, kitchen, or the counter at a local diner. Stop and observe. Take careful measure of the setting: buildings, plants, objects; people alone, walking, visiting, sitting on the grass or benches, etc. Discipline your site examination—pre-visualize your photos through an imaginary viewfinder.

YOUR STUDIO

Having selected a location, you will now define the dimensions of your studio.

Place one foot on the ground; be mindful of this simple task as once your foot is positioned you are committed. For the duration of this assignment, your foot anchors or rotates on this exact spot. The geometric body-length sphere around your anchor foot—360 degrees around, above, and below, defines your studio. Yes, tall students have the advantage over those height-challenged, as long legs define larger studios.

IMAGE CAPTURE

1. Take ten photographs—no more, no less; no re-dos; no file deletion (honor system). Each release of the shutter counts as one image towards your collection of ten.
2. Compose full-frame—the image you frame and record is exactly as you intend your final photograph, i.e., no post-production cropping.
3. Each image differs significantly from the other nine.

When watching professional photographers in the field, it is readily apparent how they make full use of their bodies while working. Paraphrasing the sentiments of photojournalist Ernst Haas: The most important lens you have is your legs—the best wide-angle is taking a step back. We were given joints for a reason—use them. Explore photographic possibilities by stretching, turning, bending, stooping, shrinking, twisting, and straining your body. Change your point of view: bird's eye; worm's eye; side, long, close; etc.

Remember as you work your site, photography is a medium of observation. Stated in slightly different fashion—photography is at once the *art of seeing* and the *art of elimination*. Zero in on your subject; leave no doubt in the viewer's mind which visual element is of greatest import to you—the heavy-lifter of your message.

Photograph for simplicity, i.e., subject + context. Include in your frame only that surrounding which connects and communicates something about your subject. Any visual element that does not advance audience understanding of your subject, must be eliminated from your photo.

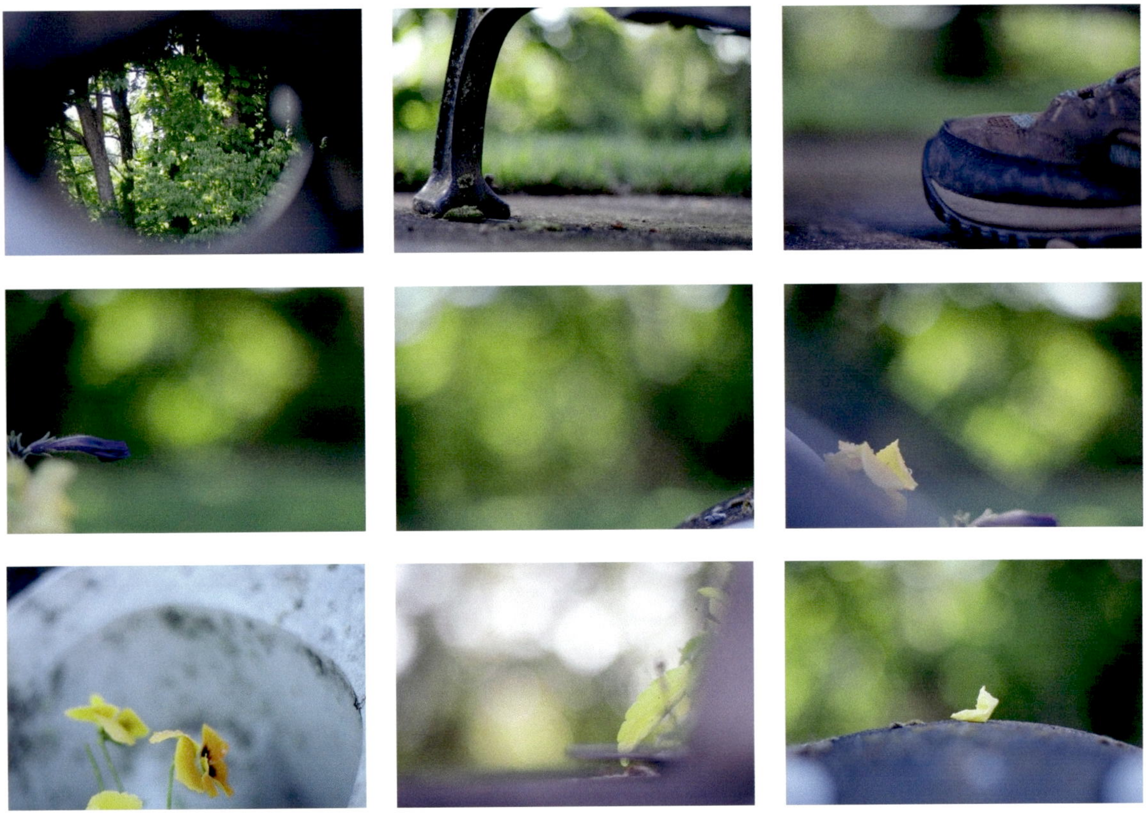

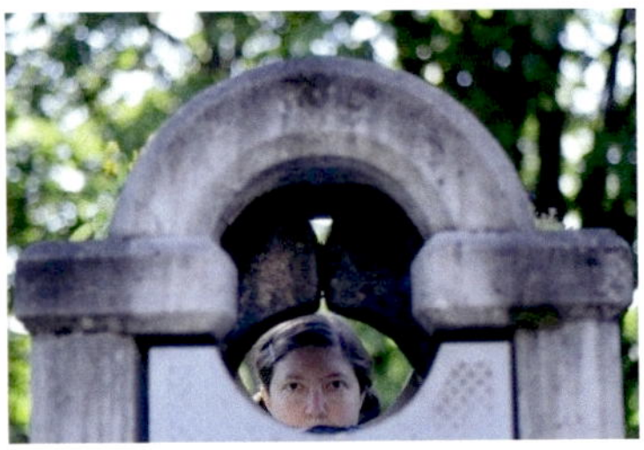

FIGURE 15.1–10 *The ten images in this collection were chosen from those submitted by Michael for his Significant Photo project. Photos by Michael Paulsen.*

ASSIGNMENT 16

Lines and Shapes

"Photographing a cake can be art"

—Irving Penn

PURPOSE: TO IDENTIFY LINES AND GEOMETRICAL SHAPES.

LINES

1. Produce a series of photographs for each of the four basic lines: horizontal, vertical, diagonal, and curved. While other lines may be present, it should be obvious to the viewer which of the three lines is dominant in the image.

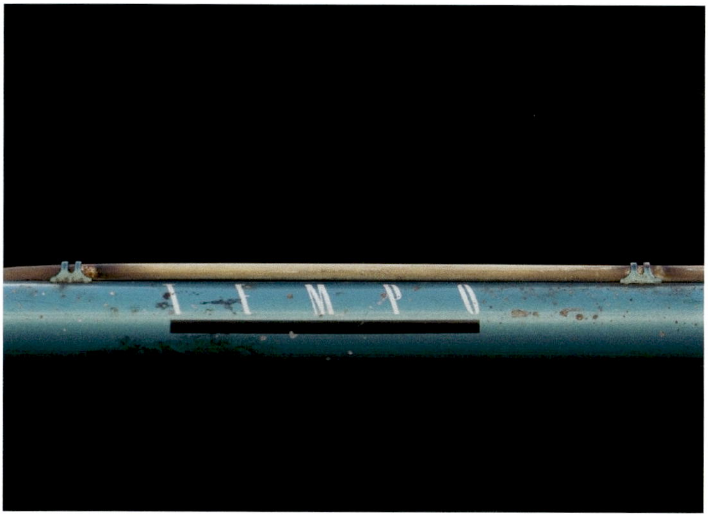

FIGURE 16.1 *Photo by Aaron Davis; 65mm lens; Canon EOS Rebel T3i.*

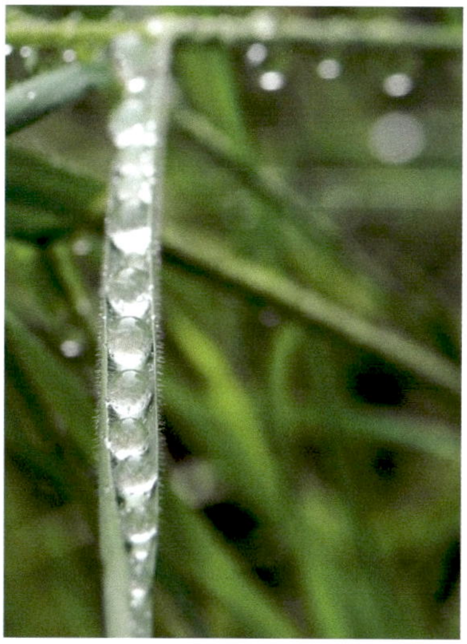

FIGURE 16.2 *Photo by Brandi Dawson; 21mm lens; Canon Coolpix P100.*

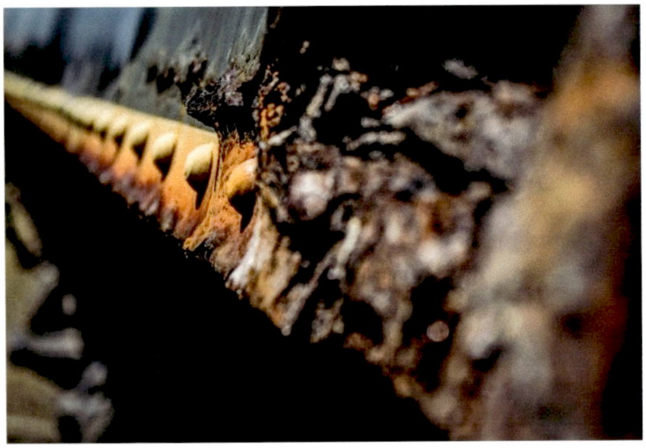

FIGURE 16.3 *Photo by Brandi Dawson; 40mm lens; Canon EOS Rebel T3.*

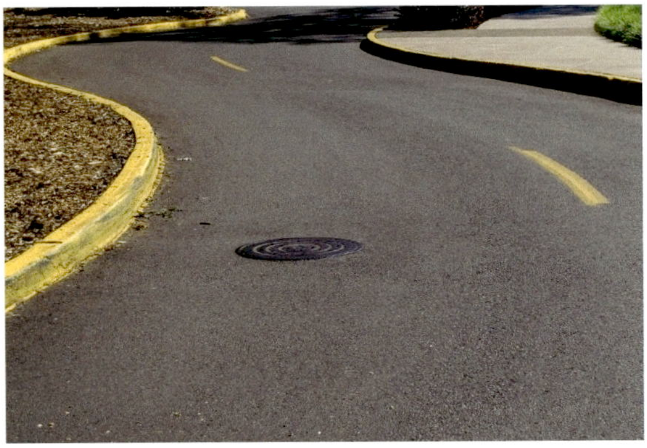

FIGURE 16.4 *Photo by Thiago Moreira Da Silva; 30mm lens; Nikon D5100.*

2. Create at least three images with implied or suggested lines.

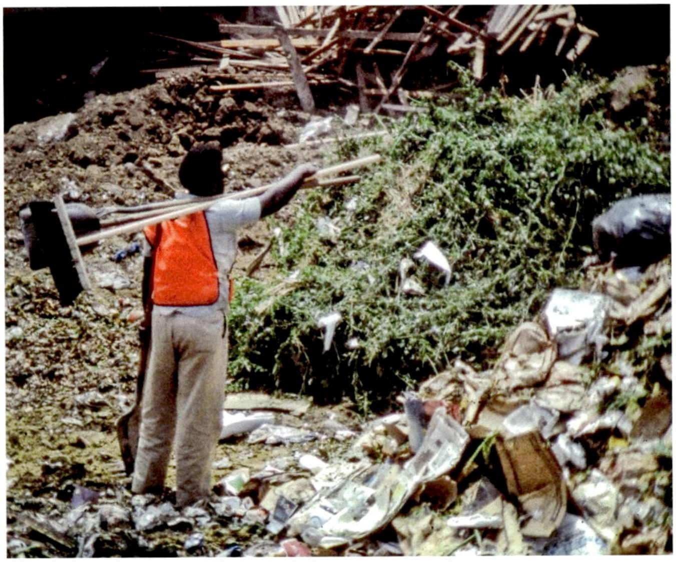

FIGURE 16.5 *The line of the broom handles lead the viewer into the image.*

REVIEW

Identify the line that you intended to be dominant in each image. Were you successful in making clear to the viewer which line was meant to be dominant?

Identify the implied or suggested line you meant to create. Were you successful in making the implied line visible?

SHAPES

1. Create a series of images that contain circles.

    - Round shapes that appear as ellipses.

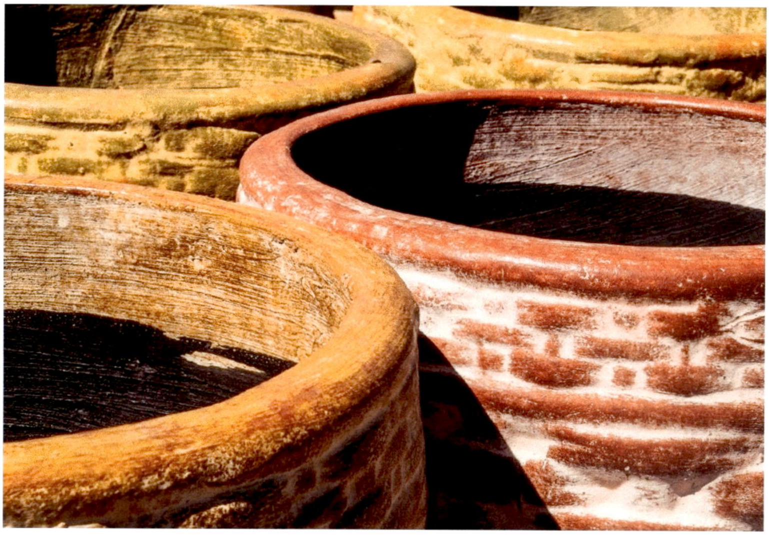

FIGURE 16.6 *Round shapes photographed as ellipses.*

- Repeating circles

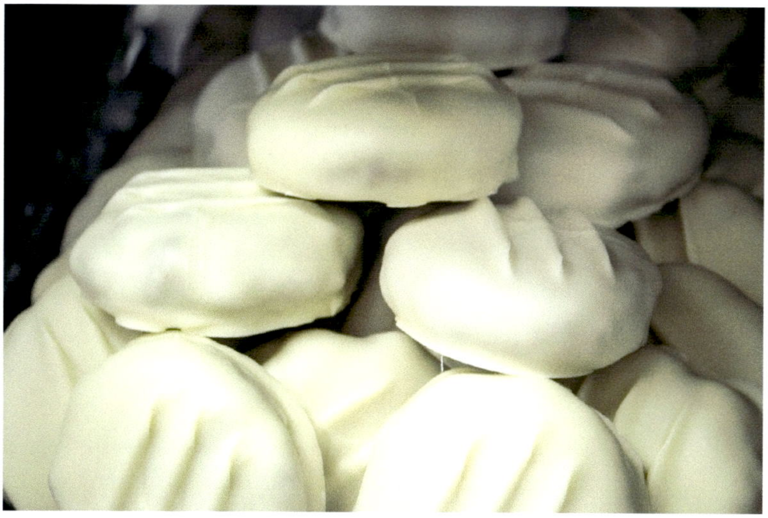

FIGURE 16.7 *Repeating Circles. Photo by Martha Baker; 55mm lens; Canon EOS Rebel T3.*

- Partially obscured

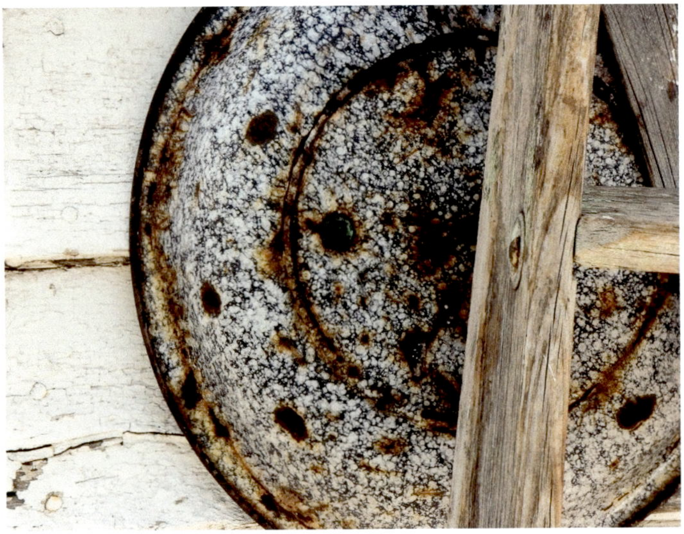

FIGURE 16.8 *Partially obscured circle.*

2. Find as many geometrical shapes as you can and create a photograph for each one that clearly shows them as the subject of the image.

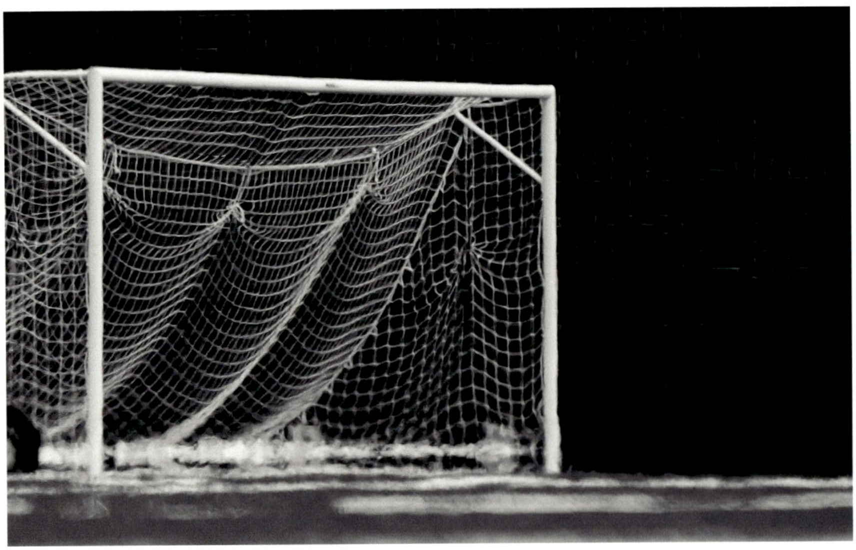

FIGURE 16.9 *Rectangle. Photo by Andie Gildersleeve; 240mm lens; Nikon D5100.*

3. Combine two or more geometrical shapes and create a photograph that clearly shows one of the shapes as being dominant.

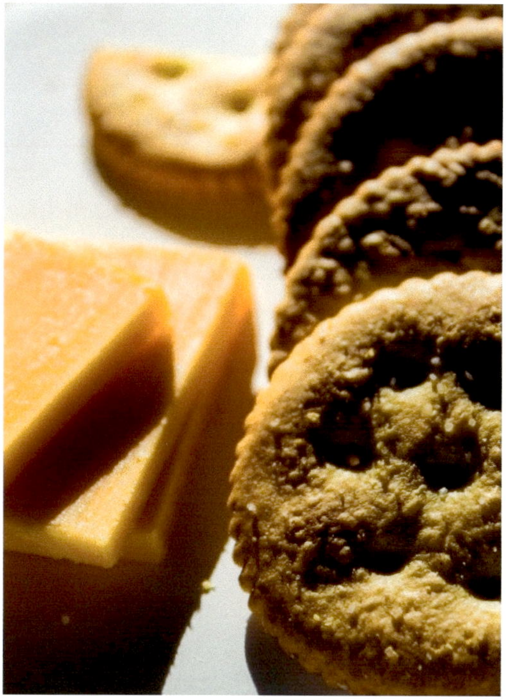

FIGURE 16.10 *Triangles, squares, and circles. Photo by Martha Baker; 55mm lens; Canon EOS Rebel T3.*

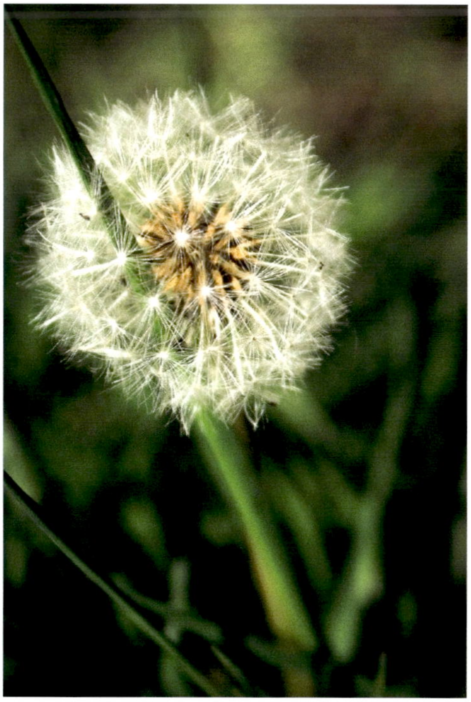

4. Create a series of photographs that feature implied shapes made from points, lines, or edges of objects.

FIGURE 16.11 *Implied circle. Photo by Dianni Freeman; 45mm lens; Canon EOS Rebel T3.*

ASSIGNMENT 17

Patterns and Textures

"When I photograph, what I'm really doing is seeking answers to things."
—Wynn Bullock

PURPOSE: TO IDENTIFY PATTERNS AND TEXTURES.

For this assignment, it is recommended that you use a zoom with macro capabilities.

PART 1—PATTERNS

Zoom the lens all the way out to the longest focal length and walk around your home or apartment. Look for as many patterns as you can on or around the structure and fill the frame with them. Avoid anything with a point-of-interest, and allow the patterns to run off the edges.

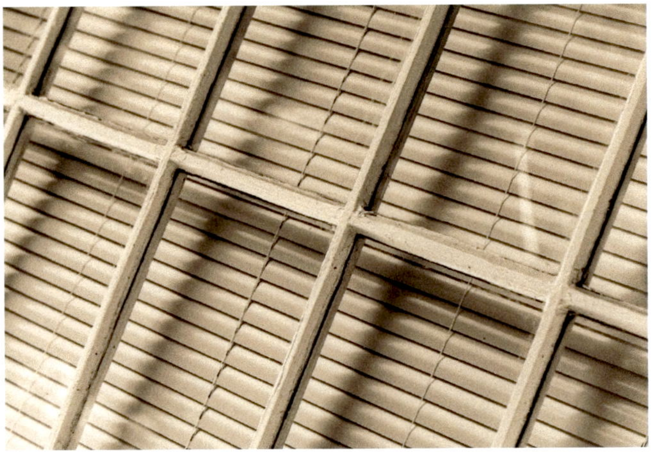

FIGURE 17.1 *Patterns exist everywhere. A diagonal pattern of window-and-blinds.*

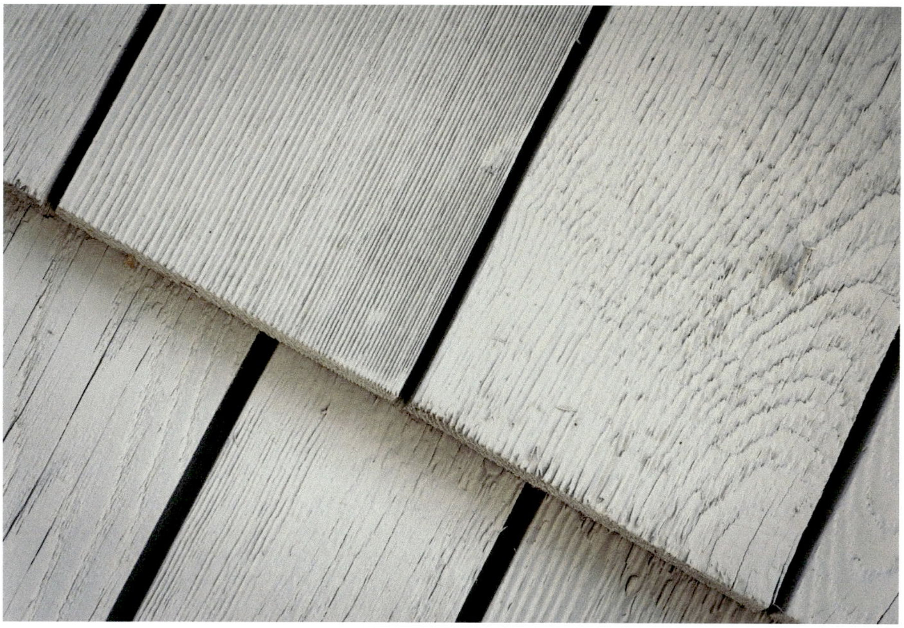

FIGURE 17.2 *Next to the window was this pattern of shingles.*

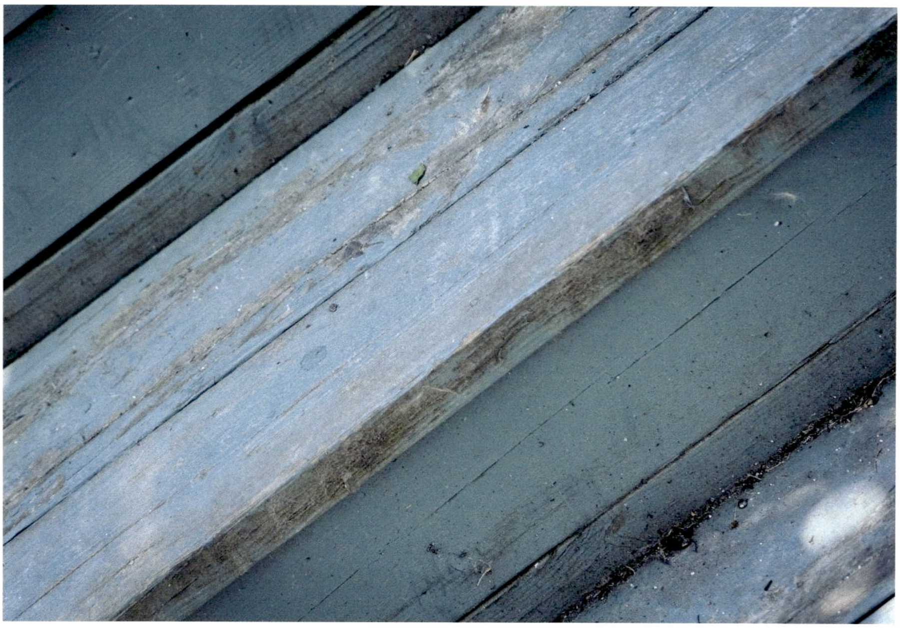

FIGURE 17.3 *A few feet away is this pattern of wooden steps.*

PART 2—TEXTURES

Repeat Part 1, only this time if the lens has macro capabilities, enable them. If it doesn't, then zoom out to the longest focal length and move in as close as you can to the subject. Look for textures that include a point of interest.

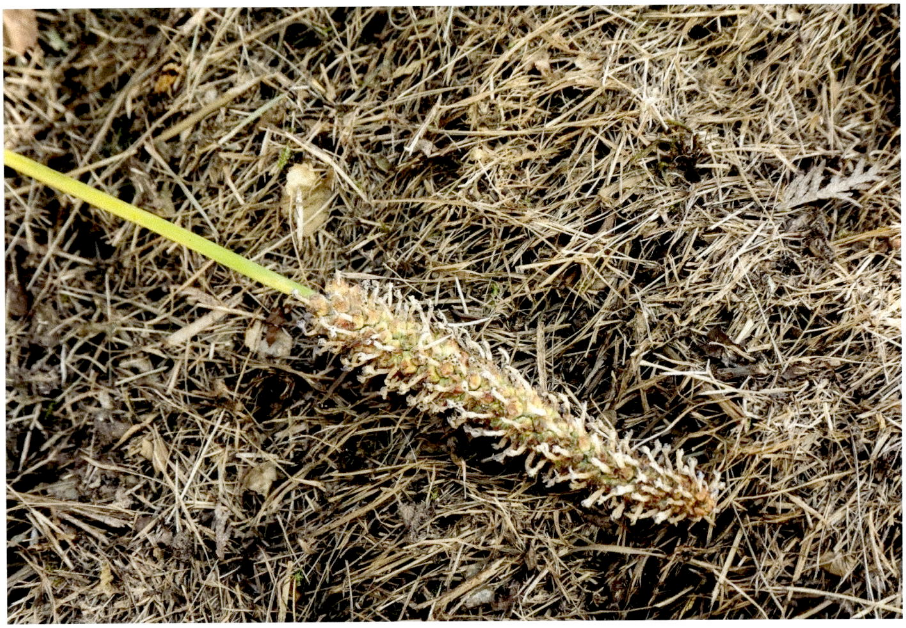

FIGURE 17.4 *This photograph of a dead primula stalk on dried grass is filled with texture.*

ASSIGNMENT 18

The Ten-Step Program

"A camera is a tool for learning how to see without a camera."

—Diane Arbus

PURPOSE: TO LEARN FRAMING AND POSITIONING.

Photography is the art of seeing. You need to slow down, look, and observe. Photographer Harry Callahan made it a practice to take his camera on a walk through his neighborhood every day. He would not return home until he had photographed something he had never seen, or photographed something in a different way than he had before.

For this assignment, start at the corner of a city block that has buildings that intrigue you. Alternatively you could begin on the corner of a street with homes—preferably not track homes that all look the same!

Slowly turn in a circle and look at everything that can be seen: buildings, plants, objects; people walking, visiting, sitting on the grass, at bus stops, etc.

Once you have completed your circle, begin photographing everything of visual interest to you. Remember that photography is the art of isolation—zero in on specific subjects; try not to include anything not connected to the subject you are photographing; try not to repeat yourself. For this assignment *do not photograph any part of yourself* (you can do that in Assignment 15—The Art of Seeing).

When you have exhausted all of the photographic possibilities, take ten steps forward along the block and do it again. Photograph as many things as possible as you photographed from the previous position, and anything new and interesting that has come into view.

As you move closer to specific subjects make it a point to kneel, sit, or lie on the ground in order to change your point of view and re-photograph them. If you pass by a bench or low wall, stand on it and make use of the new point of view.

Repeat this until you come to the end of the block to complete the Ten-Step Program.

Below are a few of the photos taken on the Ten-Step Program.

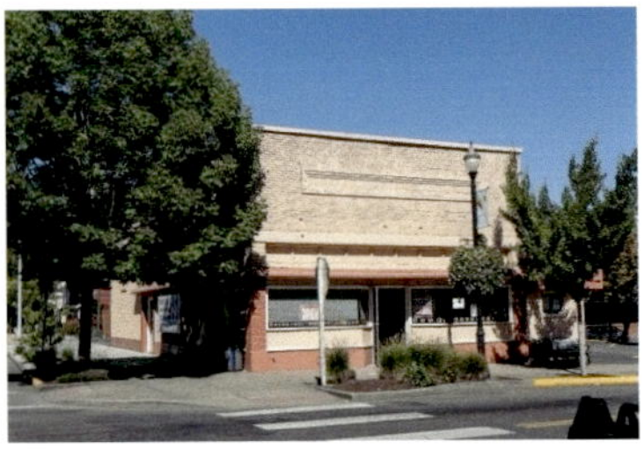

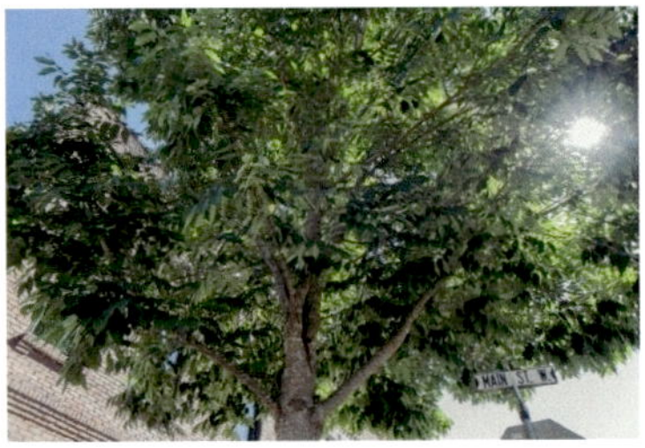

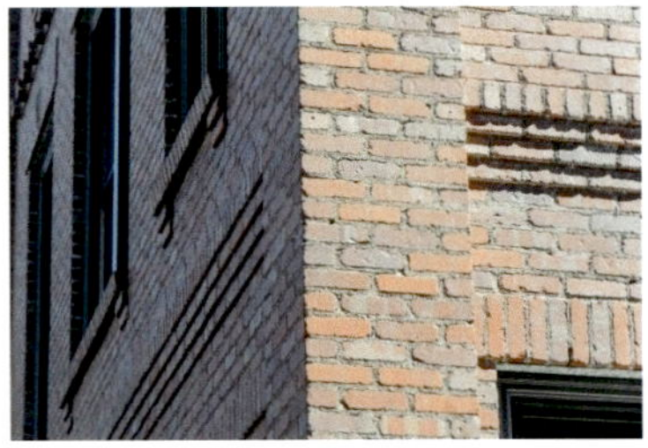

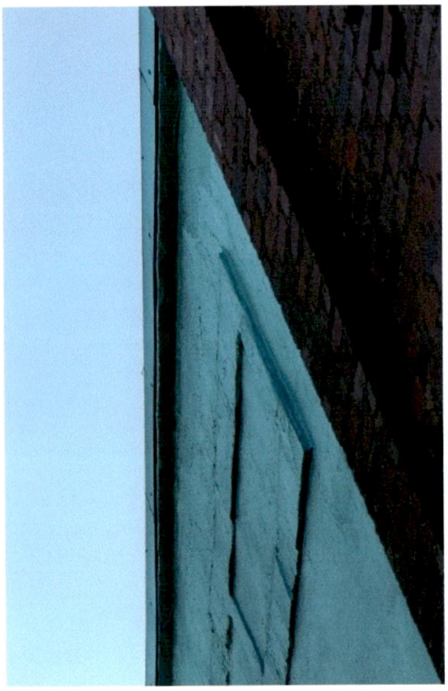

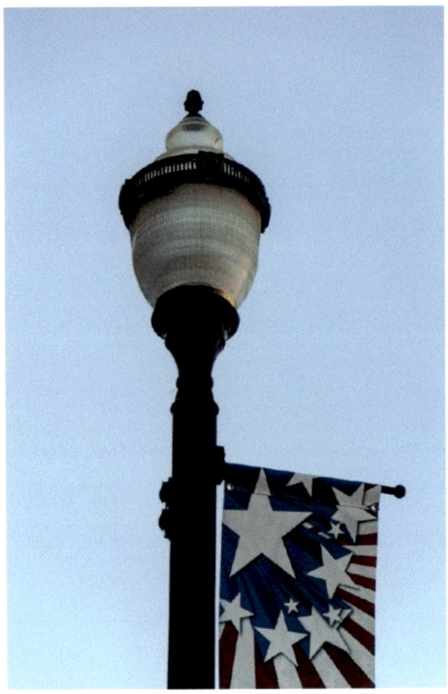

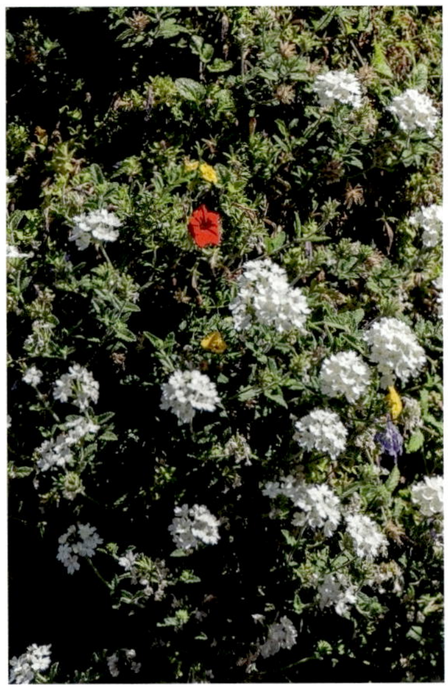

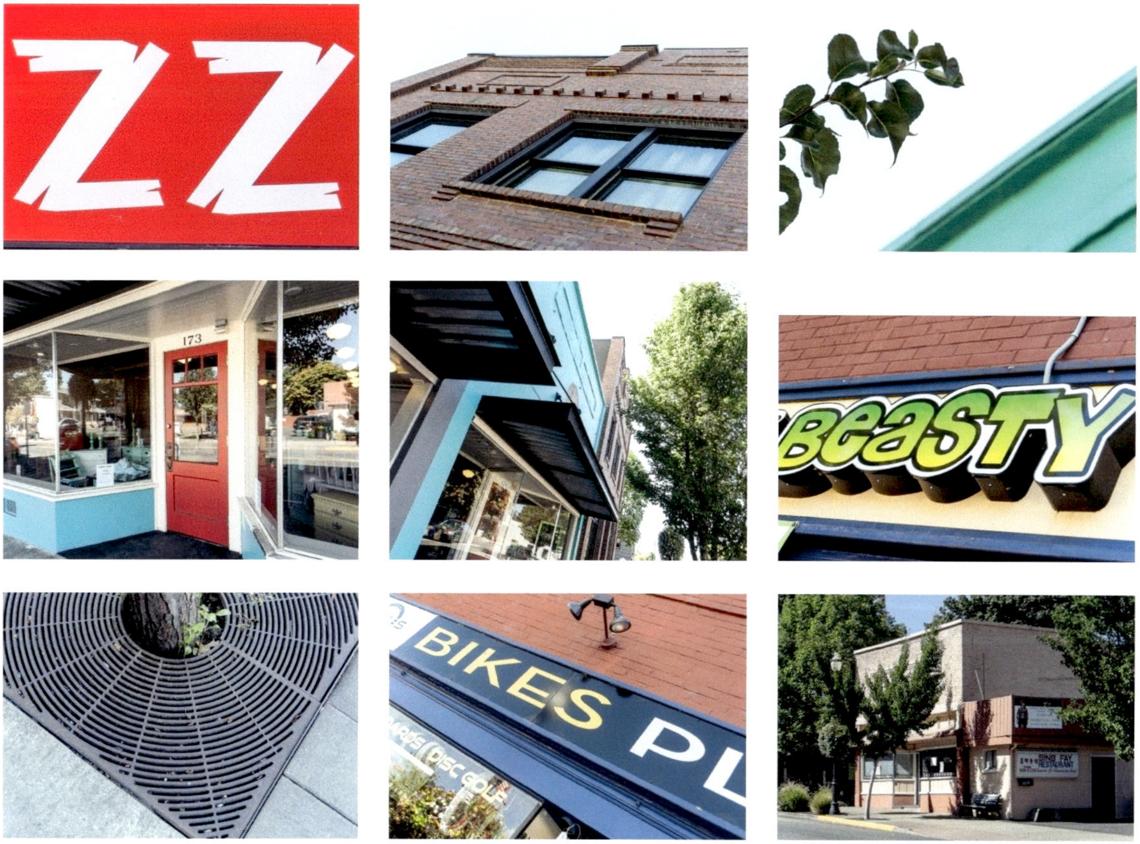
ZZ
173
BEASTY
BIKES PL
DISC GOLF

ASSIGNMENT 19

Pure Colors

"We are making photographs to understand what our lives mean to us."
—Ralph Hattersley

PURPOSE: TO RECOGNIZE AND PHOTOGRAPH PURE COLORS.

PART 1

For this assignment, you will need to locate six distinct compositions, one each of the three primary and three secondary colors: red, orange, yellow, green, blue, and violet. As much as possible try to avoid having other colors appear in each image. Retain texture and shadows so that the subject will be recognizable.

Any lens can be used for this project but you will find it easier if you can use either a macro lens or close-up diopter filters (a set of three or four filters can be purchased on eBay for $20 or less at the time of this writing) to isolate small areas.

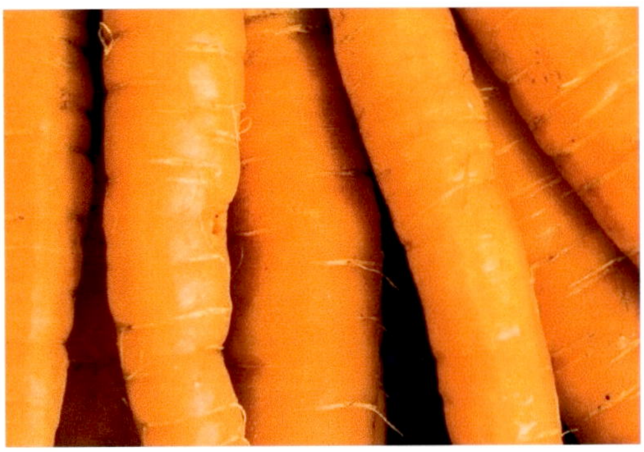

FIGURE 19.1 *By moving in close, the photographer was able to isolate the color. Photo by Megan Jaeger; 50mm lens; Canon EOS Rebel T3i.*

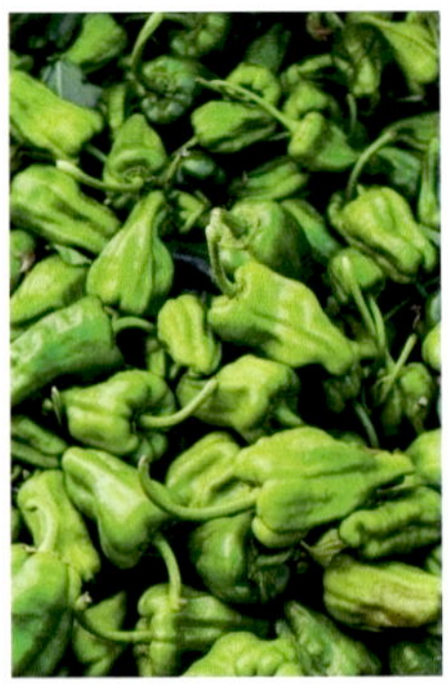

FIGURE 19.2 *Photo by Megan Jaeger; 18mm lens; Canon EOS Rebel T3i.*

PART 2

Create one photo for each of the following:

1. Dominant color. The subject should have one dominant color.

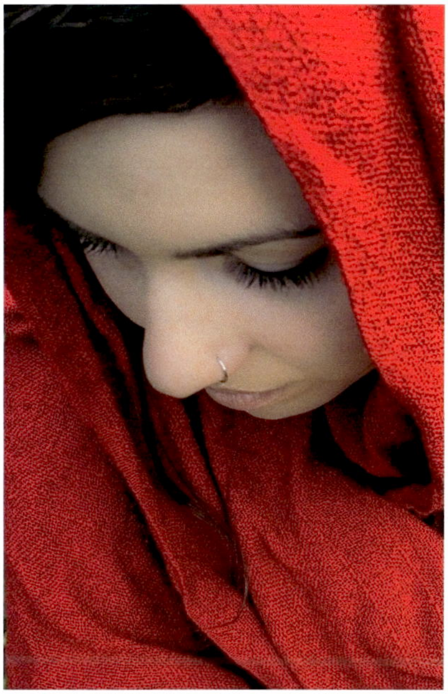

FIGURE 19.3 *Red is clearly the dominant color in this image. Photo by Megan Jaeger; 18mm lens; Canon EOS Rebel T3i.*

2. Juxtaposition. Juxtapose two complementary colors (red and green; blue and yellow, etc.).

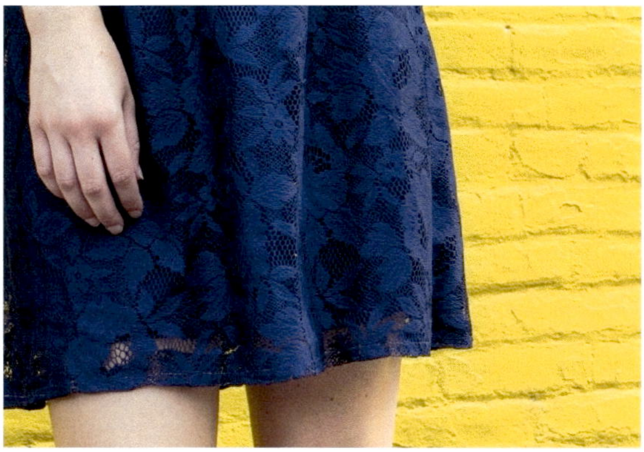

FIGURE 19.4 *Even though the color blue appears in the foreground, the saturated yellow bricks appear to move forward and dominate. Photo by Megan Jaeger; 40mm lens; Canon EOS Rebel T3i.*

3. Color harmony. Find two colors that work together harmoniously.

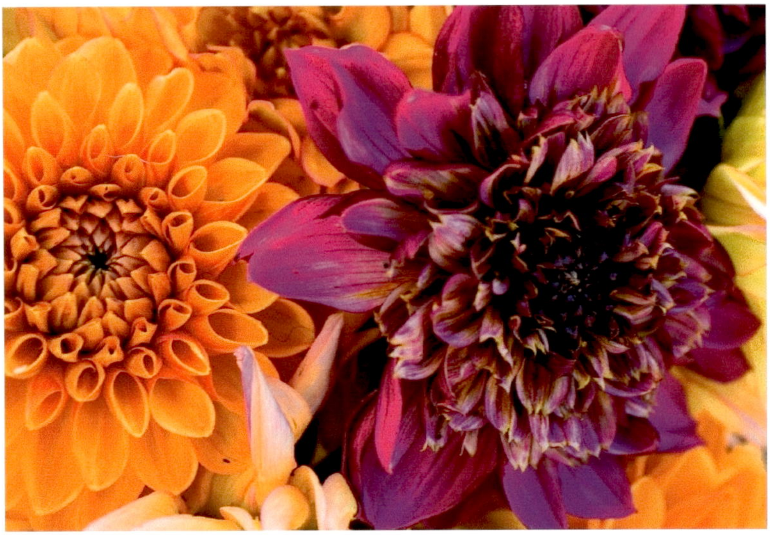

FIGURE 19.5 *Orange and fuchsia are close enough on the color wheel that they harmonize in this photo, with the orange slightly dominant. Photo by Megan Jaeger; 30mm lens; Canon EOS Rebel T3i.*

4. Color accents. Place colorful elements in two or more of the golden sectors, or on the intersection of the lines created by the rule of thirds.

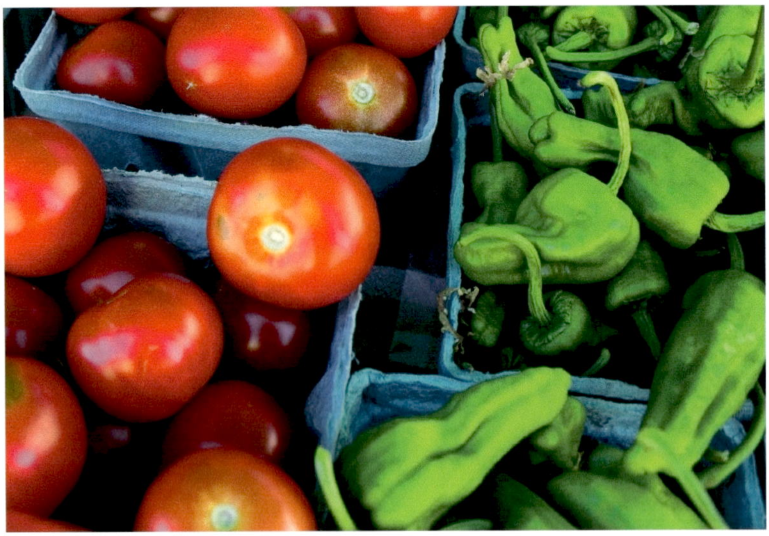

FIGURE 19.6 *Red and green have been placed on the intersections of the rule of thirds and within the golden sectors. Photo by Megan Jaeger; 18mm lens; Canon EOS Rebel T3i.*

ASSIGNMENT 20

Neutral Colors

"I think good dreaming is what leads to good photographs."

—Wayne Miller

PURPOSE: TO RECOGNIZE NEUTRAL COLORS.

Black, white, and gray are no-hue colors. Black is a low-value, no-hue color; gray is an intermediate-value, no-hue color; and white is a high-value, no-hue color. Developing a visual awareness of color needs to include an awareness of these three no-hue colors.

For this assignment locate as many subjects as you can that are predominantly black, white, or gray. Other colors may be present, but the three neutrals should predominate. Try to include some areas of gray as reference for white subjects, and as transitional tones for black subjects.

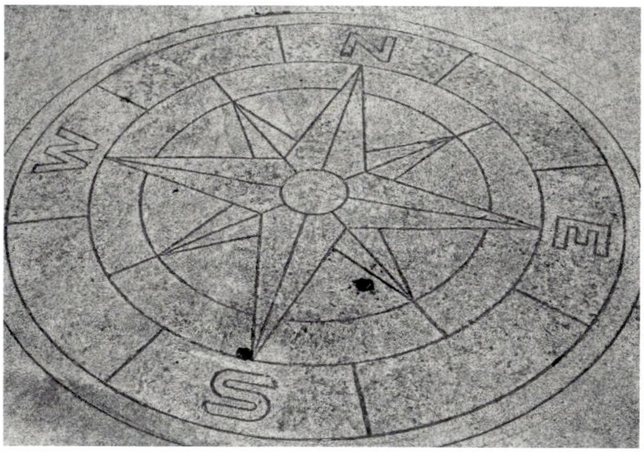

FIGURE 20.1 *Photo by Martha Baker.*

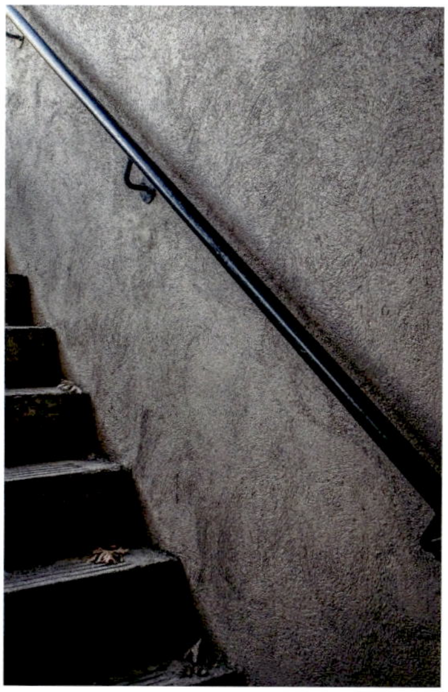

FIGURE 20.2 *Photo by Brandi Dawson.*

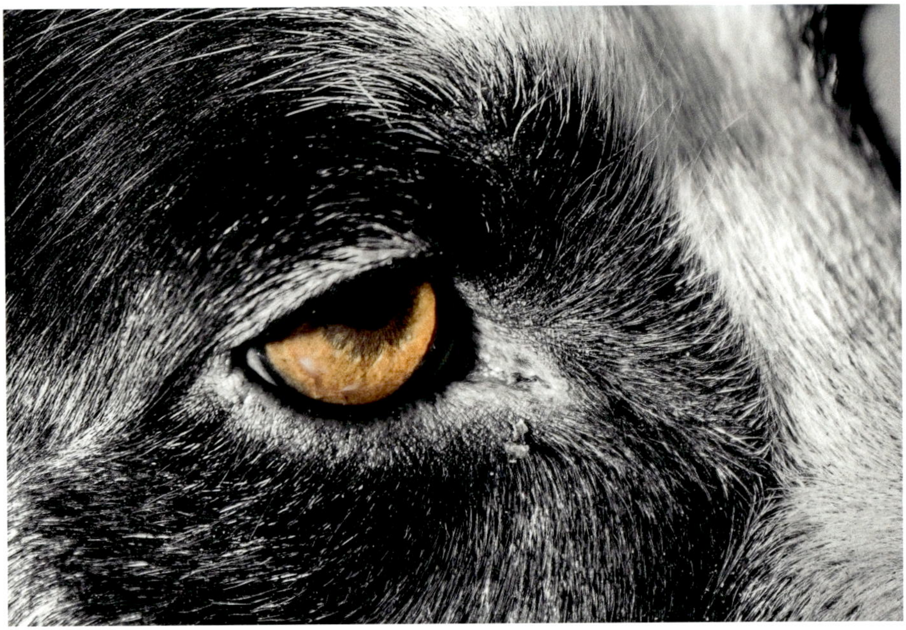

FIGURE 20.3 *Photo by Brandi Dawson.*

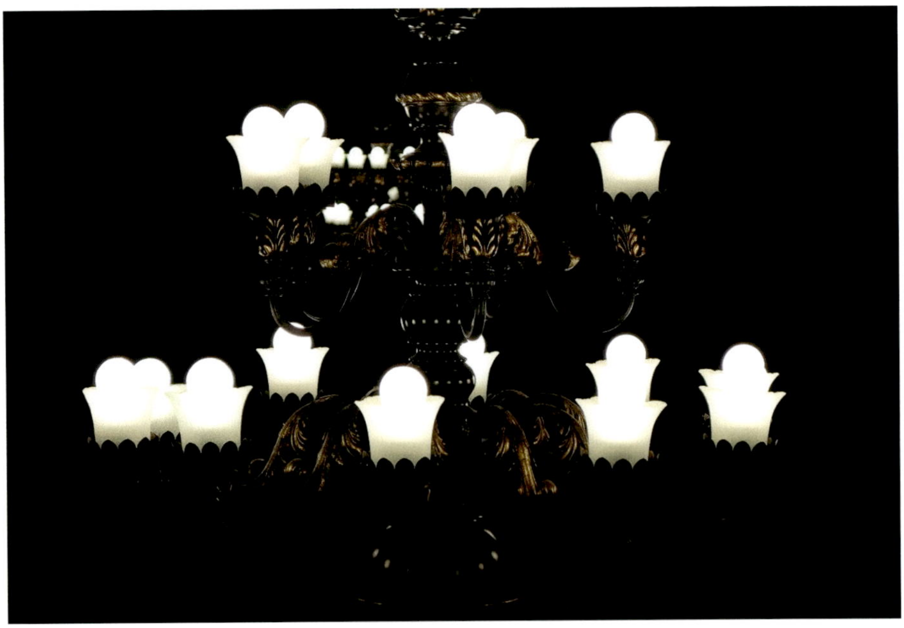

FIGURE 20.4 *Photo by Thiago Moreira Da Silva.*

ASSIGNMENT 21

Symbols

"Photography is truth."

—Jean-Luc Godard

PURPOSE: TO RECOGNIZE AND USE SYMBOLS TO COMMUNICATE AN IDEA.

PART 1

Find and photograph as many symbols as you can to illustrate each of the following themes:

1. Power.
2. Wealth.
3. Patriotism.
4. A symbol of your choice.

Try to be as original as possible in order to avoid clichés.

PART 2

Choose one or more symbols from Part 1 and associate them with a product. Create a photograph of the product in a way that associates it with the symbol (Jaguar has already been taken—find something else). You can do this in-camera or by creating a composite with software such as onOne.

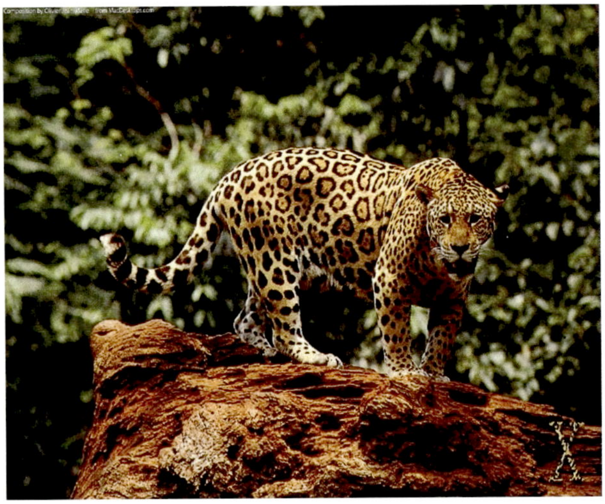

FIGURE 21.1 *The jaguar cat is sleek and a symbol of power and speed.*

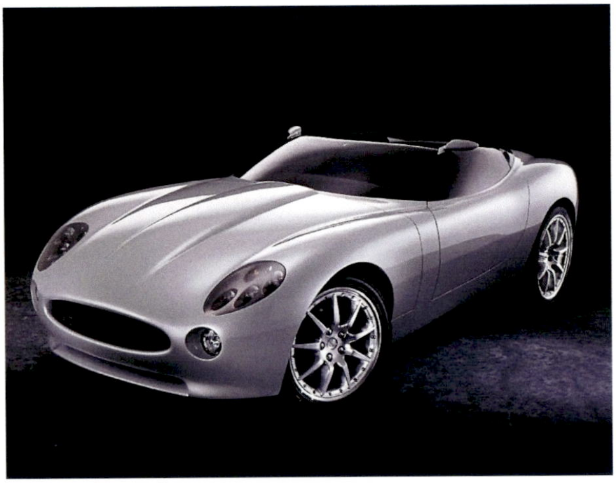

FIGURE 21.2 *By itself the Jaguar car is just another cool car photographed on a dark background.*

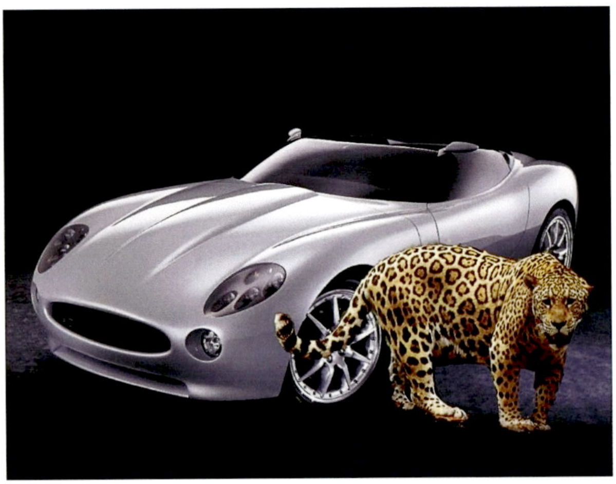

FIGURE 21.3 *Associating the car with the cat suggests that both are sleek, powerful, and fast.*

SECTION 3

Advanced

Junior

ASSIGNMENT 22

Sunrise/Sunset

"Photograph: a picture painted by the sun without instruction in art."
—Ambrose Bierce

PURPOSE: TO OBSERVE AND PHOTOGRAPH SUNLIGHT AT DIFFERENT TIMES OF DAY.

The color of daylight shifts from red/orange to blue to red/orange. These three shifts peak at sunrise, midday, and sunset.

- For this assignment, you will need to locate an outdoor scene that you can return to at least three times, and a composition you can repeat. You should scout out the location ahead of time.

To complete this assignment you only need three photographs. However, don't waste the opportunity. If it is a good location, find as many subjects as you can after you have taken the photo for the assignment.

1. Arrive as near as you can to sunrise and choose a subject/composition for your three photos. Make certain it is not a moving subject and that it will be there for the next two photos.
2. Return at or around noon and retake the same composition as in #1.
3. Return at or around sunset and retake the same composition as in #1.

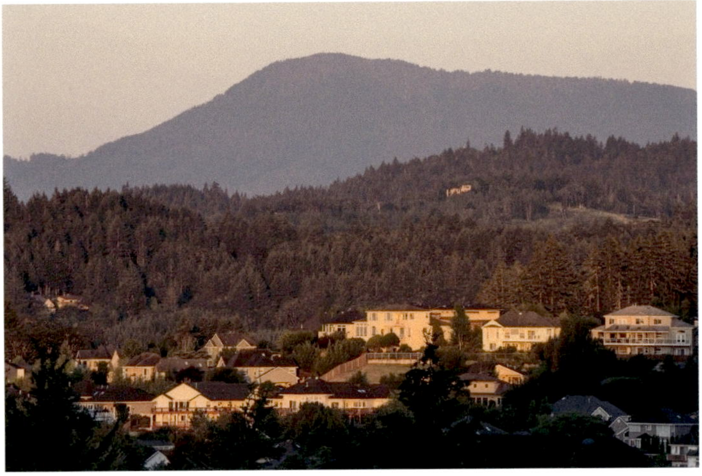

FIGURE 22.1 *Sunrise. Photo by Jacqueline Dover.*

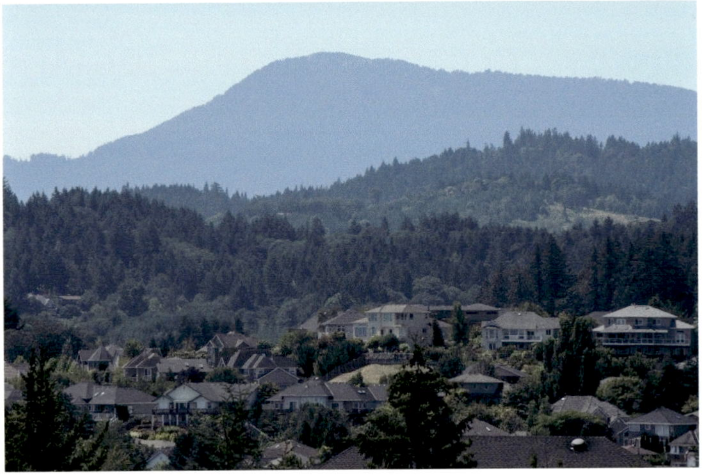

FIGURE 22.2 *Noon. Photo by Jacqueline Dover.*

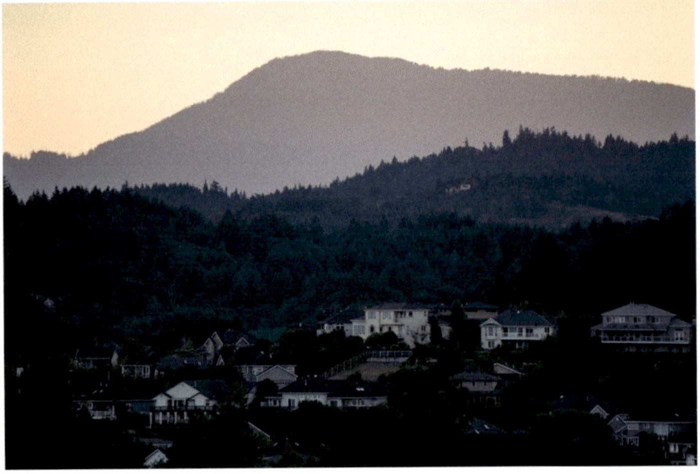

FIGURE 22.3 *Sunset. Photo by Jacqueline Dover.*

Metering Hint #1: If you do find yourself aiming into the sunrise or sunset, set your meter on manual, aim straight up at the sky, and use the meter reading you get for the scene.

Hint #2: If you are using a hand held incident light meter with a white dome, shield the dome from direct sunlight. You can do this by casting a shadow with your finger over the sun spot in the dome.

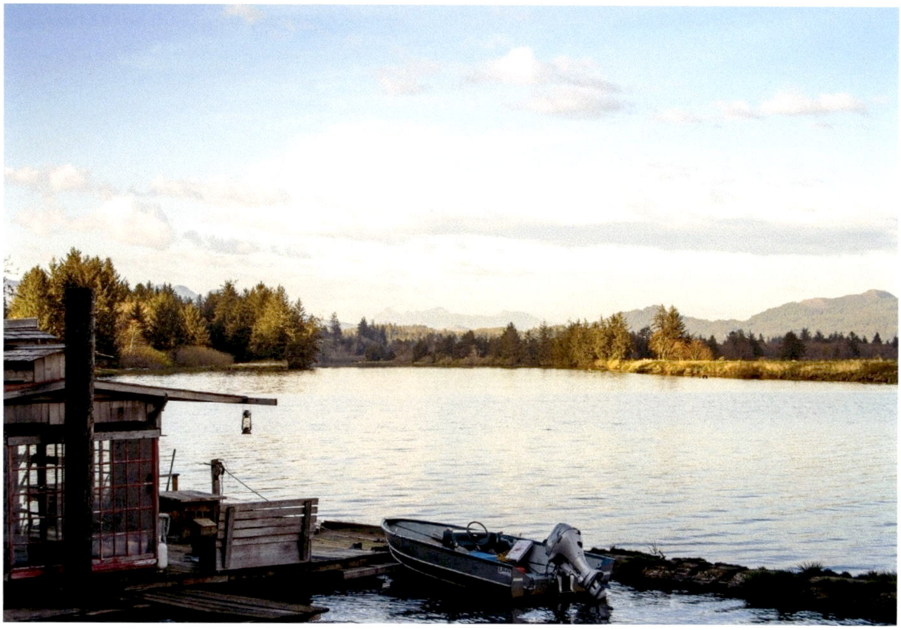

FIGURE 22.4 *The low slant of early morning light warms the grass and treetops, shadows the lake, and creates a slight magenta cast to the clouds.*

ASSIGNMENT 23

360-Degree Light

"Photography is a way of feeling, of touching, of loving. What you have caught on film is captured forever. . . It remembers little things, long after you have forgotten everything."

—Aaron Siskind

PURPOSE: TO BECOME AWARE OF LIGHT, BASED ON THE MOVEMENT OF THE SUN.

For this assignment, you need to identify a subject that doesn't move and you can walk completely around at any time of the day. It must also be in an open area where it is exposed to the sun all day long.

Anything come to mind? How about the statue of Dr. Ugodda B. Kidden, founder of your *alma mater*?

1. Arrive as soon as you can after sunrise and photograph Dr. U.B. Kidden's statue with the sunlight shining on it.
2. Move your vantage point so that the rising sun is behind Dr. Kidden. From your vantage point make a series of exposures using the following metering methods.
    a. Expose with the camera set on evaluative (matrix) or center-weighted metering.
    b. Use the exposure-compensation control on your camera to overexpose by one stop.
    c. Use the exposure-compensation control on your camera to overexpose by two stops.
    d. If your camera has a spot meter, make a fourth photo using spot metering.
    e. For the fifth photo, set the exposure mode on manual, take a meter reading of the sky directly overhead and use that reading to expose *Herr Doktor*.

3. Return when the sun is directly overhead. That would be noon without Daylight Saving Time, one p.m. during Daylight Saving Time. Photograph Dr. Kidden from a position in front, with his face showing.
4. Prior to sundown return and photograph U.B.K. from the same positions as in the morning.

REVIEW

1. Compare the four exposures—five if you used a spot meter for the fourth image. Which vantage point shows the doctor in the best light? (That was a joke; if you didn't get it, you gotta be kiddin'.)
2. What differences do you see in the backlit photograph using the different metering systems?

ALTERNATIVE

If you live in an area that has limited sun days, such as the Pacific Northwest, you can try an alternative to the above by using an artificial light source and move it to simulate the movement of the sun, Figures 23.1, 23.2, 23.3.

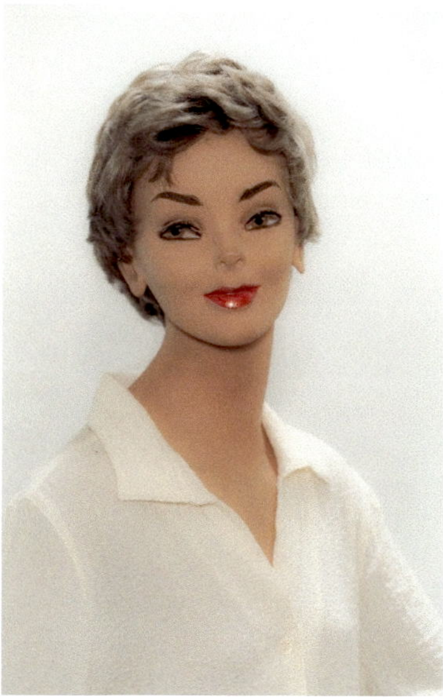

FIGURE 23.1 *Using artificial light as if it were behind the camera position and low on the horizon.*

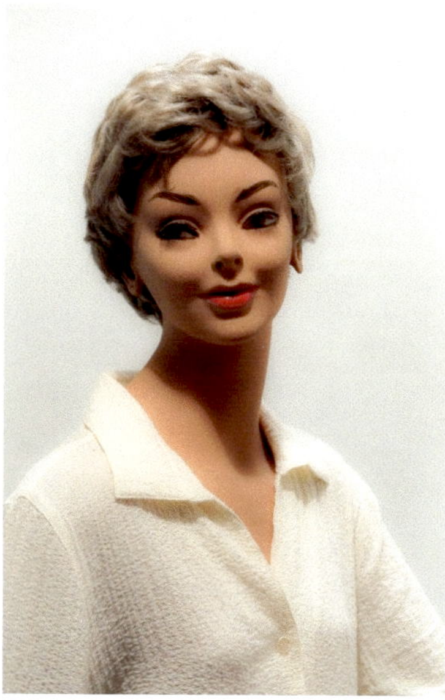

FIGURE 23.2 *The "sun" is directly overhead.*

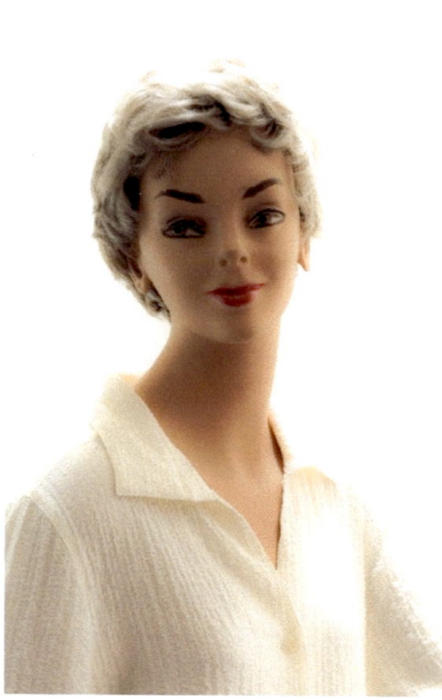

FIGURE 23.3 *The "sun" is 45 degrees behind the subject.*

ASSIGNMENT 24

Low-Light Photography

Contributed by Kay Kenny
Photography Instructor, New York University

> *"Wherever there is light, one can photograph."*
>
> —Alfred Stieglitz

PURPOSE: TO CREATE SUCCESSFUL IMAGES UNDER LOW-LIGHT AND NIGHT CONDITIONS.

All assignments require a sturdy camera support such as a tripod, and camera set to manual modes; an electronic cable or remote release is recommended.

URBAN LOW-LIGHT PHOTOGRAPHY

- Place your camera where streetlights and car headlights will not cause flare—the camera lens should be at least twenty feet from any light sources.
- Use a long shutter speed of thirty seconds or more to capture moving traffic trails. Experiment with f/stops by bracketing but maintain an ISO setting of 400 to avoid noise.

Panning a Lighted Subject such as a Riverboat after Dark

Use a long shutter speed such as thirty seconds or more; set up your composition, anticipating where the moving subject will come into view. When the subject is in the viewfinder, click and slowly pan the camera in sync with the subject. The speed will depend on the speed of the moving object. The distance and the brightness of the object will determine the f/stop.

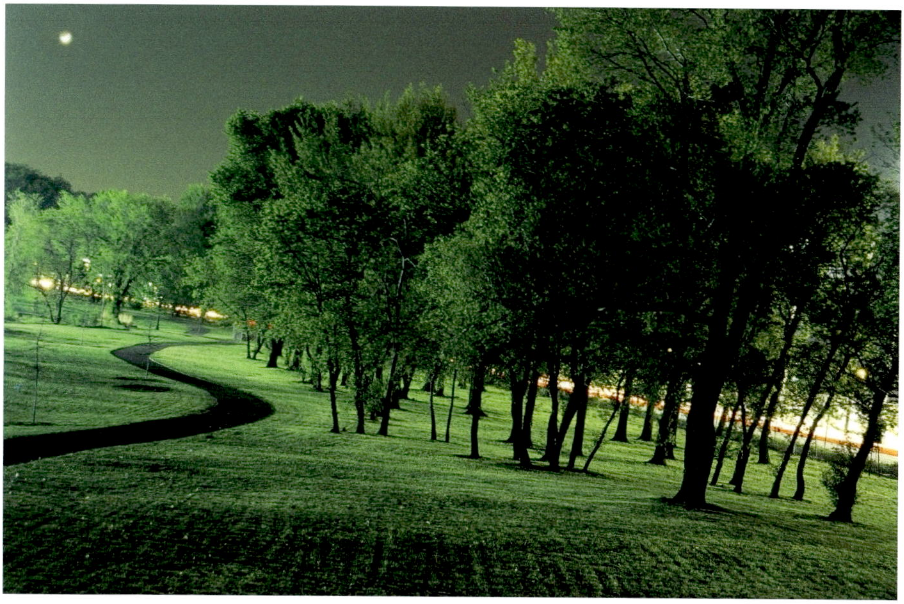

FIGURE 24.1
Lincoln Park.
© 2015 Kay Kenny.

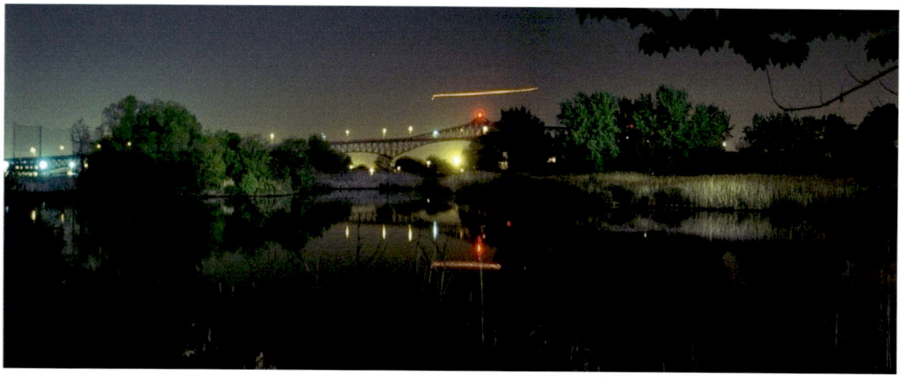

FIGURE 24.2
Pulaski Skyway.
© 2015 Kay Kenny.

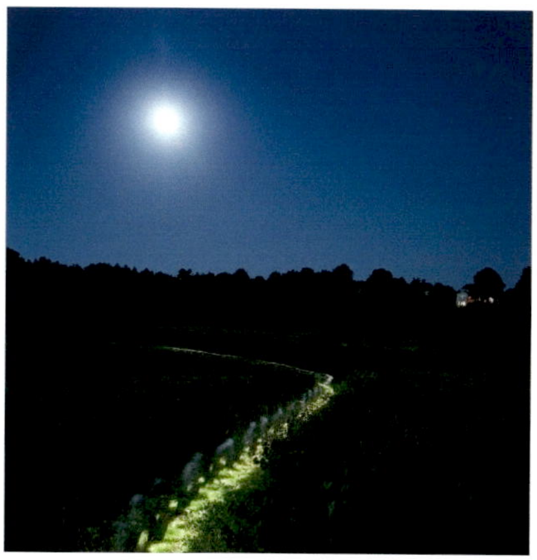

FIGURE 24.3
Peterboro Meadows.
© 2015 Kay Kenny.

Reflections from Storefronts

Be careful to set up the tripod to avoid pedestrian traffic, study the angle of lights reflecting on the storefront and focus on the glass itself. Look for an interesting montage of images or patterns and try to work with an f/stop of f/8 or above to provide some depth of field in capturing the window display behind the glass. Bracket for shutter speed: It will depend on the ambient light.

Ghosting People

Go to a public area where there is good ambient streetlight, such as a park or large arena. Set up the camera on a tripod where it will not interfere with pedestrian traffic. Use a shutter speed of thirty seconds to one minute and capture the movements of the crowd.

This assignment is best done from a higher vantage point such as steps or a hill. If possible, use an f/stop of f/8 or above. Keep in mind that each image will yield a different composition, due to the nature of the moving crowd. Flash can also be used to ghost people at night, using second curtain or rear curtain flash. This is a good technique for nighttime parades.

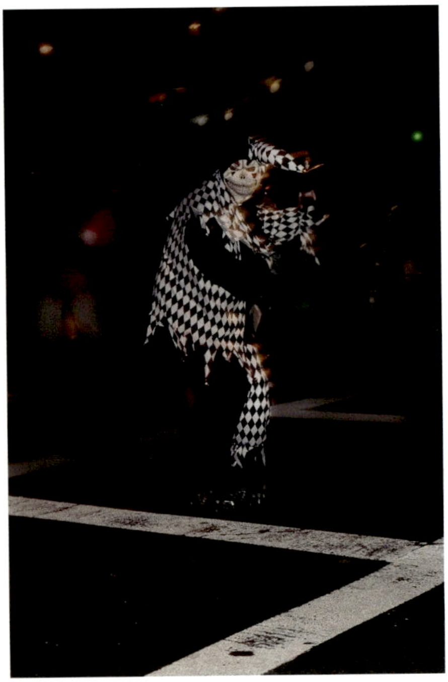

FIGURE 24.4 *NYC Halloween Parade. © 2015 Kay Kenny.*

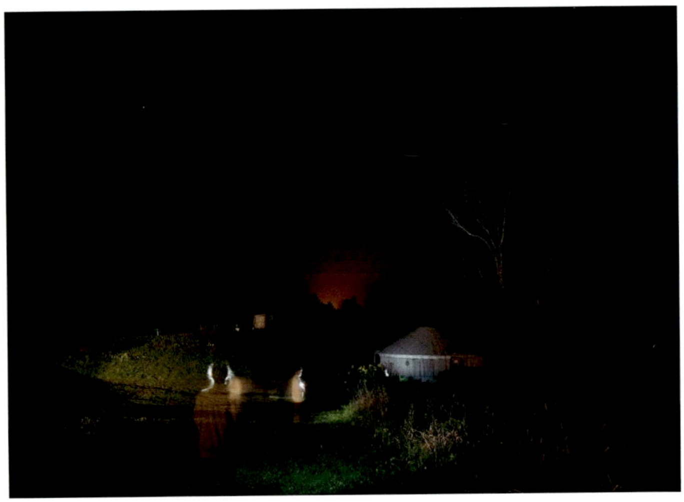

FIGURE 24.5 *Tent Meeting. © 2015 Kay Kenny.*

RURAL LOW-LIGHT EXPOSURES

Capturing Star and Moon Trails

Star trails depend on the length of the shutter speed. Scout locations in daylight and check weather conditions for moon risings and settings, cloud conditions, and dew points. To avoid loss of battery power for long star trail images use an accessory battery pack/grip.

Find a location that provides a clear vista of the sky and where there is no ambient light—a location at least fifty miles from a streetlit city or large town is a good choice.

Avoid a direct bright moon facing the lens, try different shutter speeds from five minutes to one hour using a low ISO and an f/stop relative to the shutter speed. Choose a good moonlit night to capture detail from the foreground. If possible, compose for the North Star—this will result in a circular pattern of star trails in the sky.

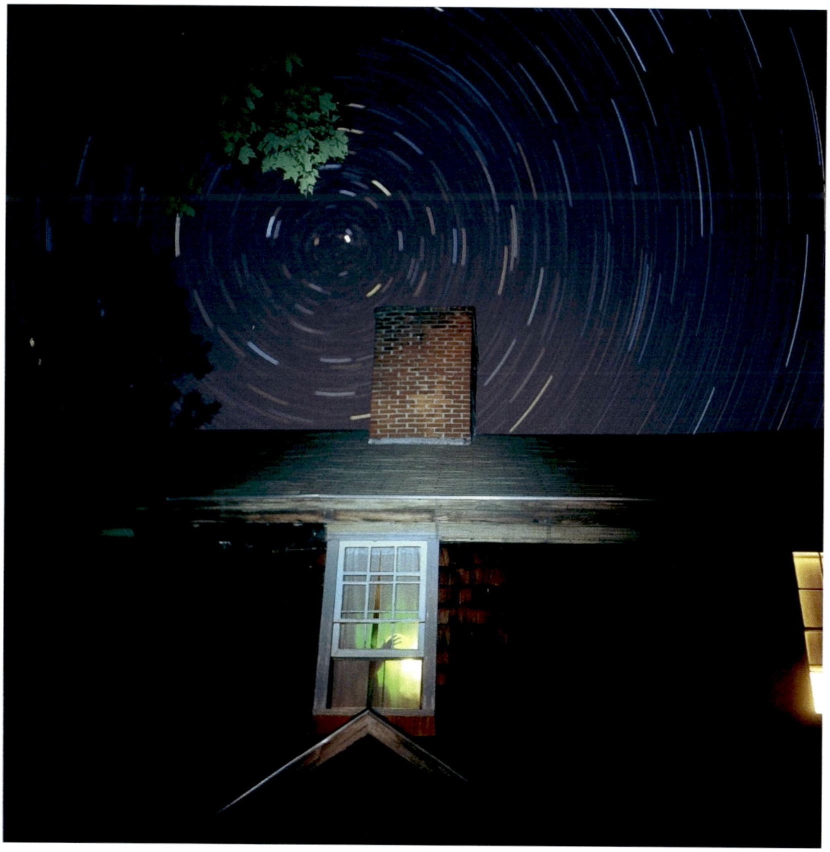

FIGURE 24.6 *Green Hand. © 2015 Kay Kenny.*

Photographing the Stars without Trails

Check for atmospheric conditions. Scout during the day and choose a location where there is no ambient light. On a night when there is little or no moon but the skies are cloud free, using a high ISO of 1200 or above, capture the night sky using a shutter speed of fifteen seconds. Use a wide-open f/stop. Look for the brightest constellations and/or stars for this assignment. Bracket with the high ISOs.

To provide some foreground image, use a flashlight or car headlights,[1] keeping in mind that the ISO is very high and lighting must be kept relatively dim for a single exposure image.

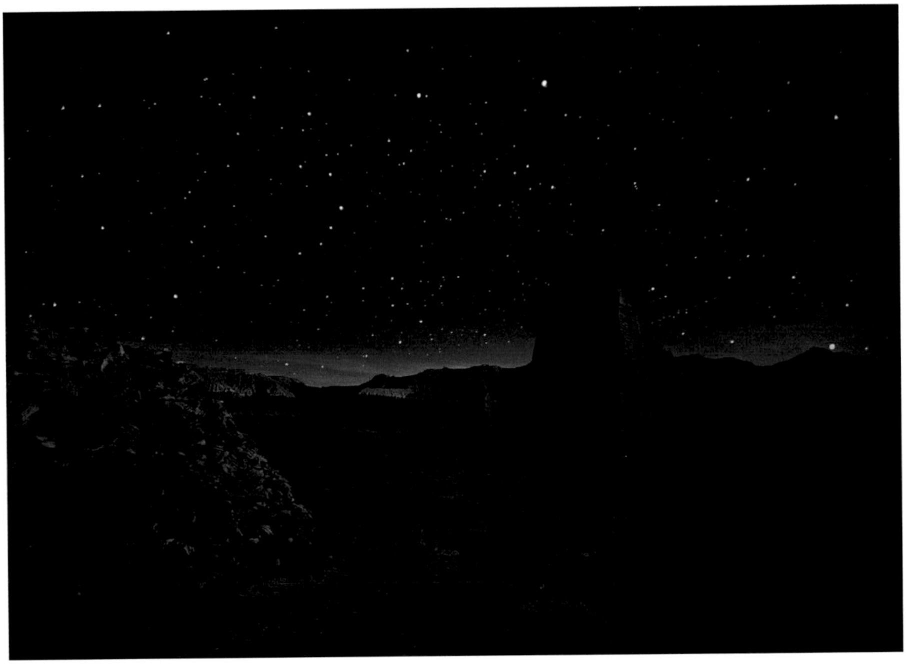

FIGURE 24.7 *Temple of the Sun & Moon.* © 2015 Kay Kenny.

Paint with Light

Use flashlights, car headlights, or off-camera flash, to capture the night sky in a long exposure of five minutes or more. Try different color filters and/or light sources on foreground subjects using short bursts of light (under ninety seconds). Experiment with moving the light sources behind and over the subjects.

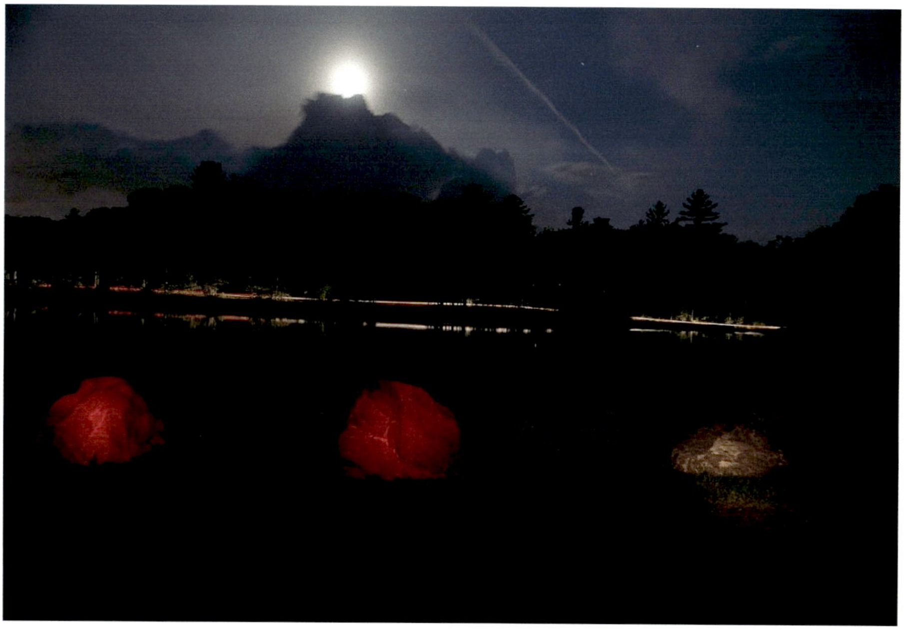

FIGURE 24.8 *Red Rocks, Lake Warren, NH. © 2015 Kay Kenny.*

Change Nighttime to Day

Use a low ISO and a very long exposure, possibly ninety minutes to two hours. This is best done with a battery pack/grip. On a brightly moon-lit night, choose a location where there is no ambient light but there are some objects with shadow depth, such as abandoned buildings. Paint the interior of the building with light, and then leave the shutter open. Try to capture the unnatural quality of the light from the moon and the lack of shadows from the light painting.

ASSIGNMENT 25

Discovering Light

"The eye should learn to listen before it looks."

—Robert Frank

PURPOSE: TO DISCOVER THE EFFECT OF LIGHT ON A SUBJECT.

When you have worked with light for a while you will be able to anticipate the effect it will have on a subject before placing the first light. You will also find that knowledge gained in the studio will transfer to the field, even when you don't have any artificial light in your bag. Without thinking, you will move a lamp; have your subject move closer to a wall; look out a window; move back a few feet so the fluorescent lights aren't casting shadows in their eye sockets; turn so an open door creates a rim or back light. When you find yourself intuitively working with light, modifying it to suit your subject, you can truly call yourself a photographer.

It begins with discovering what one light can do. For this project you will need five or six hard-boiled eggs—you could use them raw but I'm not responsible for the results. And anyway, you can eat them when you're through.

How Boiled Is Hard Boiled?

The best method for hard boiling eggs without breakage is to place them in cold water and heat them very slowly. When the water starts to simmer—steam rising and small bubbles clinging to the side of the pot—turn the heat to high and boil the eggs for ten minutes. Immerse the eggs in cold running water until cool.

A good way to keep the eggs from moving is to use modeling clay, available from art suppliers and many school bookstores.

- Use only one light.
- If possible, work with a handheld incident light meter. From the subject position, aim the light reading dome at the light source.
- Use no reflectors unless instructed to do so.

PART 1

Place the eggs on an all-white background.

1. If you have access to a boom stand, use it. Otherwise, hold the lamp in one hand as close to the lens as possible and release the camera shutter with the other.

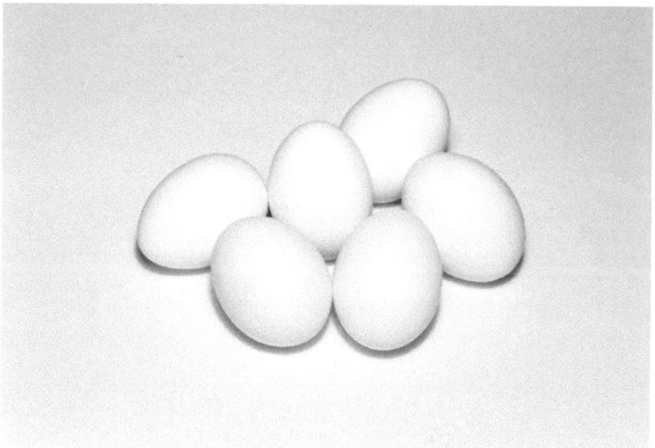

FIGURE 25.1 *Front lighting: The light is above and as close to the lens as possible.*

2. Move the light to the left or right side of the table and the same level as the eggs.

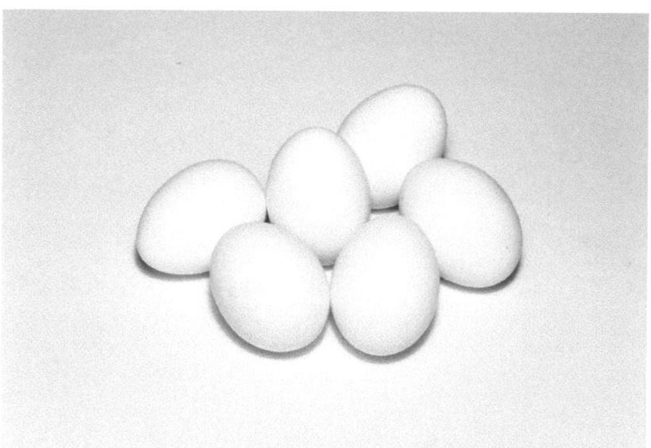

FIGURE 25.2 *Direct side light: The light has been moved to the right side of the table and lowered to the same level as the eggs.*

3. Turn the light so that it is bouncing off either a white wall or white reflector from the right or left side.

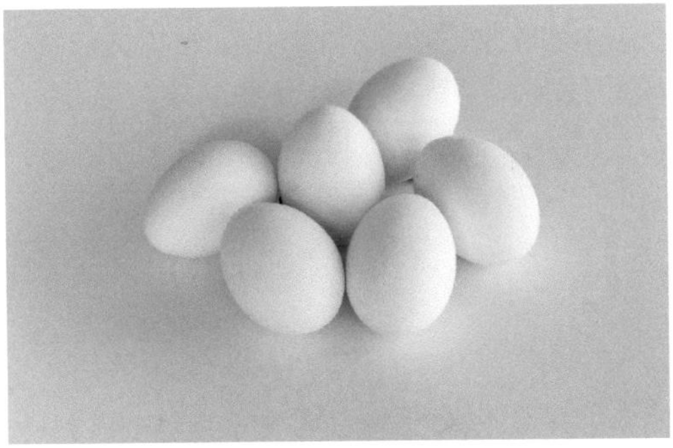

FIGURE 25.3 *Bounced side light: The light has been turned to bounce off a white wall.*

4. Turn the light towards the eggs and raise it until it's at a forty-five-degree angle to the eggs.

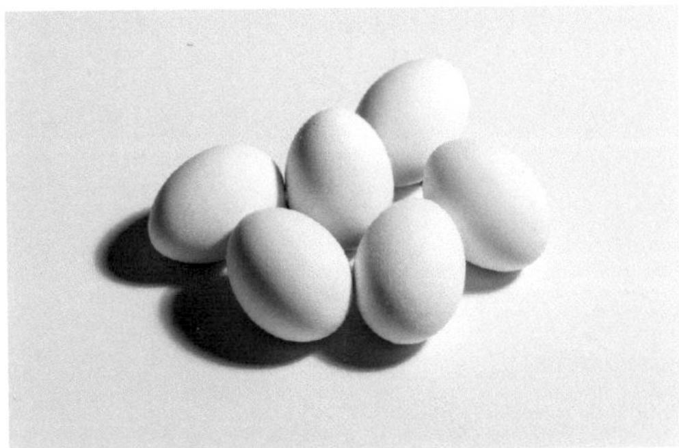

FIGURE 25.4 *Forty-five-degree side light.*

5. Place a white card directly opposite the light, one edge resting on the table, and as close to the eggs as possible.

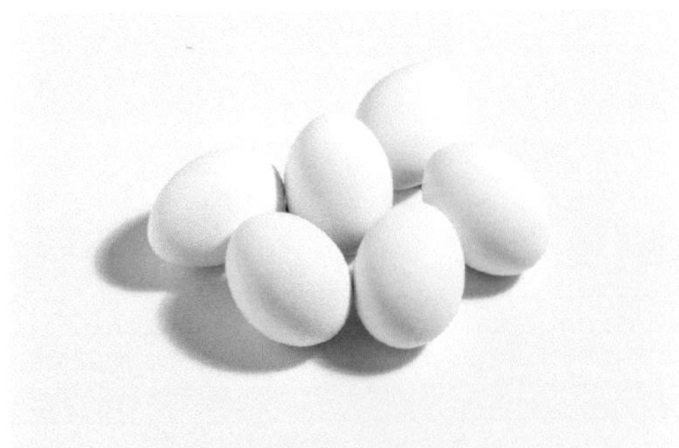

FIGURE 25.5 *Forty-five-degree side light with a white card reflector on the opposite side.*

6. Place a black card directly opposite the light, one edge resting on the table, and as close to the eggs as possible.

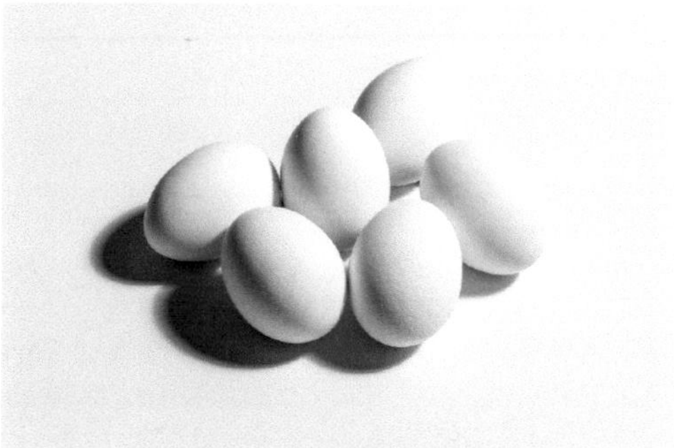

FIGURE 25.6 *Forty-five-degree side light with a black card reflector on the opposite side.*

7. Move the light so that it is shining directly from above.

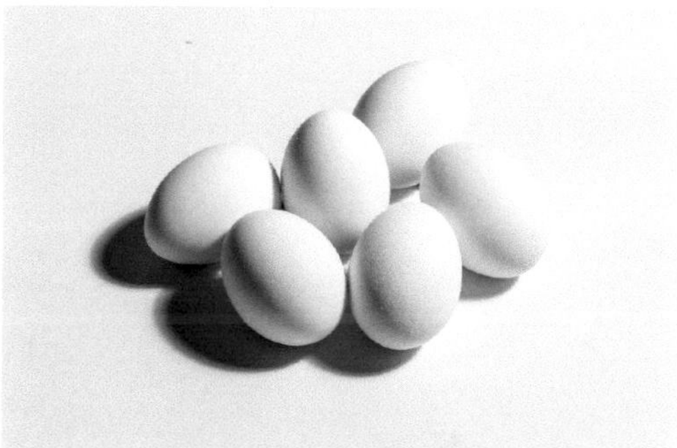

FIGURE 25.7 *Light directly from above.*

8. Move the light so that it is at a forty-five-degree angle directly behind and above the eggs.

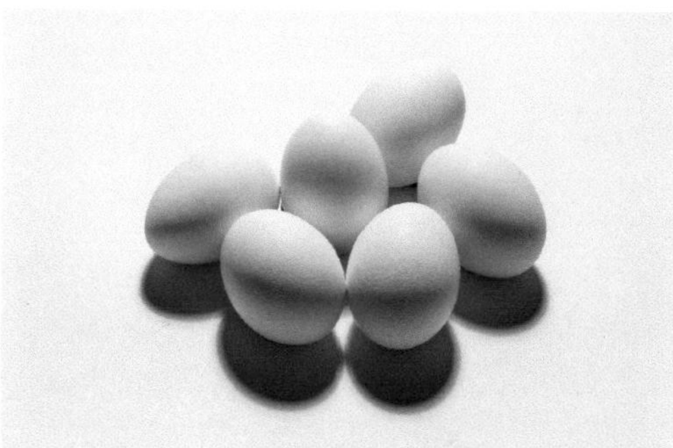

FIGURE 25.8 *Forty-five-degree back light.*

9. Keep the light at the same height as number seven but turn it around so it is bouncing off either a white wall or white reflector behind the eggs.

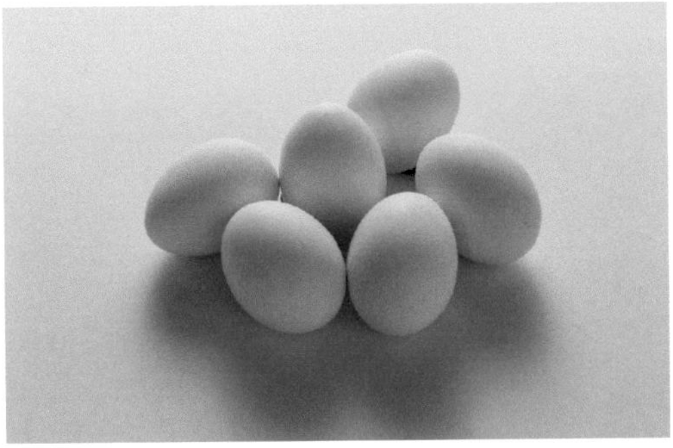

FIGURE 25.9 *Forty-five-degree back light bounced off a white wall.*

10. Move the light to the front left or right corner and lower it until the center is even with the edge of the table.

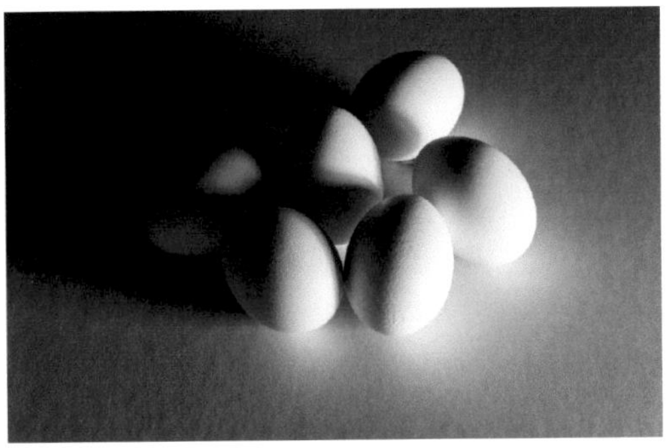

FIGURE 25.10 *Light placed at front right corner level with the subject.*

11. Keep the light even with the edge of the table and move it to the front and center, below the lens.

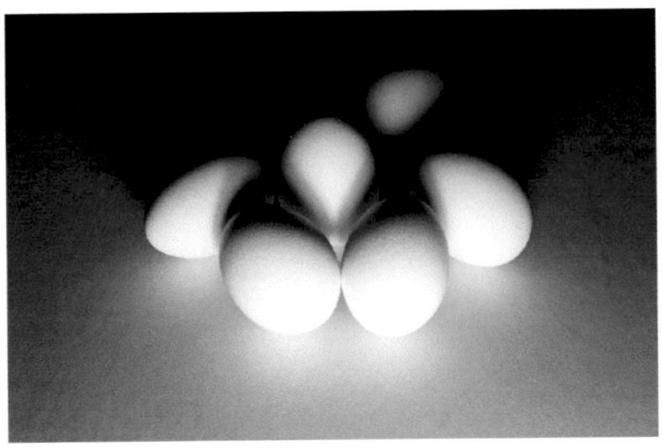

FIGURE 25.11 *Light front and center, placed below the lens.*

Rim Light

Aim the light at the white wall behind the eggs. Move the light up or down until you have a rim light similar to the one in the accompanying photos, Figures 25.12–14.

1. No reflector.

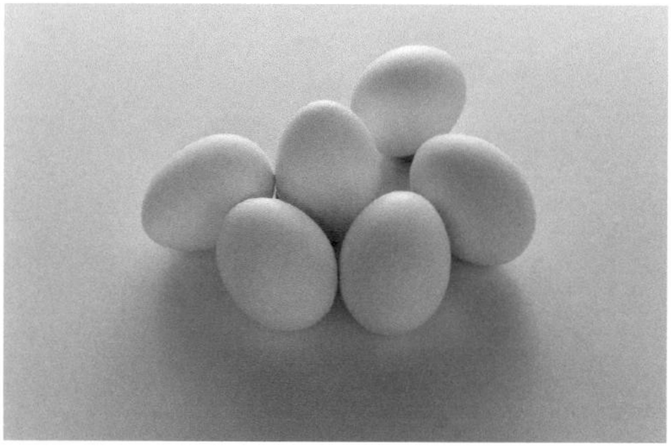

FIGURE 25.12 *Rim light bounced off the wall. No reflector in front of the subject.*

2. Place a white reflector straight up and down against the front edge of the table. Slide the reflector up or down until the top edge is just below the viewfinder image.

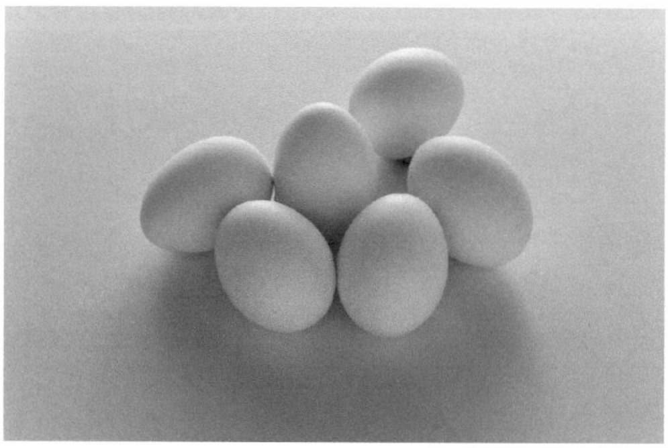

FIGURE 25.13 *Rim light bounced off the wall. White reflector in front of the subject.*

3. Place a black reflector straight up and down against the front edge of the table. Slide the reflector up or down until the top edge is just below the viewfinder image.

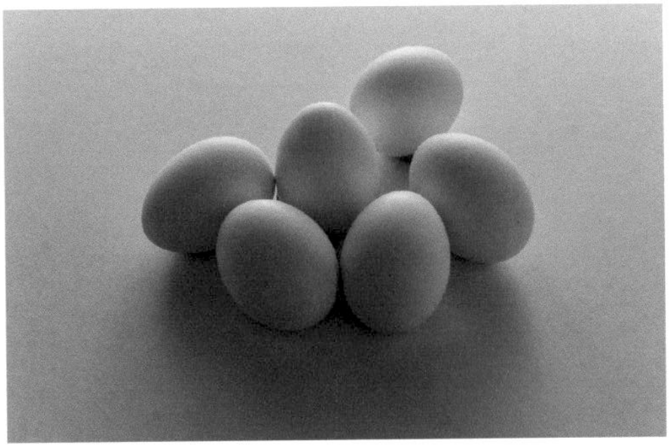

FIGURE 25.14 *Rim light bounced off the wall. Black reflector in front of the subject.*

REVIEW

Pay special note to each element of the photo: the angle of the light; the shadow; the highlight; even the reflections, if any.

1. Notice the black rim created by the front light in the first image.
2. Notice the effect on each egg caused by the shadows resulting from the side light in #2.
3. Pay special attention to the differences in the shadows in the third through fifth images using forty-five-degree side light.
4. What is the source of the rim light in numbers 10 and 11?
5. What else do you notice?

PART 2

This is a repeat of Part 1, only this time paint the eggs with matt black or glossy spray paint. Glossy paint will show up better in lighting tests, but matt black is easier to work with.

- Place the eggs on an all-black background.
- Two more photos have been added to Part 2.

1. Begin with the light above and as close to the lens as possible.

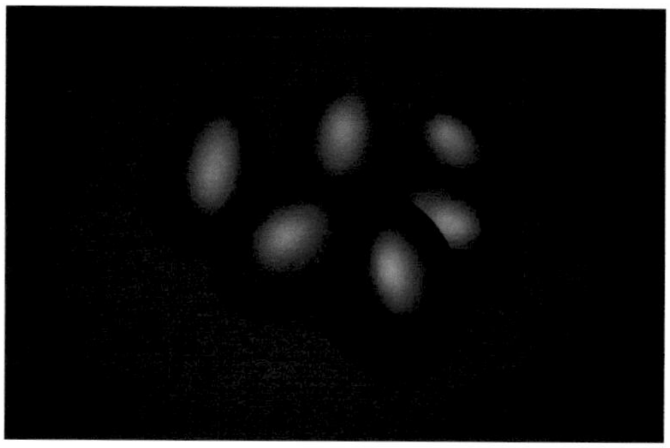

FIGURE 25.15 *Front lighting: The light is above and as close to the lens as possible.*

2. Move the light to the left or right side of the table and on the same level as the eggs.

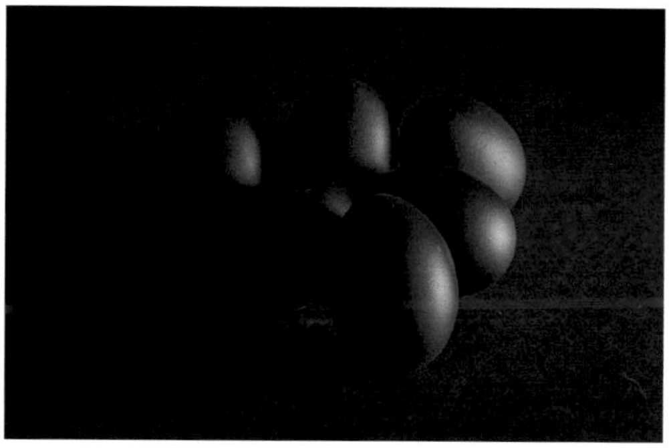

FIGURE 25.16 *Direct side light: The light has been moved to the right side of the table and lowered to the same level as the eggs.*

3. Turn the light so that it is bouncing off either a white wall or white reflector.

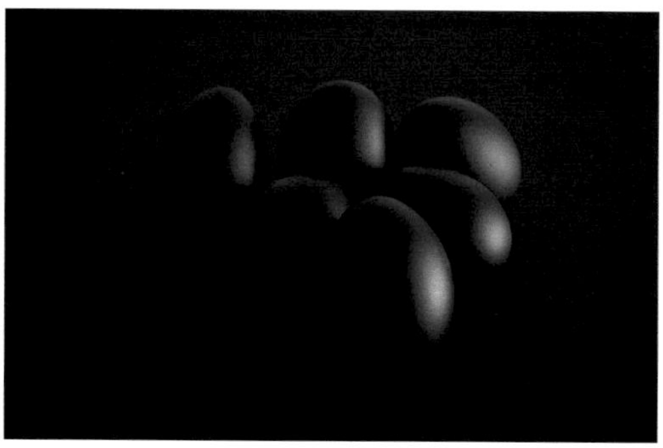

FIGURE 25.17 *Bounced side light: The light has been turned to bounce off a white wall.*

4. Turn the light towards the eggs and move it straight up from the side until it is at a forty-five-degree angle to the eggs.

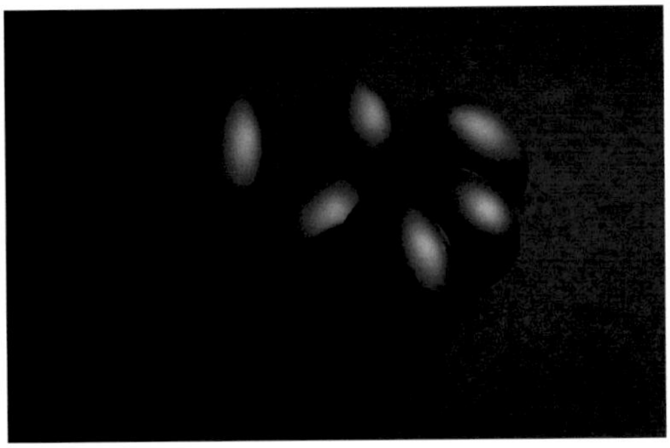

FIGURE 25.18 *Forty-five-degree side light.*

5. Place a white card directly opposite the light, one edge resting on the table, and as close to the eggs as possible.

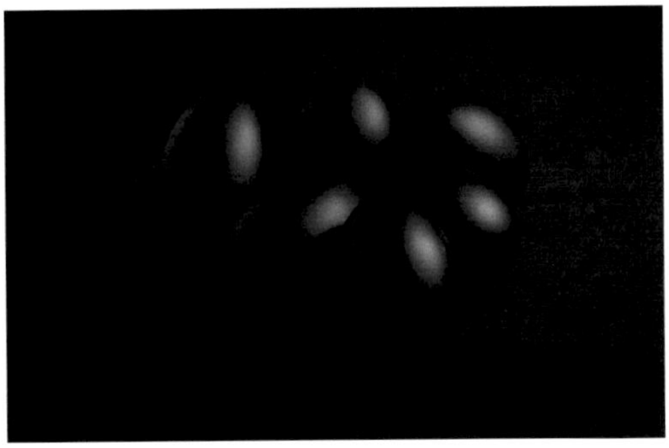

FIGURE 25.19 *Forty-five-degree side light with a white card reflector on the opposite side.*

6. Place a black card directly opposite the light, one edge resting on the table, and as close to the eggs as possible.

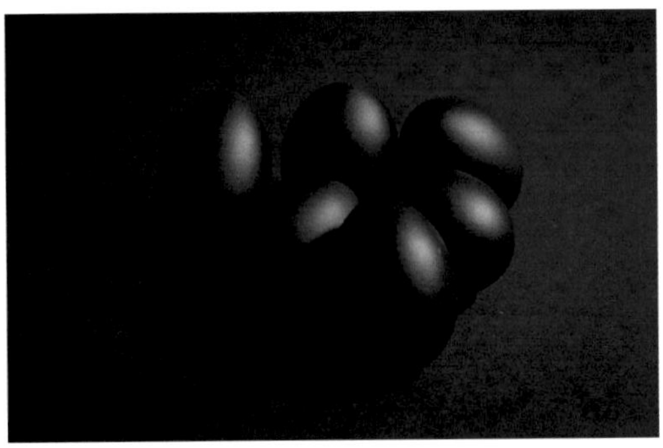

FIGURE 25.20 *Forty-five degree side light with a black card reflector on the opposite side.*

7. Move the light so that it is shining directly from above.

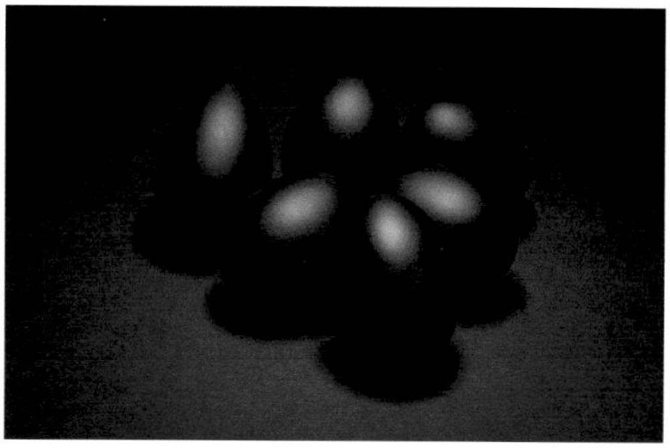

FIGURE 25.21 *Light directly from above.*

8. Move the light so that it is at a forty-five-degree angle directly behind and above the eggs.

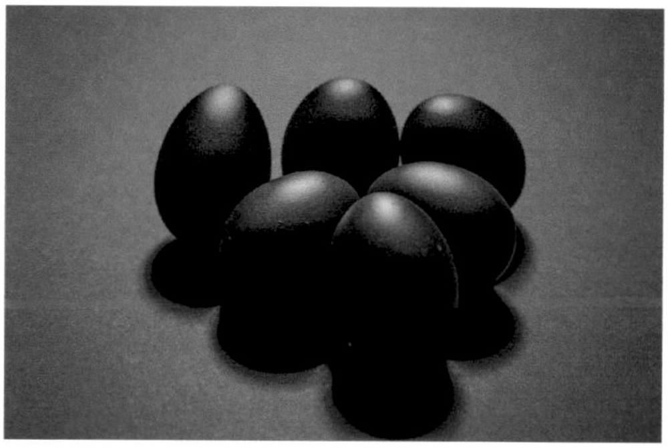

FIGURE 25.22 *Forty-five-degree back light.*

9. Keep the light at the same height as number eight but turn it so it's bouncing off either a white wall or white reflector behind the eggs.

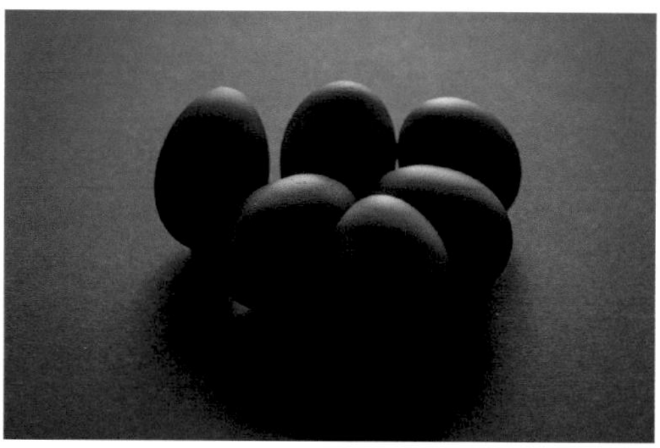

FIGURE 25.23 *Forty-five-degree back light bounced off a white wall.*

10. Place a white card at the front edge of the table. Slowly lower it until the top of the card is not visible in the camera viewfinder. Use the same set-up as in #9.

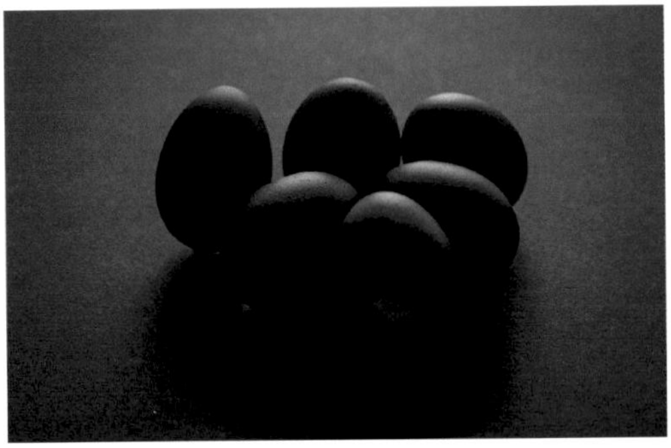

FIGURE 25.24 *Forty-five-degree back light bounced off a white wall with a white card reflector in front of the subject.*

11. Move the light to the front left or right corner and lower it until the center is even with the edge of the table.

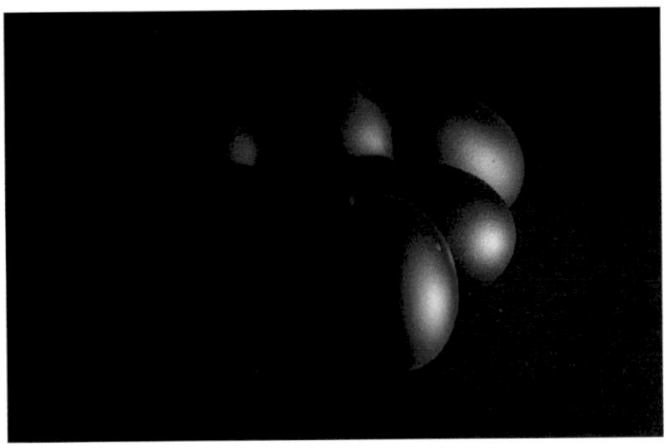

FIGURE 25.25 *Light placed at front right corner level with the subject.*

12. Place a white card at the opposite edge of the table. Use the same exposure as in #11.

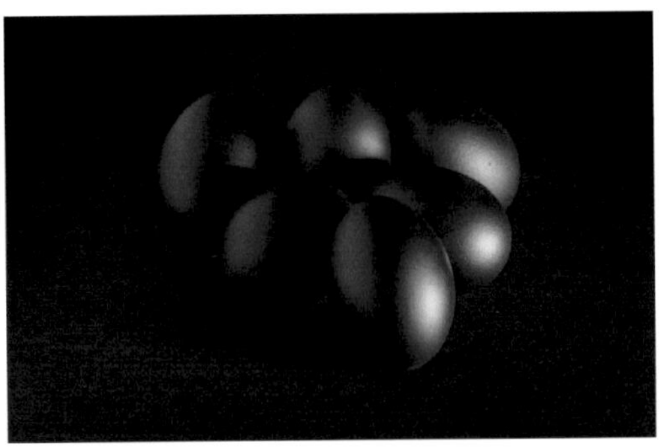

FIGURE 25.26 *Light placed at front right corner level with the subject, with a white reflector at the opposite edge of the table.*

13. Keep the light even with the edge of the table and move it to the front and center, below the lens.

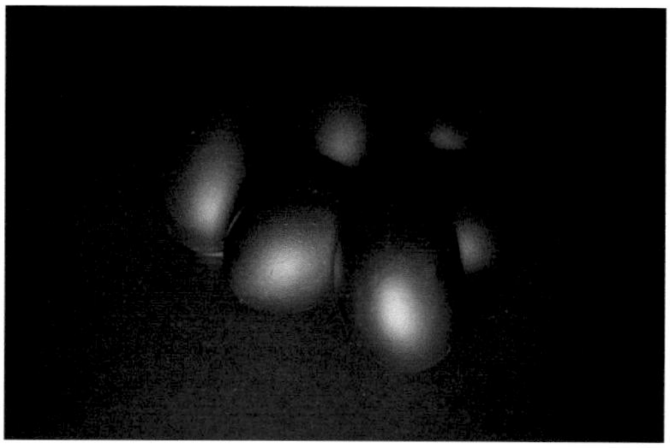

FIGURE 25.27 *Light front and center, placed below the lens.*

Rim Light

Aim the light at the white wall behind the eggs. Move the light up or down until you have a rim light similar to the one in the accompanying photos.

1. No reflector.

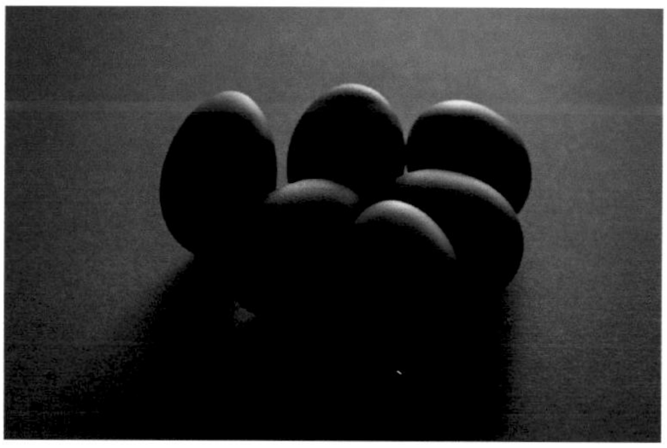

FIGURE 25.28 *Light placed at front right corner level with the subject.*

2. Place a white reflector against the front edge of the table. Slide the reflector up or down until the top edge is just below the viewfinder image.

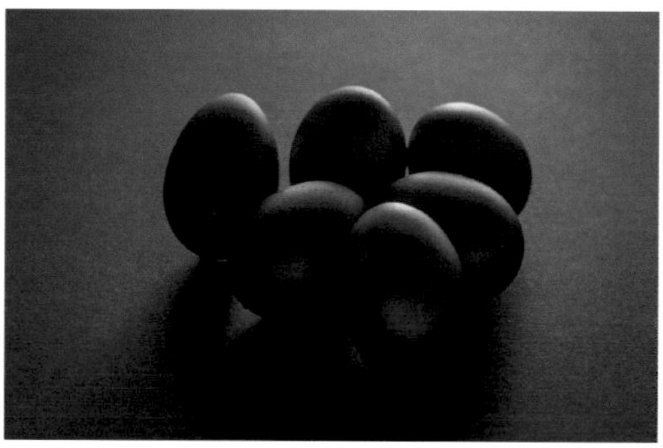

FIGURE 25.29 *Rim light bounced off the wall. White reflector in front of the subject.*

3. Place a black reflector against the front edge of the table. Slide the reflector up or down until the top edge is just below the viewfinder image.

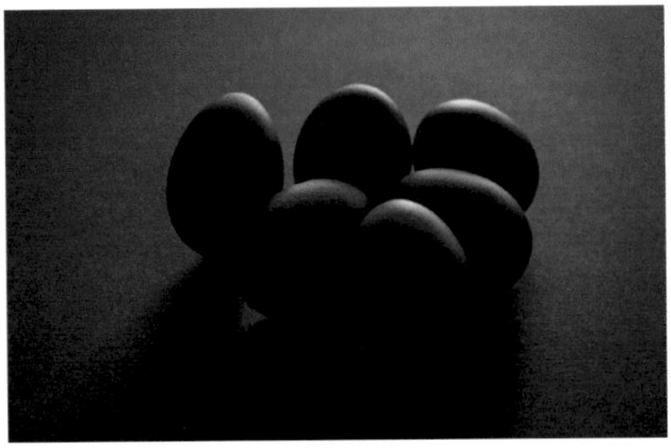

FIGURE 25.30 *Rim light bounced off the wall. Black reflector in front of the subject.*

AFTER-PROCESSING

- Convert all of the images in both Part 1 and 2 to black and white.
- Make individual 5 x 7-inch prints. Write the lighting position on the back of each card.
- Shuffle the cards and try to identify the position of the light for each card.
- Compare the white images to the corresponding black images.

REVIEW

The three most important thing you will learn from this assignment are:

1. When you work with light subjects, you light to create shadows.
2. When you work with dark subjects, you light to create highlights.
3. The eggs are still good to eat even with the shells painted black.

ASSIGNMENT 26

Lighting a Cube

"If you want to be a better photographer, stand in front of more interesting stuff."

—Jim Richardson

PURPOSE: TO CREATE THE ILLUSION OF THREE DIMENSIONS THROUGH THE USE OF LIGHT.

There are many ways to create the illusion of three dimensions in a two-dimensional photograph. One is through the use of geometry: converging lines; larger objects in relation to smaller objects; and so on. Another is through the use of color: bright colors advance; dark colors recede. A third method is through the use of shadow and light.

According to Leonardo Da Vinci, in order to produce depth in a painting, you must have three brightness levels: the true brightness of your subject; a brightness that is brighter than the true brightness; and a brightness that is darker.

Simply put, an object is given dimension by having one side darker and one side lighter than the metered brightness. Learning to light a cube will provide you with the skills and knowledge to effectively use light to create three dimensions in your image. This applies to location as well as studio photography.

The true brightness of a subject is always subjective. It is determined by identifying the area/subject of most importance, and the nature of the light. Once determined, true brightness is up to the artist to interpret correctly.

For this assignment you will light the cube in five steps in order to learn where and how to place lights and the use of modifiers.

The true brightness of the cube is the one that falls in the middle. The other two sides are either highlight or shadow.

THE SETUP

- Locate an area where there is no extraneous light—a corner of a room without windows, etc. If you cannot find a room without extraneous light, then do the project at night.
- The base should be a black card. For the examples in this book a piece of 2 x 3-inch foam board was used.
- The background should be white. If you don't have a white background, tape a piece of white foam core or paper to the wall.
- You will need a white cube at least six inches square—larger is okay. In the examples shown, a six-inch-square plastic cube, that contained a trivia card game, was spray-painted white. Place the cube so that the bottom half is on the black base as shown in Figure 26.2.

GROUND RULES

- Use only one light; it doesn't matter if it is diffused, directional, or bounced. It can be strobe or continuous light (tungsten, fluorescent). Move the light to whatever position is needed to create the lighting effect.
- Use as many flags (black cards) and reflectors (white cards) in as many configurations as you need to create the lighting effect.
- Do not allow any shadows, even that of the cube, to fall on the white background.

Hint: The black base should be placed on a table and at least two feet from the white background.

AFTER-PROCESSING

After importing the images into your image-editing program, convert them to black and white.

For all of these images the same editing correction was applied in Lightroom: Black –100%; White +50%. No other corrections were used.

SETUP 1—MAKE IT BLACK

Using any combination of flags and reflectors, light the cube so that all three sides and the base are black. The background should be white.

FIGURE 26.1

SETUP 2—WHITE ON WHITE

Using any combination of flags and reflectors, light the cube so that all three sides and the background are white. The base should be black.

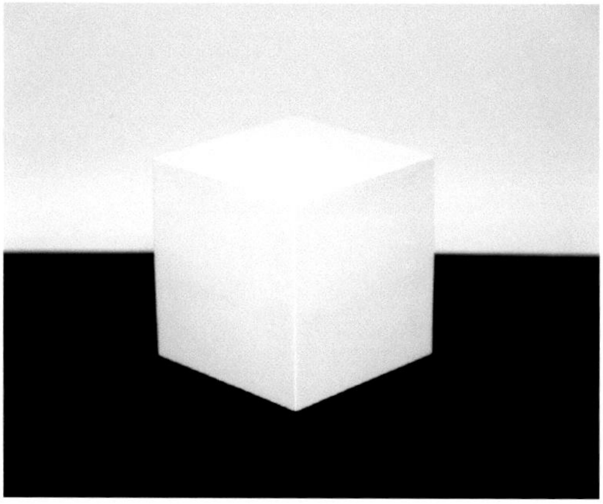

FIGURE 26.2

SETUP 3—BLACK AND WHITE TOGETHER

Using any combination of flags and reflectors, light the cube so that two sides are white and the third side is black. The background should be white and the base black.

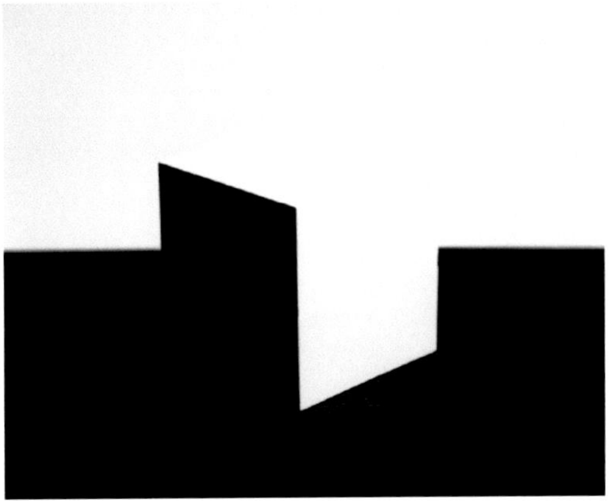

FIGURE 26.3

SETUP 4—ALMOST HOME

Using any combination of flags and reflectors, light the cube so that two sides are white and the third side is middle gray. The background should be white and the base black.

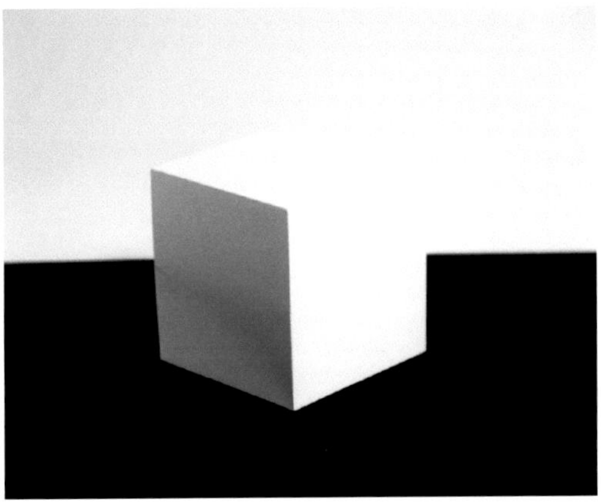

FIGURE 26.4

SETUP 5—THE MOTHER SHIP HAS LANDED

Using any combination of flags and reflectors, light the cube so that one side is white, one is middle gray, and the third is dark gray. The background should be white and the base black.

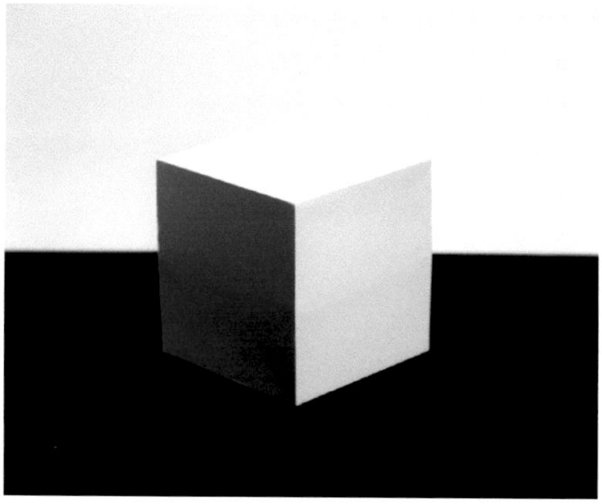

FIGURE 26.5

OBSERVATIONS

The importance of this assignment is learning how to place and modify light to achieve a variety of effects on a single object; and how varying shades of gray can create the illusion of three dimensions.

1. Black on Black

The bottom of the cube is lost against the black base. The result is a two-dimensional shape.

2. White on White

While the object is clearly white; form, space, reality, and dimension are missing.

3. Black and White Together

Due to the tonal merger of the white side and top with the background, and the extreme contrast of the black side, the cube doesn't appear to be real.

4. Almost Home

By making the left side gray, the cube looks less stark and more realilstic than the last image.

5. The Mother Ship Has Landed

By creating three distinct planes of brightness, the cube appears white and three-dimensional.

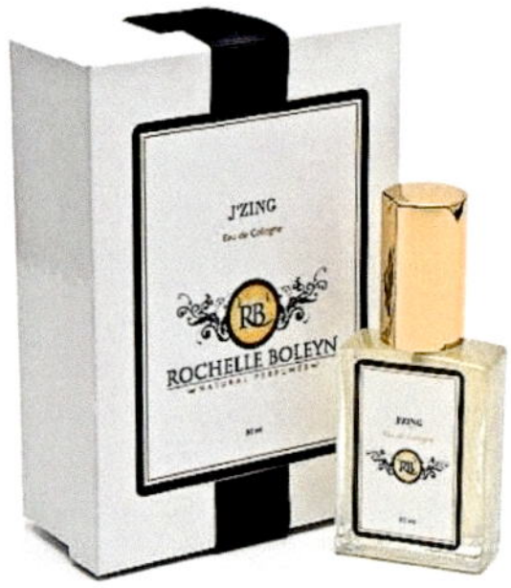

FIGURE 26.6 *Practical application of lighting a cube.*

ASSIGNMENT 27

Synchro-Sunlight

"The picture that you took with your camera is the imagination you want to create with reality."

—Scott Lorenzo

PURPOSE: TO LEARN HOW TO SYNCHRONIZE HANDHELD FLASH WITH THE SUN.

It's really quite simple. Use your flash to illuminate the subject, and the sunlight to illuminate everything else.

For this assignment you will need a willing subject.

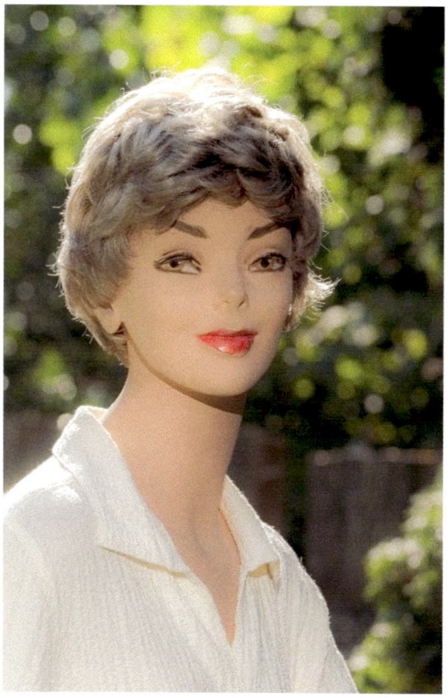

FIGURE 27.1 *Nikon D700, 155mm lens, f/10 at 1/60.*

PART 1—FORCED-FLASH

1. Have your subject stand so that they are backlit by the sun.
2. Take a meter reading of the background, set the exposure on your camera.
3. Move the flash to the distance required to match the f/stop on the camera according to the flash dial or LED.
4. If the distance is too great (e.g., your arm or flash cable isn't long enough), set a slower ISO on the camera and re-meter the scene, Figures 27.1 and 27.2.

FIGURE 27.2 *If your arm or flash cable isn't long enough set a slower ISO on the camera and re-meter the scene.*

PART 2—DARKEN THE BACKGROUND

1. Have your subject wear a hat and stand in full sunlight with their face towards the sun. The hat brim will shield their eyes so they don't squint.
2. Take a meter reading of the background, set the exposure on your camera. Move the flash to the distance required to match the f/stop on the camera, Figure 27.3.
3. Next, set the shutter speed on your camera one full stop faster, being careful not to exceed the maximum synch speed. This will underexpose the background by one stop, Figure 27.4.

PART 3—PARTIAL FILL

1. Have your subject remain in the sunlight, remove their hat, and face three quarters or half to the sun.
2. Take a meter reading of the subject and set the exposure on your camera. Move the flash to the distance required to match the f/stop on the camera, Figure 27.5.

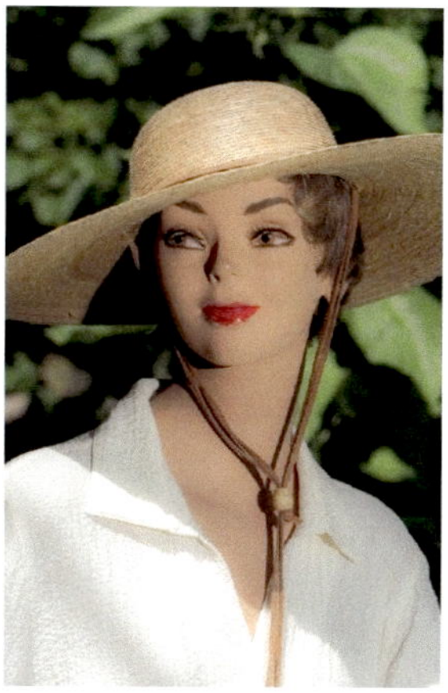

FIGURE 27.3 *Nikon D700, 145mm lens, f/13 at 1/100.*

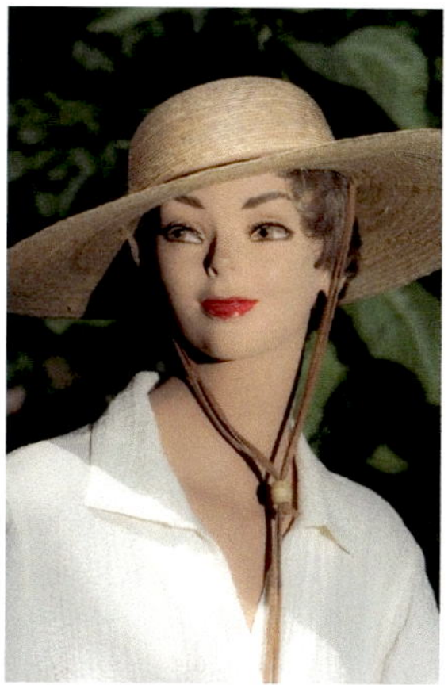

FIGURE 27.4 *Increasing the shutter speed by one stop darkens the background causing the model to stand out. An even more dramatic effect can be achieved with a two stop reduction. Nikon D700, 145mm lens, f/13 at 1/250.*

3. Change the ISO setting *on the flash* one to two stops higher (ISO 100 to ISO 200 or ISO 400). The sensor in the flash will "assume" that you are using a faster ISO. *Or* move the flash further away from the subject, approximately half the original distance (e.g., if the suggested distance for full fill is nine feet, move the flash to about twelve or thirteen feet) Figure 27.6.

PART 4—PRACTICE

Do a number of variations of the above until you are comfortable with the technique.

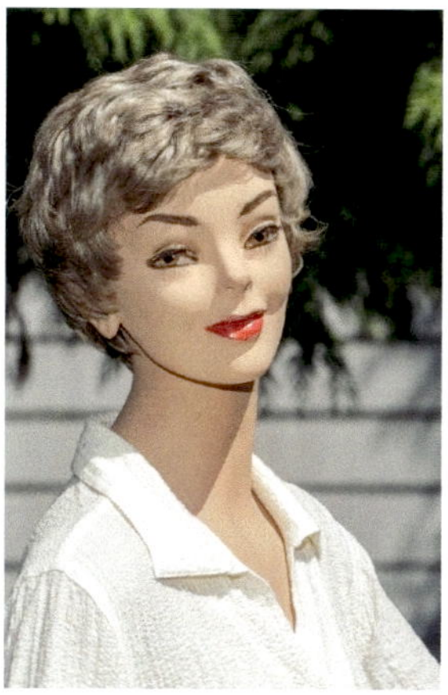

FIGURE 27.5 *Normal exposure using synchro-sunlight. Nikon D700, 145mm lens, f/13 at 1/125.*

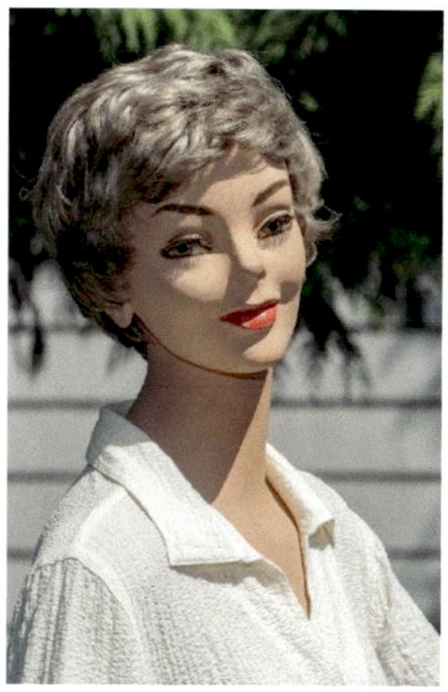

FIGURE 27.6 *The flash has been moved half the original distance further away. The shutter speed has been kept the same. Nikon D700, 145mm lens, f/13 at 1/12.*

ASSIGNMENT 28

Glow

Contributed by Mary Ellen Wortham
Photography Instructor, Fillmore High School

"Essentially what photography is, is life lit up."

—Sam Abell

INTRODUCTION

The word *photography* is derived from Greek roots *phos* (light) and *graphy* (to draw or paint). Simply stated, *photography* is *drawing or painting with light*. In this assignment, students are given literal understanding of the craft as they use glow sticks to create original light drawings.

LEARNING TARGETS

- To understand the etymology of the word *photography*.
- To demonstrate effective use of the exposure triangle, i.e. the interplay of aperture, shutter, and ISO for correct exposure.
- To understand creative options of shutter speed (i.e., control the look of movement in the photograph).
- Pre-visualization and storyboard skills.
- To demonstrate working knowledge of the camera tripod.

PRE-PRODUCTION

Your studio space must be dark and roomy enough for several students to occupy at once. Darkrooms are ideal if configurations allow. If finding appropriate indoor space proves to be challenging, assignments can be executed outside at night away from building lights. Before beginning this assignment, you need to familiarize yourself with basic tripod handling, operation, and safeguards.

- Camera settings: manual; auto-focus; shutter at thirty seconds minimum.
- Determine the correct aperture and ISO settings at a full thirty-second shutter speed.
- Pre-visualize. Where called for, sketch out each idea on paper in a single-frame storyboard format. Poses should be simple and flat (i.e., think 2-D shadow or pencil outline of someone holding a pose while on floor).
- Work in teams of three (one holding a pose; two working the glow sticks). Each member must participate as both *poser* and *drawer* for every light-drawing assignment. Teams should take the time to devise a strategy and practice approach to drawing before camerawork commences.

PRODUCTION

Outline Pose

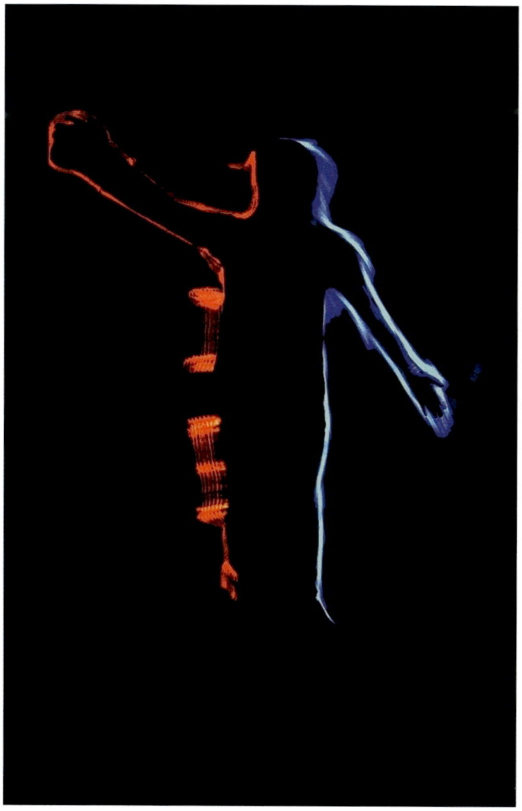

FIGURE 28.1 *Outline Pose. Fillmore High School, Photography Archives 2007–14.*

Storyboard required. Do not alter.

Assignment: Outline the human form by tracing a physical pose using glow sticks.

Do not alter the pre-production storyboard to fit the production pose; through trial and error you will strengthen your pre-visualization skills.

Challenges: Light strokes applied in smooth, even fashion; entire pose outlined within thirty-second time limit; effective teamwork and problem-solving.

Fantasy or Mythical Creature

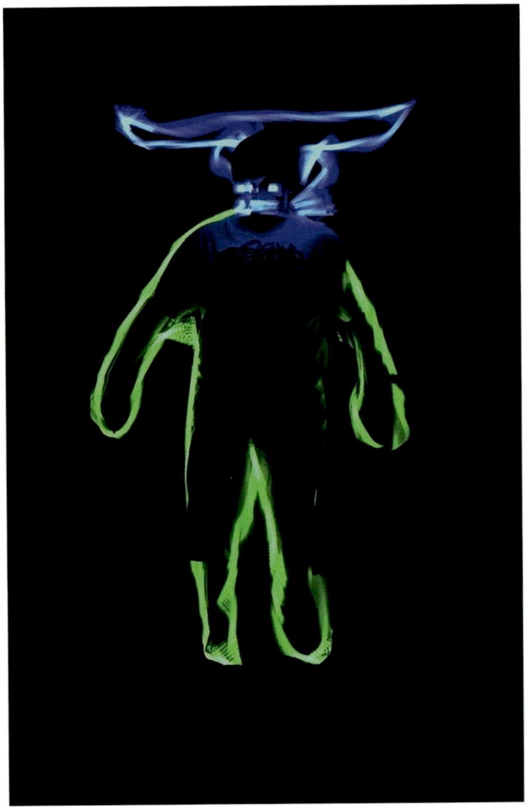

FIGURE 28.2 *Mythical Creature. Fillmore High School, Photography Archives 2007–14.*

Storyboard required for Assignment A. Do not alter.

Assignment A: Create a fantasy or mythical figure by elaborating a physical pose; extend drawing into surrounding empty space.

Challenges: As light is fleeting, you must visualize what and where you paint; this assignment requires effective timing, problem-solving, and teamwork.

Assignment B: Create a Tasmanian Devil.

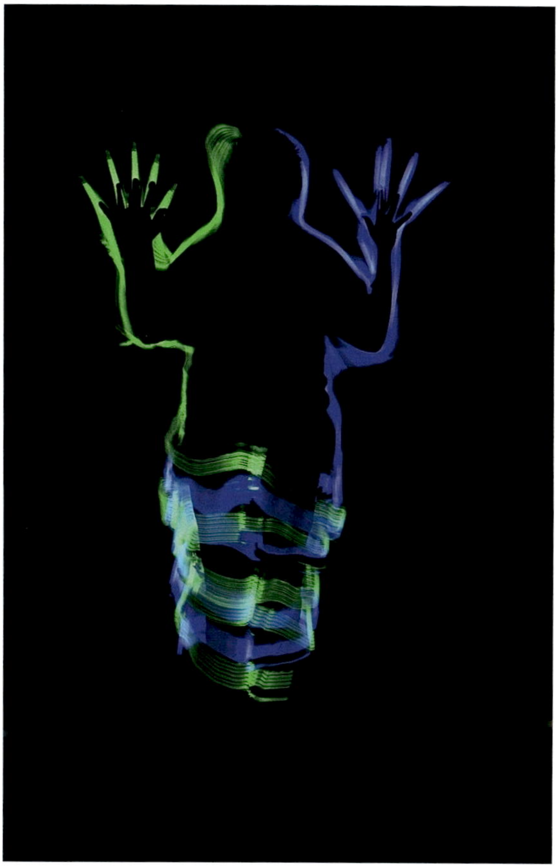

FIGURE 28.3 *Tasmanian Devil. Fillmore High School, Photography Archives 2007–14.*

Challenge: Funnel coverage from waist to feet.

Silhouette

Storyboard optional.

Assignment: Pose two to three students together in an interesting arrangement. Fill the background light to create a group silhouette.

Challenges: Relating subjects in an interesting group pose; smooth, even background coverage; effective teamwork.

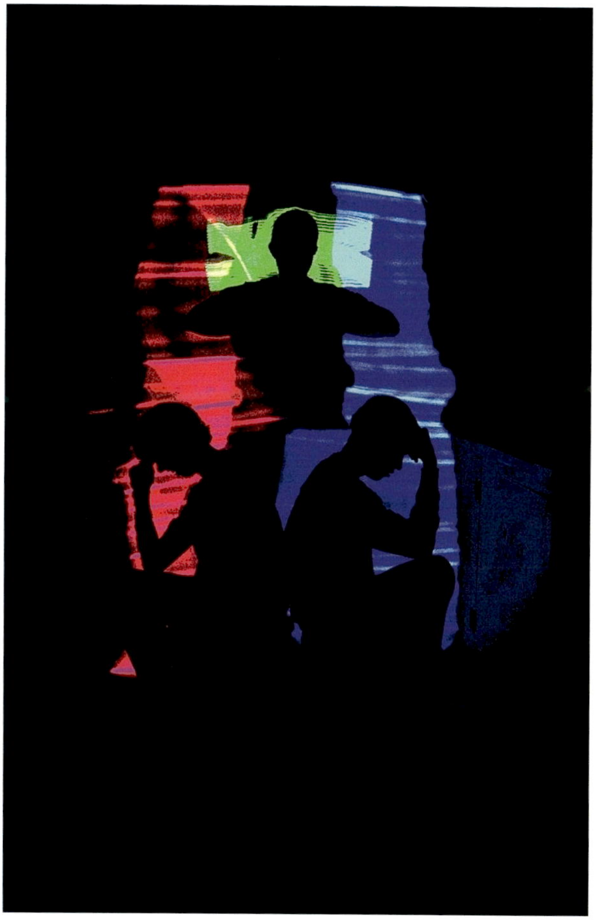

FIGURE 28.4 *Silhouette. Fillmore High School, Photography Archives 2007–14.*

Free Hand (Solo)

No storyboard required.

Assignment A: Draw simple figures.

- Girl with curly hair wearing a dress/skirt.
- Boy with baseball cap wearing shorts.
- Dog or cat.
- Type of tree.

Challenges: Strategies for blocking/releasing light to the camera; visualizing your drawing as you paint in empty space.

Assignment B: Write your name.

Challenge: Writing in mirror image (egami rorrim).

Free Hand (Group)

No storyboard required.

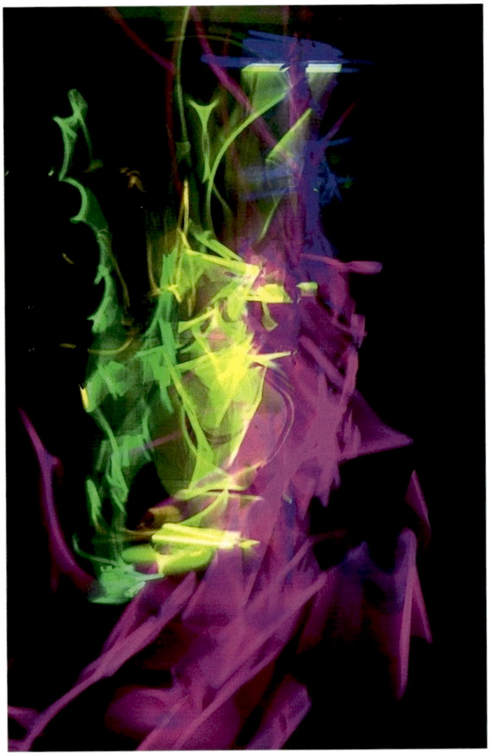

FIGURE 28.5 *Freehand. Fillmore High School, Photography Archives 2007–14.*

Assignment A: Tic-tac-toe game—draw a grid and play a game of Xs and Os.

Challenges: Visualization in empty space; strategies for controlling flow of light; coordinated teamwork.

Assignment B: Fountain—repeatedly pick up and toss the glow sticks gently to each other, in the air, on the floor, etc.

Challenges: Avoiding overexposure hotspots; glow sticks traveling in varied pathways; to register in-camera, glow sticks must travel slowly.

ASSIGNMENT 29

Selfies

"The best thing about a picture is that it never changes, even when the people in it do."

—Andy Warhol

The *Oxford Dictionary* online defines selfie as follows:

> Selfie (also selfy): sel·fie \ selfē\ n. (plural selfies): A photograph that one has taken of oneself, typically one taken with a smartphone or webcam and uploaded to a social media website.

Self-portraiture is one of the oldest genres in Western European art. Almost, if not all, great artists have turned their eye on themselves—perhaps out of curiosity; perhaps for immortality. Photographers are no less interested in portraying themselves through their medium.

The cell phone is the ultimate device for self-portraiture. You always have it with you, and you can record yourself anywhere, any time, doing anything. That's the good news. The bad news is you always have it with you, and you can record yourself anywhere, any time, doing anything, *ad nauseam*.

The challenge for you, the artist, is to find ways to use your cell phone to portray yourself in ways that are unusual and thought provoking.

Your assignment is: Using a cell phone, create three selfies in which you find a way to make yourself disappear or become unobtrusive. The viewer should have to search for your image.

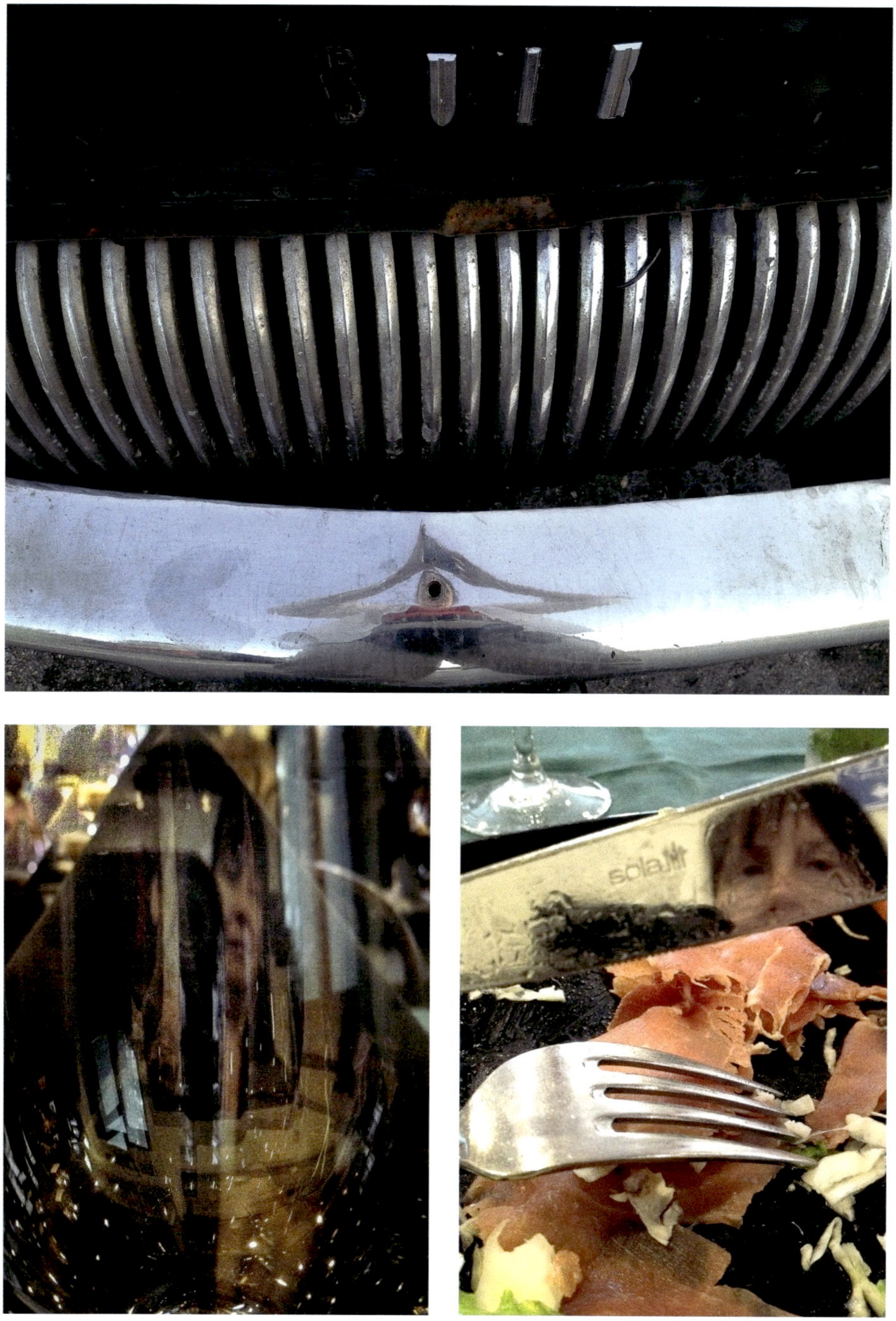

FIGURES 29.1–3 *iPhone camera selfies. Photos by Donna Conrad.*

ASSIGNMENT 30

Portrait Lighting Styles

"It's one thing to make a picture of what a person looks like, it's another thing to make a portrait of who they are."

—Paul Caponigro

PURPOSE: TO LEARN TO USE LIGHTING STYLES AND POSITIONS.

PART 1

The following seven portraits were part of a joint project between OSU and Western Oregon University in which OSU photo majors, Tomas Patlan and Jerome Stretch, photographed WOU graduating music majors. Using one light and white card reflectors, replicate each of the following seven lighting styles. You won't be able to achieve the back and hair light effects with one light so only try for the basic style, forty-five, butterfly, modified or side butterfly, side, rim, long, and short.

1. Forty-five

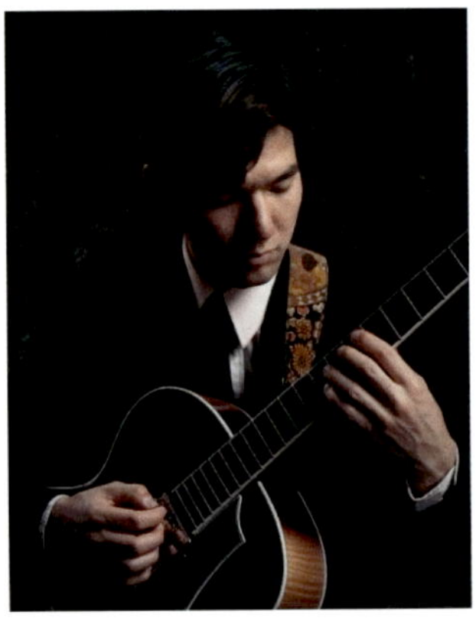

FIGURE 30.1 *Forty-five lighting. Erik Moulton. Photo by Jerome Stretch.*

2. Butterfly

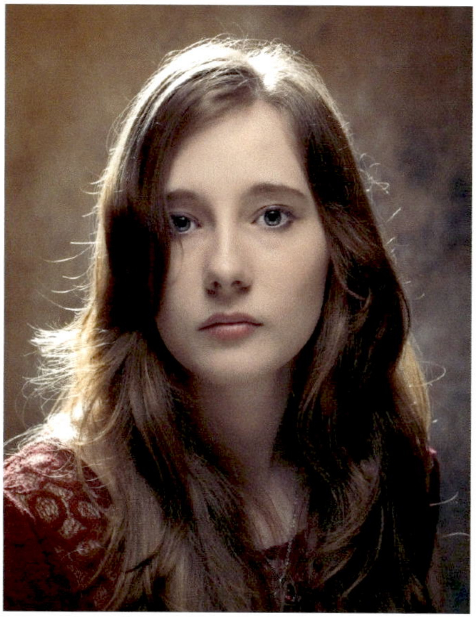

FIGURE 30.2 *Butterfly lighting. Megan Johnson. Photo by Tomas Patlan.*

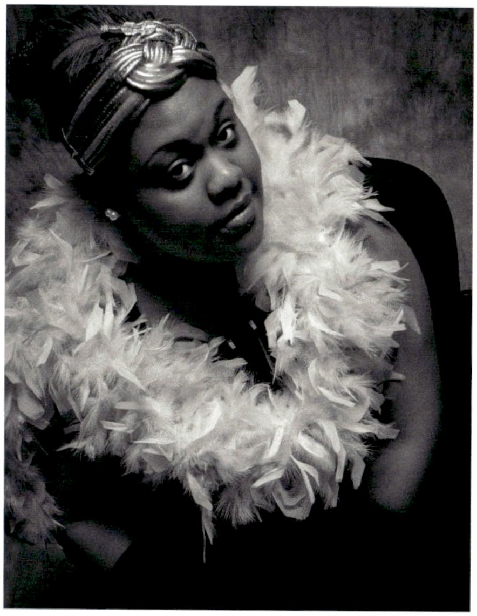

FIGURE 30.3 *Butterfly from the side. Jessica Peterson. Photo by Tomas Patlan.*

3. Side

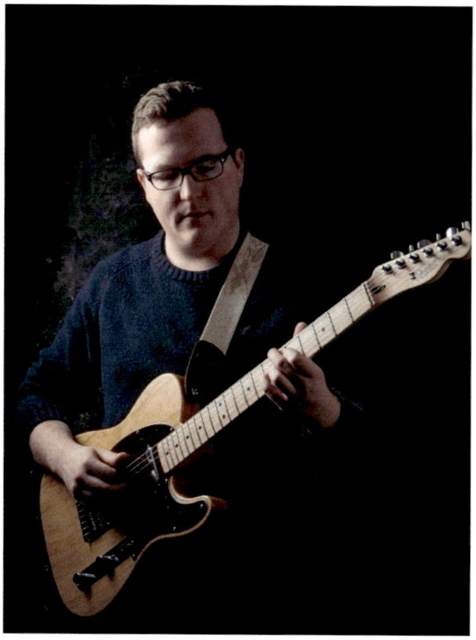

FIGURE 30.4 *Side lighting. Shawn Thornhill. Photo by Jerome Stretch.*

4. Rim

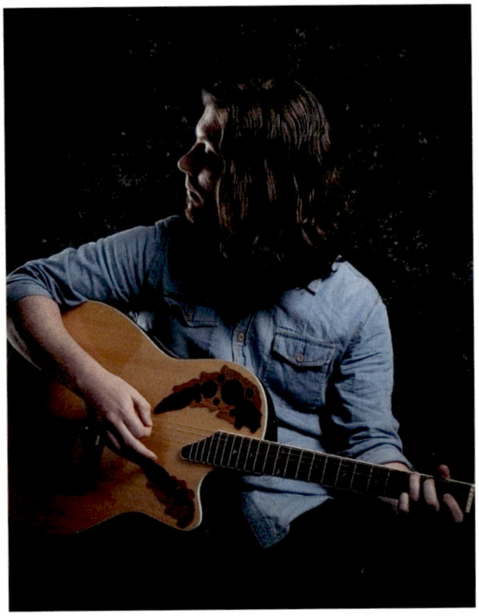

FIGURE 30.5 *Rim lighting. Ethan Wilson. Photo by Jerome Stretch.*

5. Long (broad)

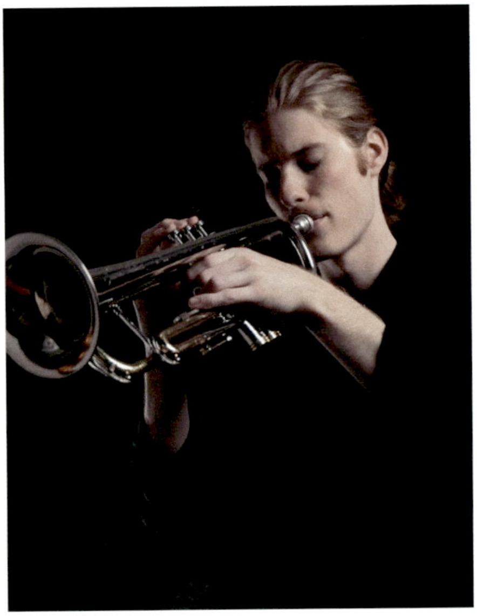

FIGURE 30.6 *Long lighting. Kylan Berger. Photo by Jerome Stretch.*

6. Short

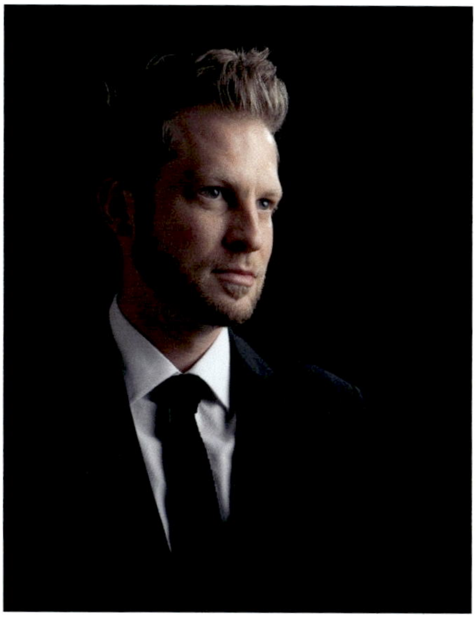

FIGURE 30.7 *Short lighting. Jason Wenger. Photo by Jerome Stretch.*

PART 2

Once you have familiarized yourself with the different styles and light positions in a controlled environment, it is time to take it outside. You will need to find a subject to model for a few hours.

Walk around campus, downtown, or your neighborhood and try to find examples of the seven lighting styles and positions from above.

Butterfly and forty-five should be fairly easy using sunlight. For side, rim, short, and long lighting a good bet would be a window. You can position your model next to the window facing the camera for side lighting; turn facing the window for side profile; move so the window is behind and to their side for rim; turn their head away from the window and halfway towards the camera for long. I'll let you figure out short.

ASSIGNMENT 31

20 Frames

"Only photograph what you love."

—Tim Walker

PURPOSE: THIS PROJECT IS DESIGNED TO TEACH YOU TO DISCIPLINE YOURSELF NOT TO OVERSHOOT.

For this assignment cover the LCD screen on the back of your camera using black photographer's tape, white drafting tape, or a piece of cardboard. Do not look at your image previews or histogram. Set the exposure and create your compositions without the aid of the preview.

When you begin your career as a photographer you want to identify things that interest you and learn how to photograph them in ways that interest other people. As you progress in skill and vision, you learn to photograph things that *don't* interest you—or anyone else for that matter—in order to make them interesting to other people.

For this assignment think about what kinds of things interest you: sports; people in enclosed spaces (e.g., coffee house, concert, keggers); street scenes; your pets; your children, boyfriend, girlfriend, spouse; collection of dolls, toy soldiers, or stuffed animals; arboretums; zoos; landscape; old buildings.

Choose one as your subject.

Expose *exactly* twenty frames from as many different vantage points and points of view as you can. If the subject is moveable (e.g., a stuffed-animal collection), then create as many different compositions as you can. Don't delete anything—include misfires and mistakes.

To get the most out of this assignment either move to a new vantage point or rearrange the composition after each exposure—don't take two images in a row from the same position or of the same composition.

If your subject can't be moved (e.g., a landscape or building), then photograph it from as many angles/positions as you can: from the base of the hill or building; from the top; out of a window. Come back later, or earlier the next day, and photograph it in a different light.

ASSIGNMENT 32

Event Photography

"A good photograph is one that communicates a fact, touches the heart, and leaves the viewer a changed person for having seen it; it is in one word, effective."

—Irving Penn

PURPOSE: TO RECORD AN EVENT IN PHOTOS.

For this assignment, you will need to locate an event that interests you. It could be a county fair; strip mall carnival; concert; parade; festival of any kind; work party; Renaissance Faire; sporting event; etc. Plan ahead and read up about the event, whether it is a blurb in the local paper or an event website.

Using the information you have gathered (assuming there is some), make a list of the performances and highlights. For example, for a Renaissance Faire you will want to know when the Queen of the Faire will be crowned, when there will be a joust, and any other events that may sound interesting to photograph.

What you are going to do is record the event so those who could not be there can participate vicariously; and those who were there can relive it. If you get really good at doing this you may even be able to sell photos to the organizers and/or photograph future events as a paid photographer.

Attempt to contact the event organizer in advance. Tell them you are learning photography—if you are at university, mention that—and request behind-the-scenes access. If you can't obtain access, it simply means you must photograph what everyone else sees, in ways they don't see it.

Try to arrive early, or at least prior to the first happening you intend to photograph. Walk the area if possible. Look for vantage points. You can't be everywhere at once, so you want to be in the most likely spot. If that spot turns out to be a dud, you want to know where to quickly move while the event is still in progress.

The first thing you want to photograph is an establishing shot. Photograph the poster or marquee announcing the event with the date, time, and place. You can do a close-up, but even better is to show it in context with the background: the front of the building; the sign on the gate, etc.

From that point forward constantly remind yourself: If I weren't here what would I want someone to show me so I can feel like I was? That's the key. Photograph everything you can, with emphasis on what you think will show the event to its best advantage.

Gain Access

If you happen to know the event organizers or are yourself part of the group, you should arrive before anyone else and begin photographing the space/area before people arrive.

One OSU student photographed an outdoor rock concert put on by her church group. She arrived early and photographed the empty field where the concert was to take place. She photographed the first arrivals, who came to build a temporary stage; the sound crew when they arrived; the other participants; then the audience; the musicians arriving; then the performance; and then the breakdown. At the end of a long day she had in-depth coverage of the event, and a record of something that had meaning to her and her community.

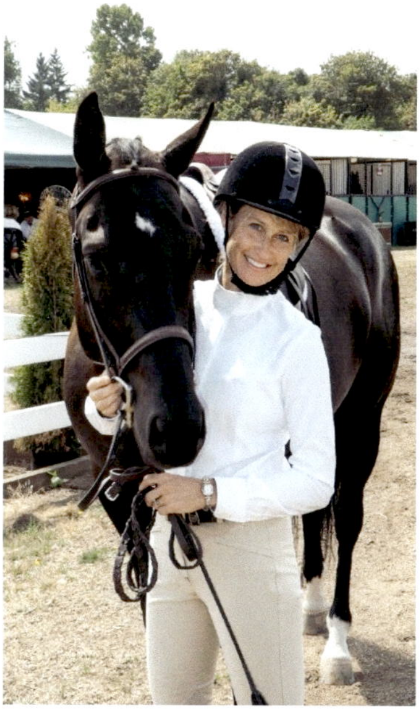

FIGURE 32.1 *Photograph before the event . . .*

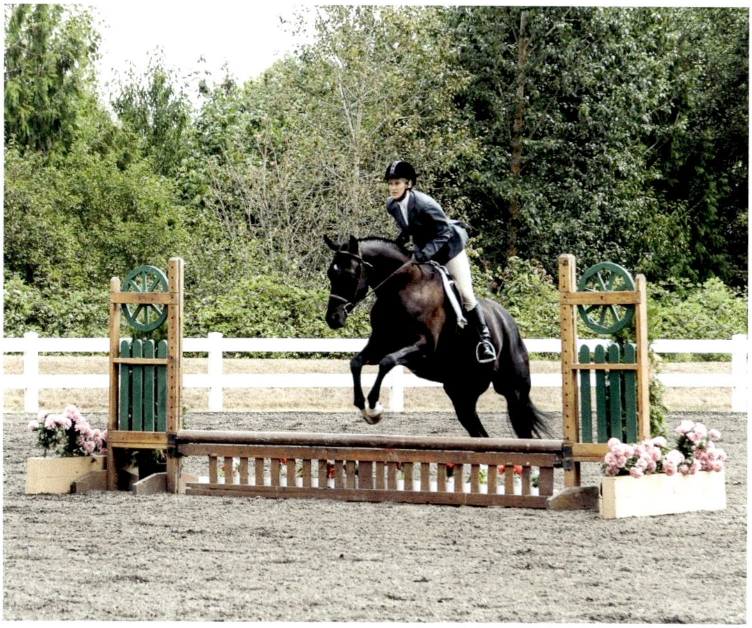

FIGURE 32.2 *. . . during the event . . .*

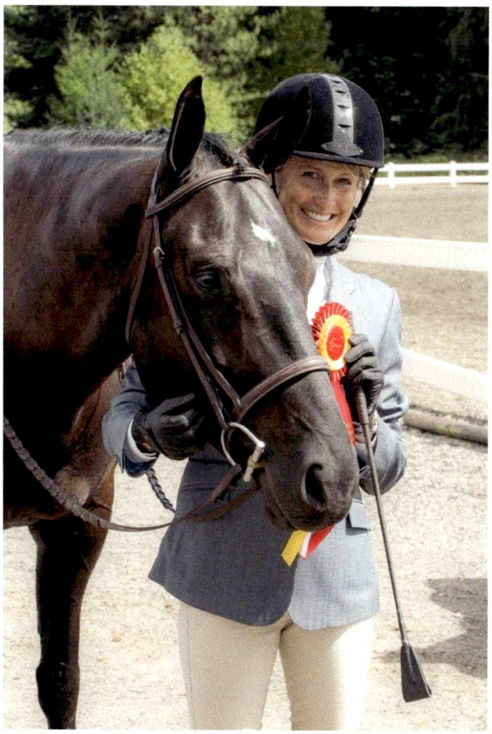

FIGURE 32.3 *. . . and after the event.*

ASSIGNMENT 33

A Day in the Life

"The camera is an excuse to be someplace you otherwise don't belong. It gives me both a point of connection and a point of separation."

—Susan Meiselas

PURPOSE: TO BECOME ACCUSTOMED TO PHOTOGRAPHING PEOPLE.

For this assignment you need permission from someone to follow them around and photograph their activities. It could be a relative, best friend, or your significant other. It could be a political candidate or someone you admire for other reasons.

The subject needs to clearly understand that you need access to the fullest extent during the time you are together, including their private moments. You will then follow and photograph them for an agreed period of time. It could be an entire day, from waking to retiring, or it could be a three- to four-hour period when they are most active.

At first they will be self-conscious and strike poses—let them. Take a photo of their pose—it will make them feel more comfortable. Then take another photograph right after the pose ends and they go back to what they were doing. Some subjects will become irritable. Back off, stay out of their way, but stay in the game. After a while they will simply forget you're there—sooner or later everyone does. That's when you'll get your best photos.

Although this is a "day" in the life, it can actually be photographed over several days and the images sequenced later. If this is the case, be certain that the subject wears the same clothes. An example is a day-in-the-life story by an OSU student who photographed a Marine back from a tour in Iran but still on active duty.

Obtaining permission from his superior officer, she photographed the Marine over several days, from waking to retiring; wearing his uniform to and from the duties he performed each day. When she had what she needed, she sequenced the photos to appear as if they were all taken in one day.

Remember, this is photography, not reality. If you want reality, be there.

> Students should not edit on the computer if they are doing straight kinds of images [editor's note: documentary, street, event]. Pretty much all their images should be tiled with their file number and printed. The images don't need to be bigger than postcard size though they need to be cut to a uniform size. These small proofs are what they need to edit with and sequence. They can have this mini portfolio with them pretty much all the time. If they sit down for coffee they can sort and make piles, relationships, "dates and marriages" sequences.
>
> This is far more flexible than doing it on the computer. Also, as they play with these images—and I do recommend playing with them—they will SEE new correspondences and visual connections. Images will come together in ways they had not thought of.
>
> Linda Connor
> Professor of Photography
> San Francisco Art Institute

ASSIGNMENT 34

Extended Documentary

". . . we are there with our cameras to record reality. Once we start modifying that which exists, we are robbing photography of its most valuable attribute."
—Philip Jones Griffiths

PURPOSE: TO TELL A STORY IN PHOTOS.

An extended documentary is a story of a particular ethnic group, community, fraternal organization, lifestyle, social class, age group, or an individual. It could be the story of a place or culture; a city, urban renewal project, highway, or national park.

When you begin an extended documentary it's not always possible to place an end time to it. It might take a week, a month, or years to complete.

I photographed Route 66 one to two months a year for ten years; after that, I felt there was no more story to be told even though there were a lot more photos to make.

Another project I worked on was documenting people over seventy years of age in the San Luis Valley of Colorado. After three months I had not photographed everyone but I felt the story had been told, and stopped.

The individual images are not as important as the way they flow, one to the next, like the chapters in a book. You need to think of every image, every set of images, in relation to how they fit in and flow with the next set.

To be successful at documentary photography, you must find out as much as you can about the people and places you are going to include. If the people involved are open and accepting, you should interview them, individually or in groups, to find out their concerns, what motivates them, why they are doing what they are doing. This will help you get beneath the surface. If the people are hostile, you should still attempt to interview them to better understand their point of view before you photograph them.

If possible, involve yourself in some of their activities. If it is a place you are photographing, not people, then spend some time there. Don't attempt

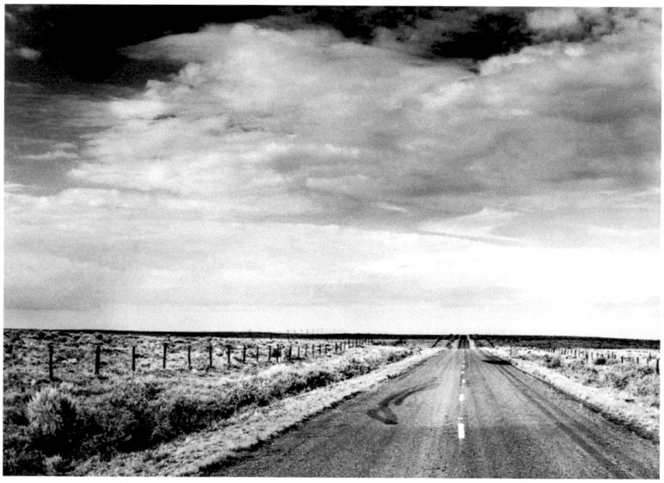

FIGURE 34.1 *Route 66 East of Navajo, Ariz.. from "Route 66" project.*

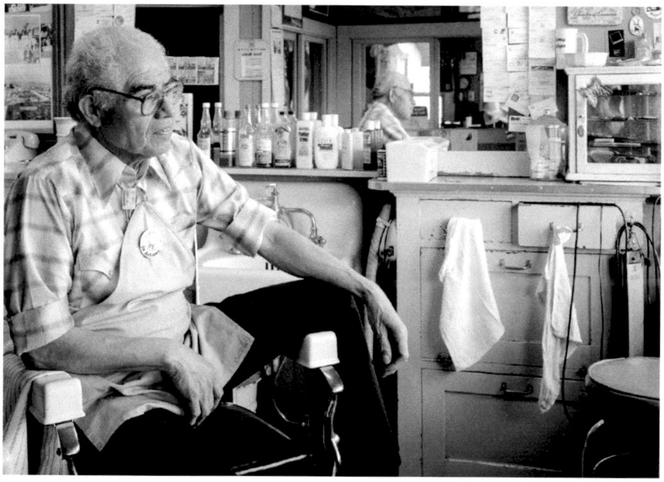

FIGURE 34.2 *Angel Delgadillo, Mayor of Seligman, Ariz., from "Route 66" project.*

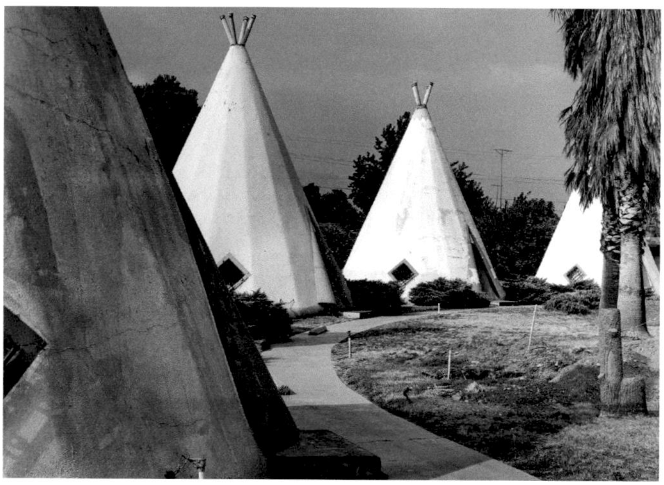

FIGURE 34.3 *Wigwam Motel, Rialto, Calif., from "Route 66" project.*

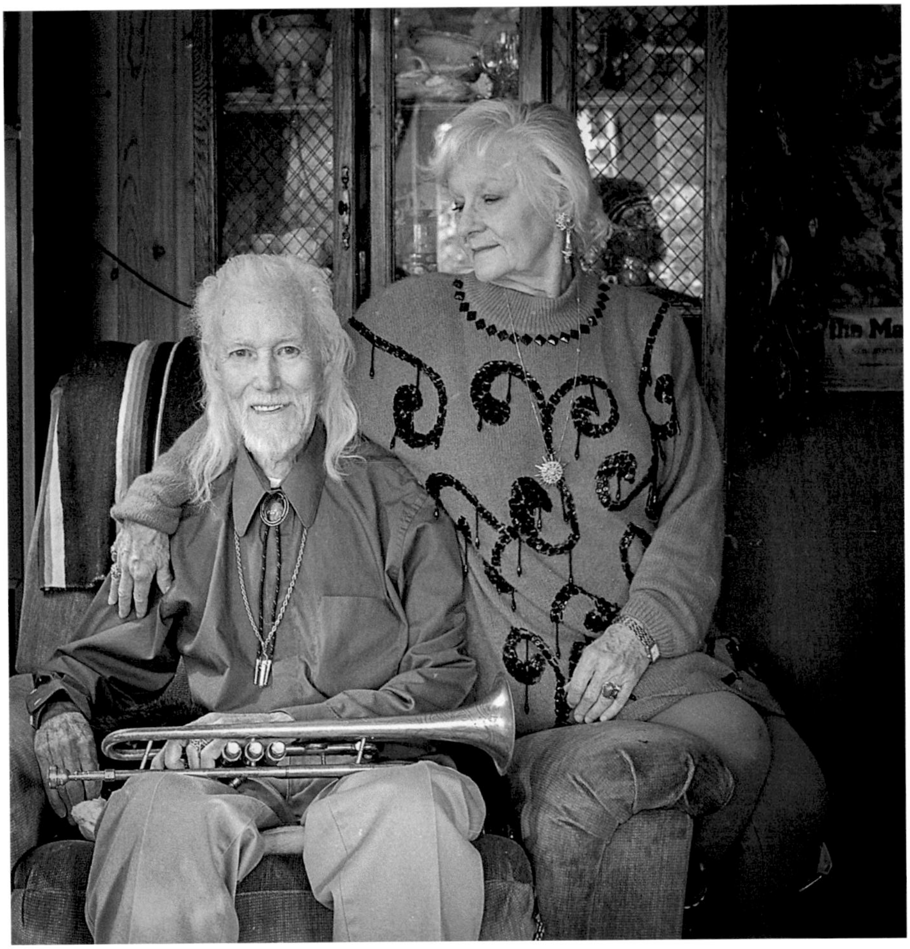

FIGURE 34.4 *Al and BG Purvis, from "Honor the Elders" project.*

to do a documentary of Zion National Park unless you have at least walked the trails and spoken with the rangers.

Once you have insight into the people or place you intend to document, you should create a storyboard. Make up a page with four to six boxes on it and sketch out the story you intend to tell in each box and how you intend to tell it. Use stick figures if you can't draw. If you can't draw stick figures, then write out the intended photo in the box. Draw or write in pencil. Allow your preconceived ideas of how the story should unfold to grow, change, and evolve as you spend more and more time with the subject.

Write inside the boxes the photos you need to advance the story or to connect the story as if it were a story of words rather than photos. Just like a written story, there may be photographs needed to bridge ideas or span time.

Then prepare to spend as much free time with the subject as possible. And take notes—lots of notes. Record everyone's name and where and when you photographed them. Keep a journal. In your down time write your impressions and how you are progressing. One of the great documentarians of the twentieth century, Dorothea Lange, kept copious notes of everything and everyone she photographed; as did many others.

As the work progresses make small prints, 3 x 5 inches or 4 x 6 inches, and lay them out on the floor. Move them around and see how they flow or if the story is making sense—if it isn't, what else do you need to photograph? Have trusted friends or family look at the story on the floor and see if they can "read" the photographs.

Photograph it until you feel the story is told and then stop.

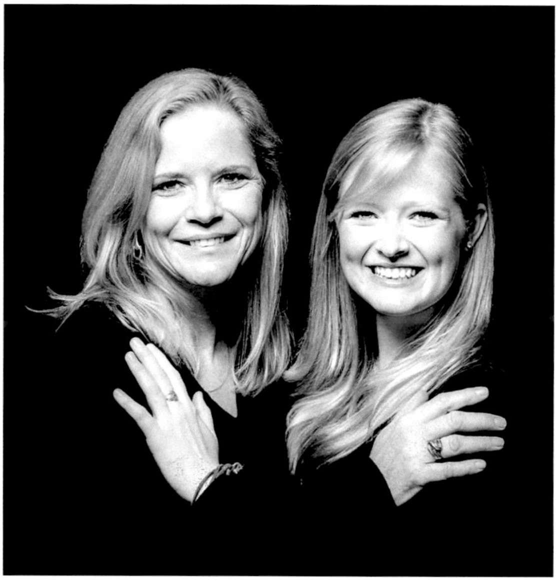

FIGURE 34.5 *Elizabeth and Brenda, from "Mothers/daughters project."*

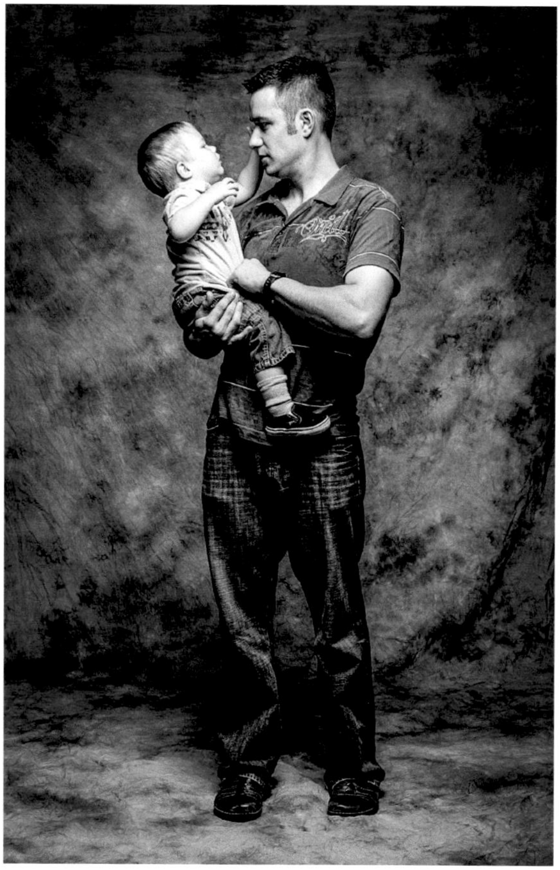

FIGURE 34.6 *Joel and Caleb, from "Fathers/sons" project.*

ASSIGNMENT 35

Editing DSLR Video

Contributed by Ford Lowcock
Professor of Photography, Santa Monica College, California

"Today everything exists to end in a photograph."

—Susan Sontag

PURPOSE: TO INTRODUCE BASIC VIDEO-EDITING SKILLS.

This assignment requires the use of an image-editing program. Current versions of Photoshop have a scaled-down video-editing program embedded. Photoshop video-editing software is not as powerful as Adobe Premiere Pro, Final Cut Pro, or Avid, but it is an excellent program to learn on. The skills you gain can be easily segued into the more professional programs mentioned.

Because of the availability of Photoshop and the ease of learning the basic video-editing program, it will be used as the software model in the following assignment.

CINEMAGRAPH

The goal is to create image content that incorporates two digital video files between 30—60 seconds in length, a still image, and background music. The final piece will be rendered as a movie.

Ground Rules

- Do not use any previously edited video that you have created. However, you may use previously recorded raw (unedited) clips.
- Don't repeat the exact or too similar POV in duplicate sequences.
- You will need a still image to use with the two video clips.

Vimeo is an online video sharing and resource site. The basic membership is free. It is recommended that you register on their site and then make use of its online resources. You can begin with storyboarding. Here's a link to storyboarding basics on Vimeo: http://vimeo.com/videoschool/lesson/4/storyboarding-basics.

Capture

- Create a story to bring to life. Write the story in an outline format. This is your script, aka treatment, that you will follow as you assemble your pieces in an image-editing program. Think and describe what images need to be static and what motion imagery works in support of the still image. Create a storyboard to follow.
- Ideally you should use a DSLR camera and a tripod with a fluid head. (There is a saying in the movie industry: No matter how good you think you are handheld, you aren't that good.)
- Think simple in terms of capture. In terms of story, be dynamic, visually appealing and give the viewer a reason to watch your movie.
- If you do not have access to a DSLR camera, you can use a cell phone with video capabilities. Your capture and output options may be limited but there is no end to the apps you can download in order to dress it up. You can also find tripod adapters online for cell phones; check out Joby at www.joby.com.
- The final video should be compelling to view. Today's culture is about constant interaction. A still image is about being alone—contemplative; intellectual; thoughtful. Motion is about today—being in touch 24/7; tweeting; iChatting; non-stop; sharing to the max.
- Remember, too, that most of today's culture views imagery on a mobile device—small and portable. Your imagery has to be more impactful when viewed small.
- Capture enough video clips from two separate situations that you are able to select the "perfect" clip from each. Think simple. Try to find situations that could be recorded as direct, uncut, unedited footage. Choose one of the two situations to be your main movie.

Process

1. Download the video files from your media card onto your hard drive.
2. Process your RAW still image in Photoshop or Lightroom as an sRGB, 8-bit file. Make note of the size of your main movie and apply that to the still image in terms of ppi (usually 72ppi) and the long-side dimension.
3. Import your two video clips into Photoshop: File > Open. Photoshop will automatically open them in the video-editing window on the same edit track as Video Group 1, Figure 35.1. You can create a second edit track at any time and drag either of the clips to it in order to overlap or for other special effects.

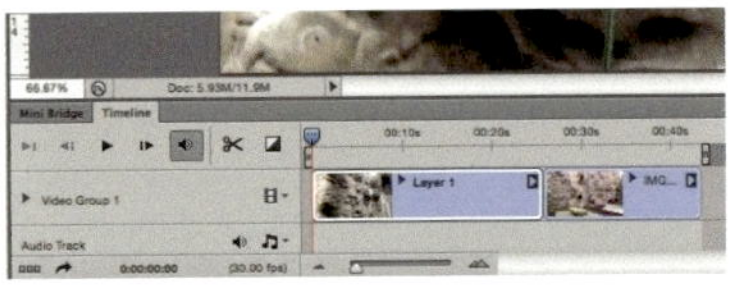

FIGURE 35.1

4. To add the still image click on the filmstrip icon to the left of the two clips and select Add Media, Figure 35.2. Navigate to your still image and click Open. Drag the image to where you want it in the video: the beginning, end, or between the two clips as seen in Figure 35.3.

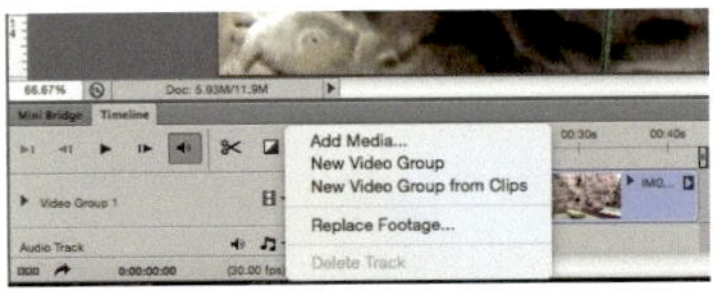

FIGURE 35.2

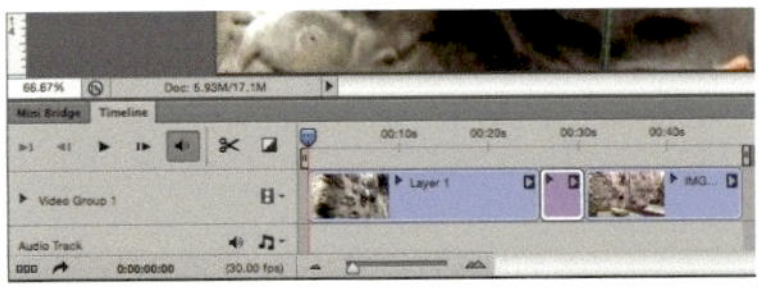

FIGURE 35.3

5. To create a fade between the clips and the still image click on the black and white icon to the right of the scissors and drag whichever fade you want to use and drop it between the two media, Figure 35.4.

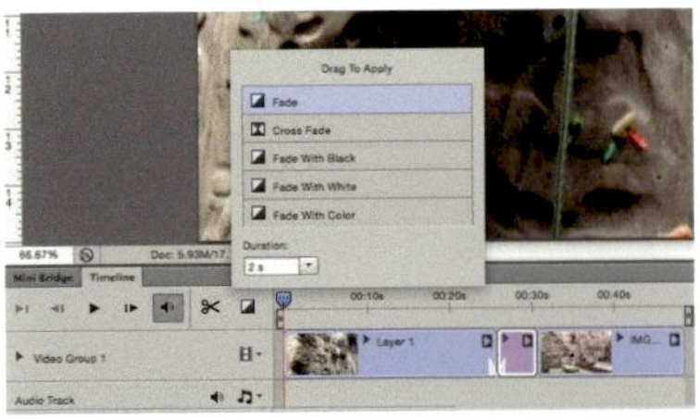

FIGURE 35.4

6. To add audio drop down to the audio track below the video track and click on the music symbol then Add Audio. Navigate to where your music is stored and select the track you want to use, Figure 35.5.

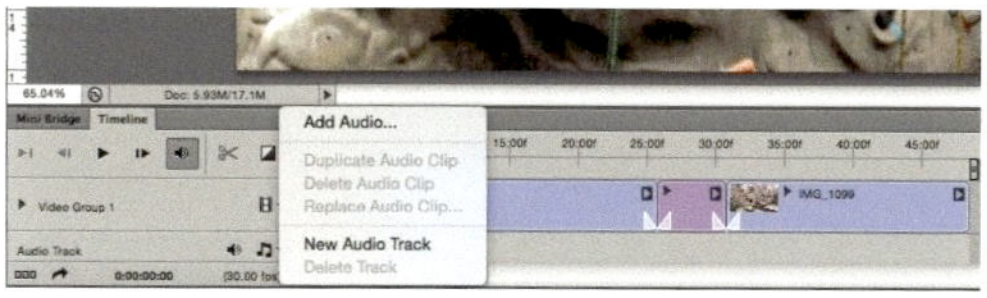

FIGURE 35.5

7. If you want to add an open or end slide, create one in a separate file in Photoshop>File>New, using the type tool and adding background color or graphics if desired. Make certain the size of the slide matches the size of the video frame, the ppi matches (usually 72 ppi), the color space is the same (usually sRGB), and the bit depth is set at 8 bit. Copy and paste the title slide onto Video Group 1. You can drag and drop it anywhere on the track, Figure 35.6.

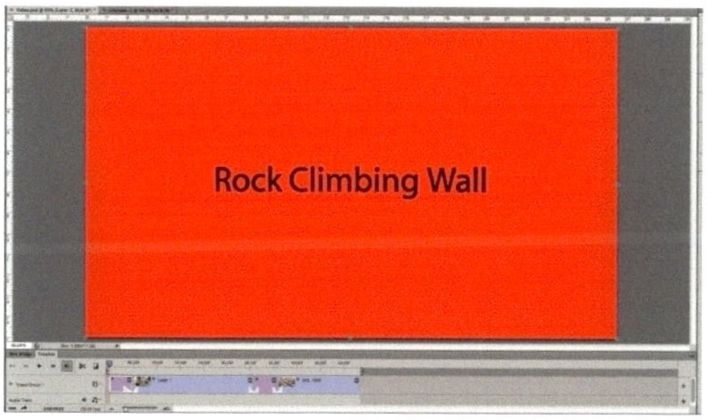

FIGURE 35.6

8. The final step is to render the video for viewing. Before you do save it as a .psd file. If you flatten it first the file will be smaller. If you don't flatten it you can open it and work on it again.
9. See After Process, below, for tips on rendering.

After-Process

Save the file then render it as a HD video, File> Export>Render Video, Figure 35.7. Look on Vimeo for their recommendations: http://vimeo.com/help/compression.

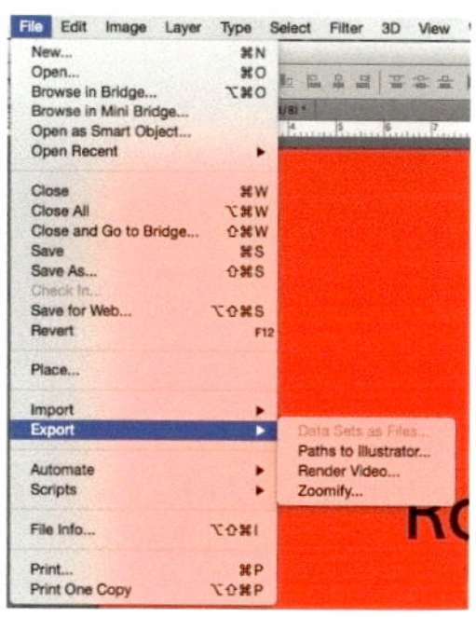

FIGURE 35.7

You can see the settings for the 5D Mark III in the screen capture illustration, Figure 35.8. While there might be slight variances, they should be more or less the same for most DSLR video cameras.

- Name and where to save.
- Select Adobe Media Encoder.
- Format: H.264.
- Preset: Vimeo, since you are going to be uploading to Vimeo.
- Size: Document Size.
- Frame Rate: Document Frame Rate.
- Field Order: Preset (Progressive).
- Aspect: Document (1.0).

Vimeo will compress what you upload, so you'll need to review it online. If the results are not what you expect, try rendering again with more appropriate export settings.

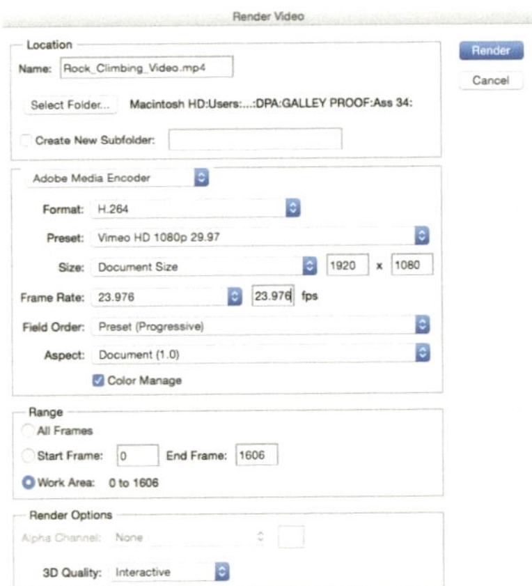

FIGURE 35.8

ASSIGNMENT 36

Prohibitions

Contributed by Dr. Shaun Huston
Western Oregon University

> *"Photographs open doors into the past, but they also allow a look into the future."*
>
> —Sally Mann

Look around. You are surrounded on all sides by prohibitions: Don't walk; don't run; no smoking; do not enter; twenty-one years or older; no shoes, no shirt, no service; wrong way; use other entrance; stop; no outside food or drink; no overnight camping; do not walk on the grass; do not leave your car unattended.

For this video project, you are to create a one- to two-minute video that illustrates not the words but the meaning of the prohibitions. You may select one theme, or multiple themes.

To be successful you should spend time reflecting on the purpose of the prohibition: Why it is in place; and the consequences of violating it—to you or to others. Is there a good reason for the prohibition, or is it someone's control issue? Think about how you can visually express the purpose and/or the consequences.

You should then write a treatment, or create a storyboard, that you can follow both in filming and in assembling the footage during editing.

In filming the video be certain not to violate any prohibitions that might endanger you or someone else, including your performers, if any.

Should you need to access private property, or violate a posted prohibition, first gain permission from the owner or the appropriate authorities. Bear in mind that all professional filmmakers take these precautions prior to filming. If they are not able to obtain permission, they find a location where they can—or they create their own location on a back lot. Creating illusion is a major part of filmmaking.

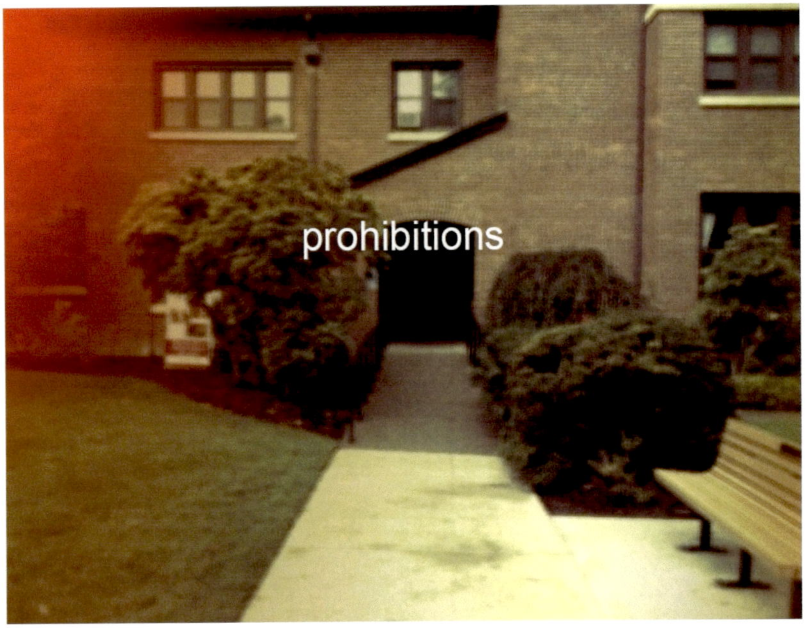

FIGURE 36.1 *This video was made with an iPhone for Shaun Huston's "Prohibitions" project. An 8mm film app was used to make it appear as if it were an old film that had begun to deteriorate.*

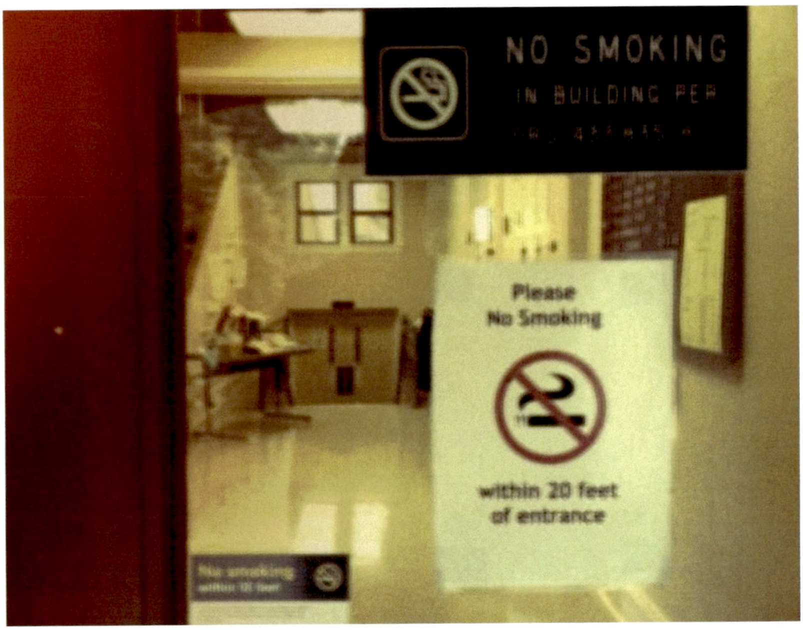

FIGURE 36.2 *The prohibition was "no smoking."*

SECTION 4

Getting Noticed

Senior

ASSIGNMENT 37

Tribute Photo

"All photographs are accurate. None of them is the truth."

—Richard Avedon

PURPOSE: REPLICATE A FAMOUS PHOTOGRAPH IN YOUR OWN UNIQUE STYLE.

All art is derivative—no one creates in a vacuum. Everyone is influenced to some extent by what has gone before. If you don't study the work of other artists—not just photographers but painters, writers, musicians—then your influences will come to you second hand from people who do, usually through billboards, ads, television, and magazine articles.

A Question of Influence

A large-format landscape photographer told me that he doesn't look at anyone else's work, as he does not wish to be influenced by anyone. I thought it circumspect not to point out that his recent work was photographing petroglyphs, one of the oldest art forms.

"The more pictures you see, the better you are as a photographer."

—Robert Mapplethorpe

The fastest way to grow creatively is to study other artists' work. Not only those you like, but also those you don't, to try and discover why some people do.

The web is an inexhaustible resource for viewing the work of others—both historical and contemporary. Libraries are a great place to find oversized books of photographers and artists. And it never hurts to visit a museum or attend a gallery opening.

For this assignment, you need to identify a commercial photograph that you really like. By commercial, I mean a photograph that was used in an ad campaign. This is because most photographs used in ads are made in a controlled environment and it will be easier for you to replicate (in the commercial industry it's called a "knock-off").

The idea is to parody the image, not copy it.

For my own tribute photo, I chose one of my alltime favorites, *Dovima with Elephants, evening dress by Dior, Cirque d'hiver, Paris, August 1955*. To see the original, go to www.avedonfoundation.net, navigate to the Archive folder and search for the photo under Fashion. My tribute photo is entitled *Dovima with 16-wheelers*, 1996.

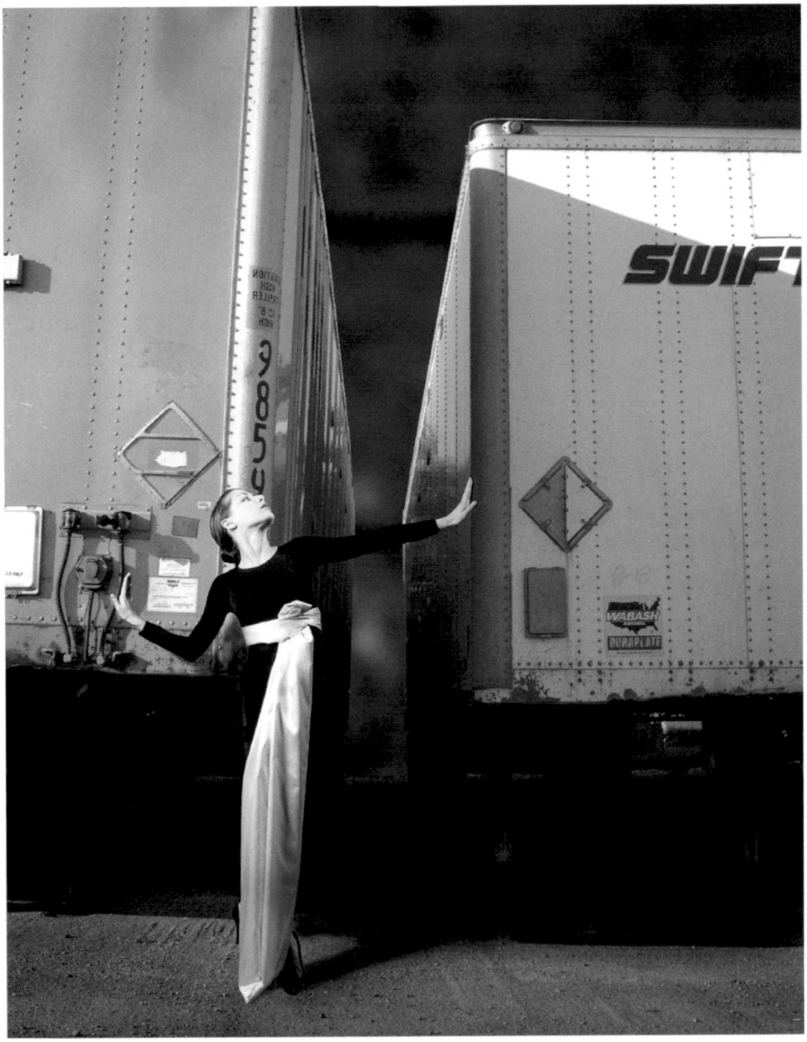

FIGURE 37.1 Dovima with 16-Wheelers, *1996. ©2014 Steve Anchell.*

My tribute photo was made by combining three photos: Kira Distler; sixteen-wheelers; background (Figure 37.1).

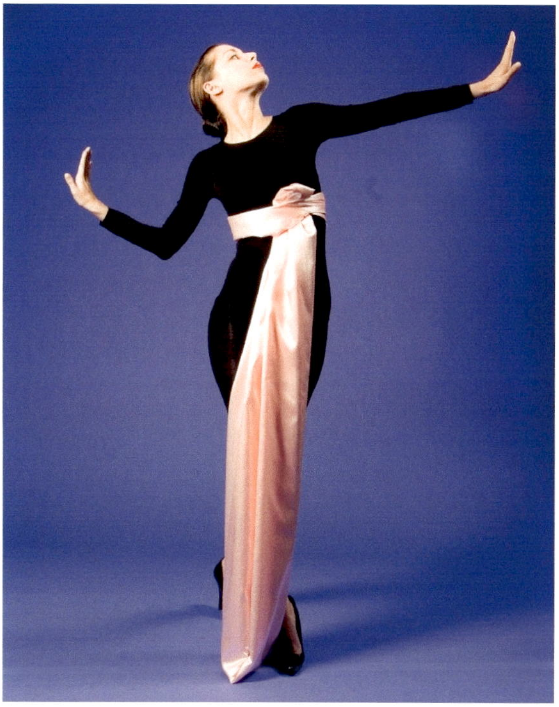

FIGURE 37.2 *Model: Kira Distler.*

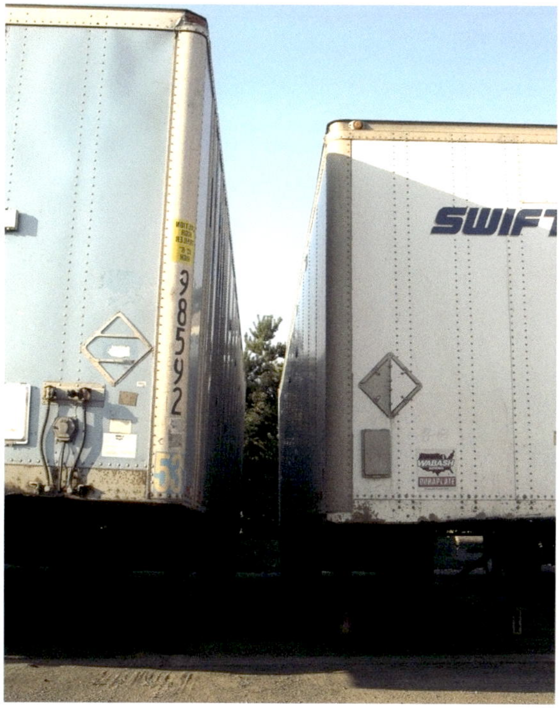

FIGURE 37.3 *The inspiration for this photo came when I passed by these two parked trailers. Being familiar with Avedon's iconic image,* Dovima with Elephants, *I immediately recognized the possibility.*

FIGURE 37.4 *The background was a photograph of a wall on a building near the trailers. It was intentionally photographed out of focus.*

ASSIGNMENT 38

Building a Portfolio

Contributed by Brent Wood
Professor of Photography, Victor Valley College

> *"Which of my photographs is my favorite? The one I'm going to take tomorrow."*
>
> — Imogen Cunningham

Your assignment is to build a portfolio of twelve unique images based on the concepts outlined below.

The portfolio you build for this project will reflect the industry in which you are going to look for work. For this assignment, select your strongest area of photographic interest to build a targeted portfolio.

- Your portfolio will consist of twelve 8 x 10-inch prints matted on 11 x 14-inch mat board.
- A mixture of color and black and white should be used—even if you only work in one or the other. This is a lesson in learning to sort, combine, and organize, as much as anything else.
- The final portfolio should be placed in a professional portfolio case, a printed copy of your resume to be included.
- Include a digital portfolio on a CD with a digital copy of your resume.

Portfolio Resource

A good source for portfolio supplies is Freestyle Photographic Sales in Los Angeles, www.freestylephoto.biz, 800.292.6137.

FIVE STEPS TO A POWERFUL PORTFOLIO

1. The work must be good. You need to be absolutely ruthless in choosing your samples.
2. The work must be relevant to the interests and needs of the client/ company.
3. Your samples must convincingly demonstrate that your work can be an advantageous choice for the client.
4. Your images must be organized so they deliver a clear message to the client of just what it is you do and what subjects, styles, and techniques you have to offer.
5. The physical form of your presentation must be efficiently designed, attractive, and easy to look through.
6. Above all, don't repeat yourself. Each of the twelve images should be unique and unlike any other in the portfolio.

ASSIGNMENT 39

Camera Phones and Apps

Contributed by Dan Burkholder

> *"Art does not depend on the tools used, but on how they are used; in the hands of an artist, the camera produces works of art."*
>
> —Paul L. Anderson

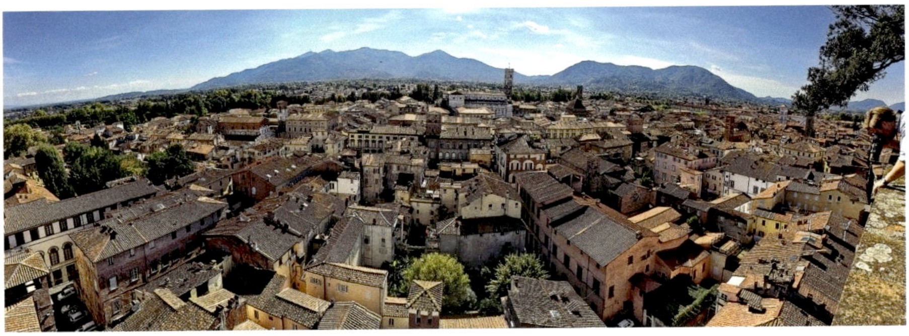

FIGURE 39.1 *Italy panorama made with the sweep panorama mode on an iPhone 5S.*

Photography is filled with an almost overwhelming array of hardware, optical, software, and esthetic choices. There are so many options that many practitioners often fall into "decision paralysis," where they are so overwhelmed by the photographic possibilities that they end up doing nothing well . . . or just nothing. I've seen this often when photographers carry more than one format camera, too many lenses, or—in a very contemporary affliction—have too many apps on their iPhones. To help avoid bogging down with our mobile photography, I've found it helpful to separate the photographic process into three sections:

1. Capturing the Image.
2. Editing the Image.
3. Stylizing the Image.

For this assignment, we'll delve into neat capture techniques and even start to tiptoe into some editing steps.

STITCHING

Stitching is the process of shooting two or more separate photos that are seamlessly combined via software into a new photo with a wider field of view. There are many apps that tackle stitching; let's look at just two of the best for creating panoramas and larger stitched images.

The Built-In Camera App Does Stitching (with iOS 7 and the iPhone 4s and newer)

Just as most of us begin our iPhoneography journey with the iPhone's built-in camera app for normal, single frame exposures, let's see how Apple's pre-installed camera app handles stitching.

Choosing Pano Mode in the iPhone's Camera App

Apple doesn't call it "stitching" but rather Pano (for Panorama).

You get to Pano mode by sliding the modes (Video, Photo, Square, Pano, etc.) left and right.

> Hot Tip: It's tedious to slide those little yellow mode labels (shown in Figure 39.2) back and forth. Instead, try sliding your finger left or right on the image area itself to select a different mode. It's much easier!

Let's examine some of the features of Pano Mode on our iPhones in Figure 39.2 below:

1. When the yellow Pano label is above the shutter button, you're in Pano mode.
2. The default *sweep* of the camera is from left to right. Tapping on the white arrow (circled in red) will reverse the pano direction.
3. Here the arrow is aimed to the left for a right-to-left sweep of the camera during pano shooting.
4. The camera app even provides helpful tips when shooting the pano; if you sweep too quickly, the suggestion to "Slow Down" will appear here.

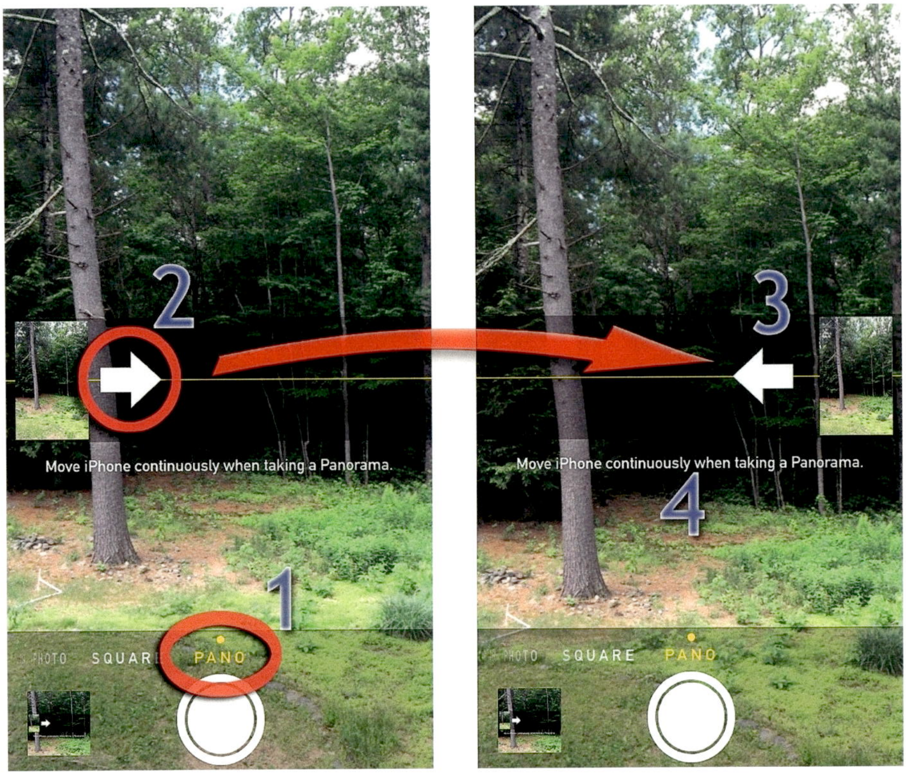

FIGURE 39.2 *The iPhone's pano mode.*

Figure 39.3 shows the final sweep panorama made with the iPhone's Pano mode.

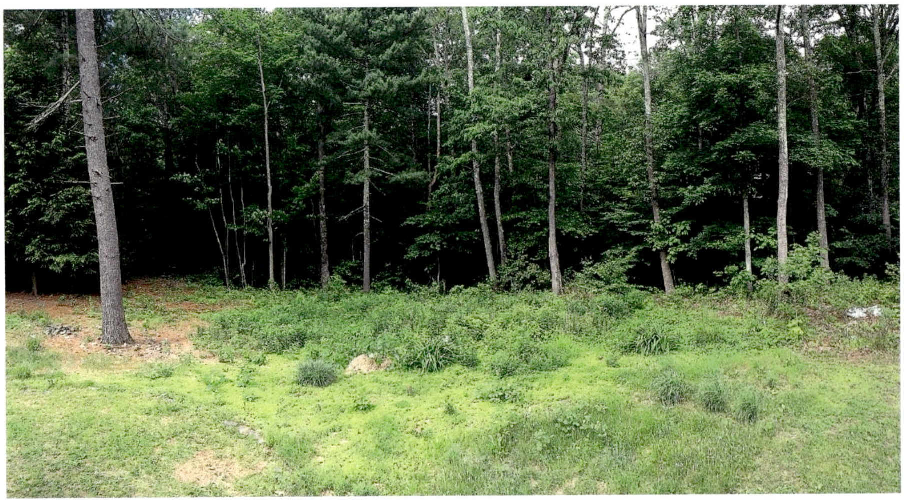

FIGURE 39.3 *The iPhone's Pano mode.*

After about five minutes of editing on the iPhone 5s, the final version is shown in Figure 39.4 below. What's most marvelous about iPhone photography is that we can start editing right on the spot instead of waiting to get back to a computer with Photoshop. It's an intoxicating workflow.

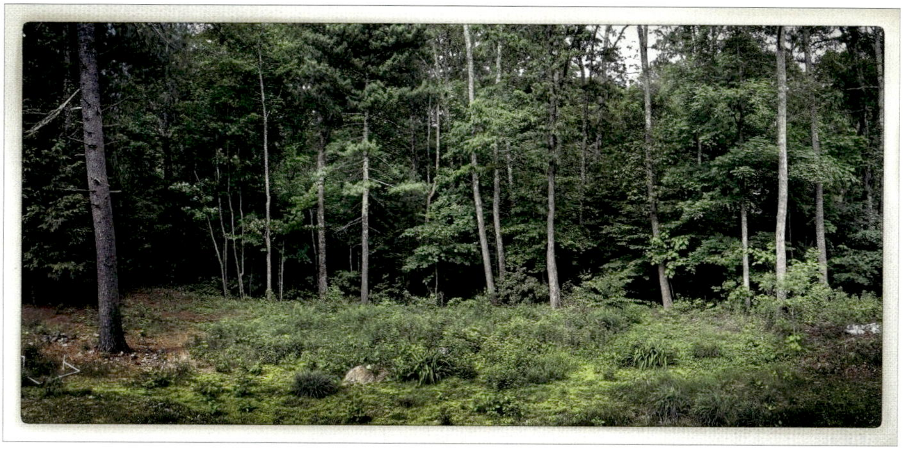

FIGURE 39.4 *After a short editing session on the iPhone.*

Camera–Time Distortions with Pano Mode

For a real bit of fun, try using the Pano mode in different ways. In Figure 39.5 I swept from right to left as a crew boat went down the river in Florence, Italy. Because the boat was traveling in the same direction as my sweep, it was rendered almost like a stretch limo, while the buildings in the background were rendered normally.

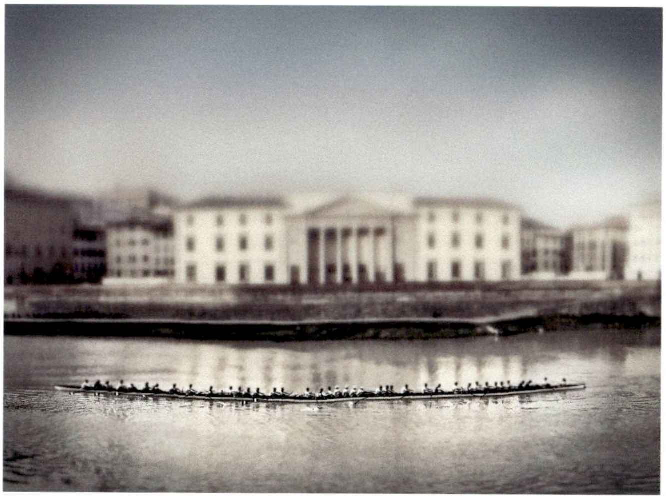

FIGURE 39.5 *Crew boat on the Arno River. Captured with the iPhone 5S sweep panorama mode.*

YOUR ASSIGNMENT (PART A)

You should photograph a scene using your iPhone's Pano mode, choosing either the sweep-right or sweep-left direction. Also, take a screen shot of your iPhone's LCD (like I did in Figure 39.2) by pressing the Power button and Home button simultaneously. This is your "honest" shot.

Here's a summation of the three images you should have on your iPhone so far for this assignment:

Image Number	What it Should Be	What it Should Illustrate
01	A Pano taken with your iPhone's Pano Mode	This image should be a wide pano. Note: you can shoot vertically with the sweep Pano mode also.
02	A screenshot of your iPhone's screen, as I did in figure 39.2.	This shows you were indeed using the Pano mode of your iPhone. Note: you do not have to markup your screenshot with arrows and circles!

AutoStitch Is a Miracle Maker

Making simple, sweep-pano stitches is great fun and often produces just the wide-frame effect we need to capture an expansive subject. But stitching can be much more. For the past five years I've explored what I call 2-D (for two-dimensional) stitching. The 2-D means we stitch not just a series of horizontal images; we also shoot up and down to capture taller compositions. We can't do this magic with the Apple camera app, however. Let's look at how easy it is to play in this 2-D stitching playground.

AutoStitch is the best $1.99 you could possibly spend if you're a photographer. It's amazing how it combines multiple images to build stunning photos with depth and intrigue.

Caution: Sometimes you'll encounter imposter apps in the App Store. When you search for "AutoStitch," the app's icon should look like Figure 39.6

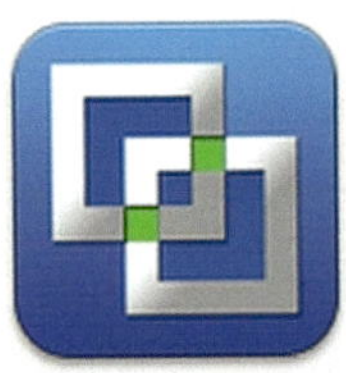

FIGURE 39.6 *AutoStitch's icon (make sure you purchase this one).*

Figure 39.7 shows an image I shot, using AutoStitch, to combine twenty-eight individual images.

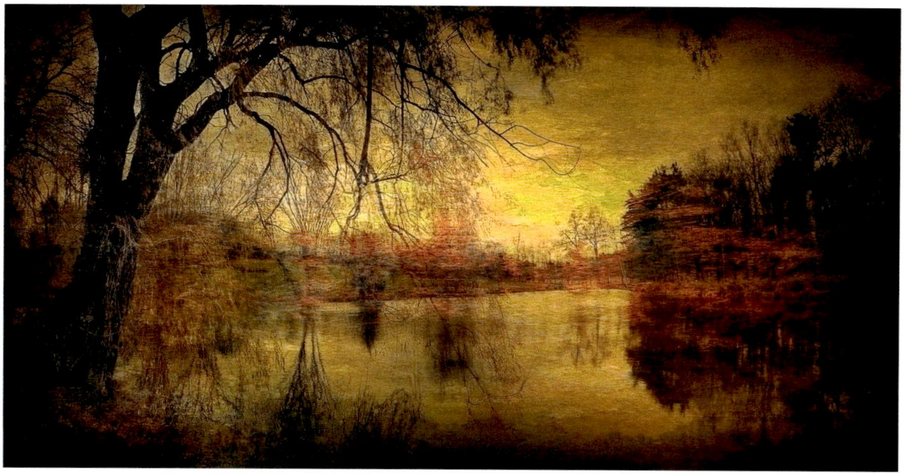

FIGURE 39.7 *The final stitched image with editing on an iPhone 3GS.*

In Figure 39.8 you see the group of individual exposures that were melded with AutoStitch. Look closely and you'll notice this was not a single row of images. Instead, I exposed two rows—one high and one low—to capture a taller image.

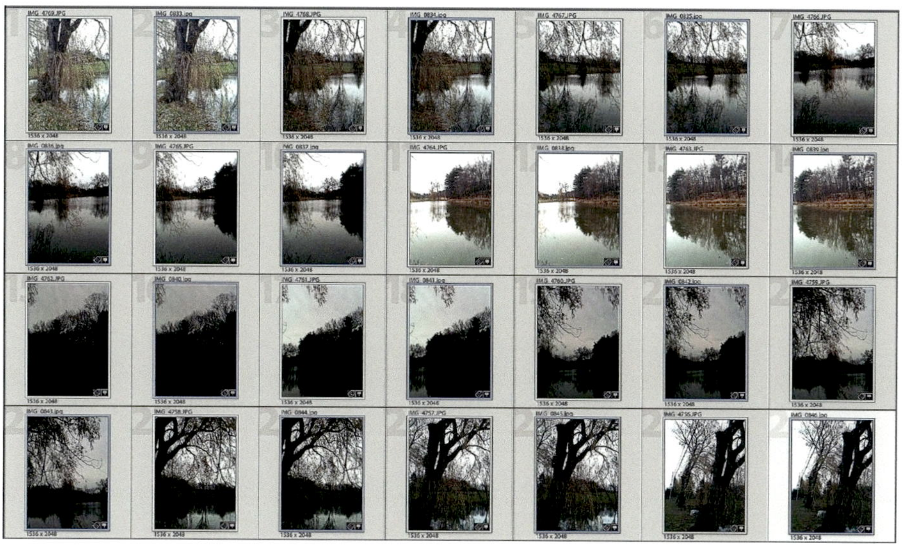

FIGURE 39.8 *Twenty-eight images combined with AutoStitch (captured with iPhone 3GS).*

AutoStitch is very forgiving about the order in which you shoot your series of images to be stitched. Still, it's a good idea to have a routine for your 2-D stitching, as in Figure 39.9. Start your series by shooting the lower left corner of the scene, and then move up to capture the upper region. Pivoting to the right, you continue with the "Square-S" pattern until you've covered the scene to be stitched.

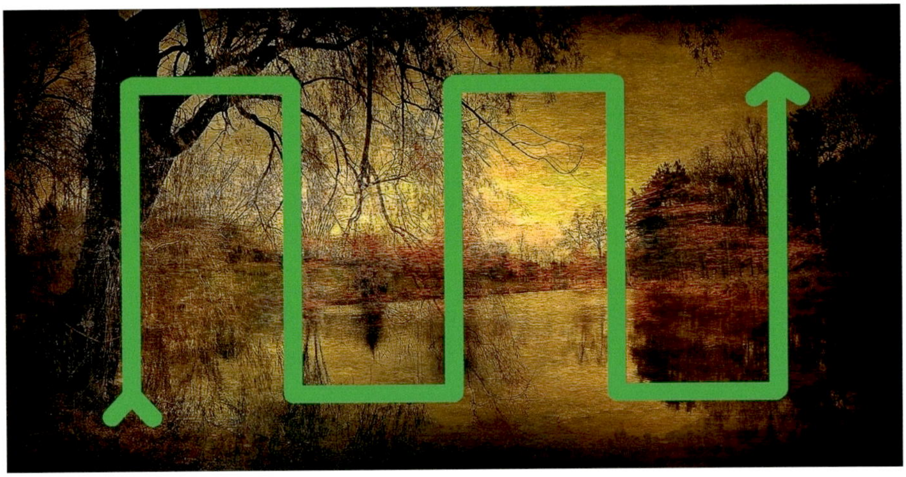

FIGURE 39.9 *The order in which Dan typically shoots a 2-D stitch series.*

Figure 39.10 shows the final "Swollen Creek" image that was stitched from about sixty images that were shot using the "Square-S" technique (starting at the lower left, going up and then over to the right and back down). In this example, I captured a much taller scene with AutoStitch. The iPhone was actually pointing down to capture the bottom of this image (my feet were just out of frame at the bottom), and it was almost pointed straight up into the trees to capture the top. Using this 2-D technique will let you create wide and tall vistas that you can't get any other way.

For sharp-eyed readers who notice the subtle crosshatch pattern in the "Swollen Creek" image, I used the SketchMee app to process a pencil-like monochrome version that was blended back into the color version using the ImageBlender app.

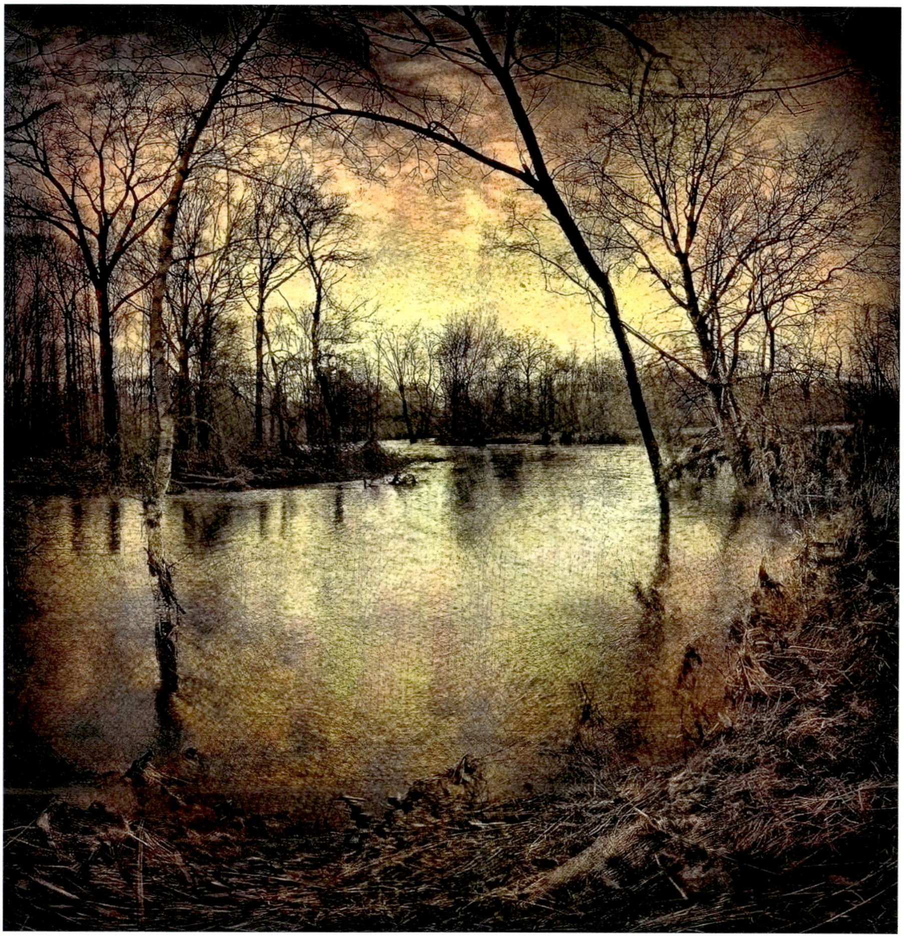

FIGURE 39.10 *A final image stitched from about sixty individual iPhone shots.*

Play with AutoStitch Settings

Just as you should check the settings in any new app (both in the app itself and checking to see if the app put a separate settings in your iPhone's iOS settings), you should experiment with the blending and auto-exposure settings in AutoStitch. You might be surprised at how your image output can vary—good or bad—according to your choices.

Check the example in Figure 39.11. Here, just for kicks, I used AutoStitch to combine two vertical panos that were made using the iPhone Pano mode. I photographed one from bottom to top and one from top to bottom; these two tall, vertical images had very different tonal renditions because of how the exposure began: either over dark foreground or bright sky. It was educational to see how simple setting changes can make a huge difference.

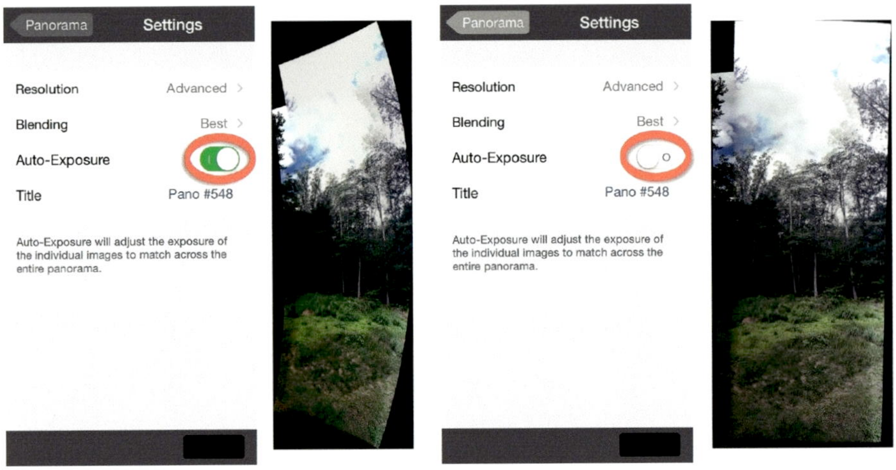

FIGURE 39.11 *Changing the auto-exposure settings changes image geometry.*

Changing just the auto-exposure setting resulted in AutoStitch's rendering a completely different image shape!

> Note: Your Volume Up button on your iPhone can be used to trip the shutter in Pano mode, just as in the regular Photo shooting mode.
>
> Another hot tip: You can "finish" your sweep pano by simply moving the camera in the reverse direction at the end of your sweep. Try it!

YOUR ASSIGNMENT (PART B)

Find a subject that lends itself to a 2-D stitch. This could be a landscape, architectural photograph, or interior. (The photo in Figure 39.13 was captured with an iPhone 4. In this example, I used a tripod to better manage pivoting the iPhone for the eighty-four separate exposures.)

Image Number	What it Should Be	What it Should Illustrate
03	Take a screenshot of your iPhone's LCD as you are ready to start taking your images in AutoStitch	This image should show just a portion of your final stitched image and there should be a green border around the image (because that's how AutoStitch frames your shots as you shoot).
04	The final Stitched-with-AutoStitch image	This image should show the benefits of stitching with a sweeping vista effect.
05	This will be a screenshot of your iPhone's screen using PhotoSize (free) to check the pixel dimensions in your stitched and saved photo (see Figure 39.12).	This "honesty" shot will show that you not only captured a nice view but that you also increased image size.

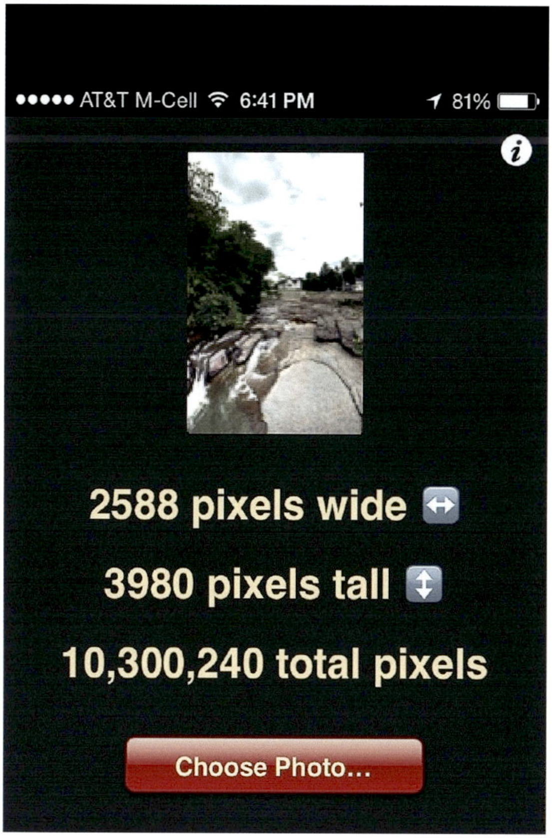

FIGURE 39.12 *Checking the stitched image size with the Photosize app.*

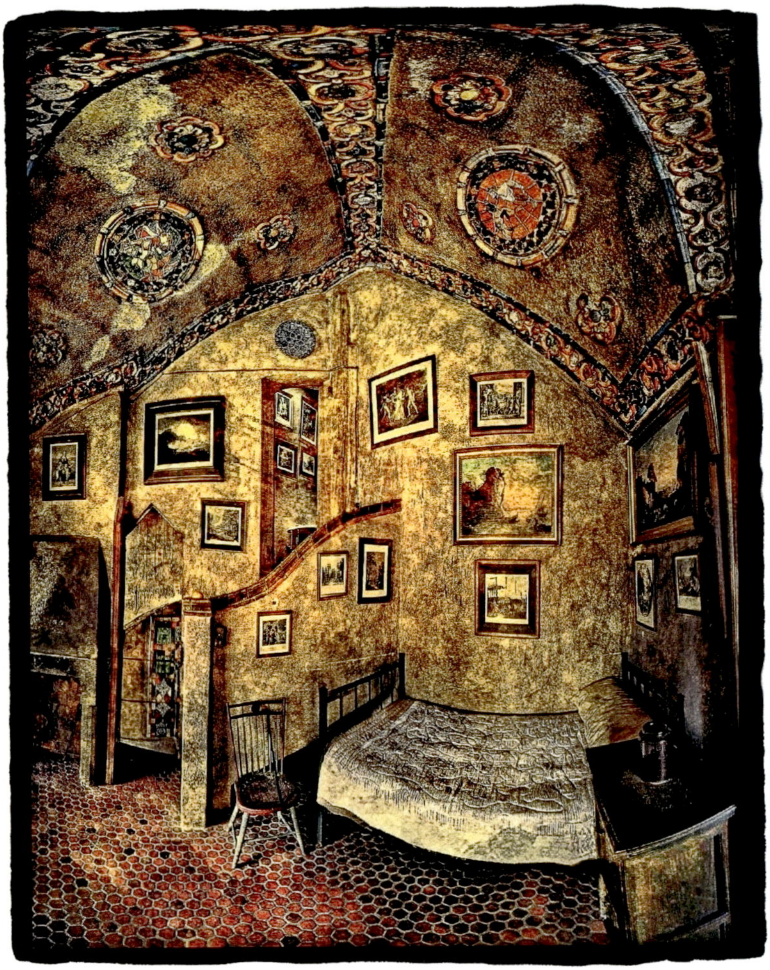

FIGURE 39.13
This interior was stitched with AutoStitch from eight-four separate exposures on an iPhone 4.

You'll never run out of fun and creative possibilities on your iPhone. Stitching—whether with the iPhone's camera app or with AutoStitch—lets you tap in to one of photography's most exciting image-making techniques. Have fun!

> Note: AutoStitch on the iPhone can create up to an 18MP image. On the iPad, that doubles to 36MP, so if making big prints is your thing, you might want to shoot with your iPhone (with its better camera) and then transfer the images to your iPad for final stitching.

ASSIGNMENT 40

Building an Online Presence

Contributed by Kayla Anchell and Charley Zheng

> *"Very few people possess true artistic ability. It is therefore both unseemly and unproductive to irritate the situation by making an effort. If you have a burning, restless urge to write or paint, simply eat something sweet and the feeling will pass."*
>
> —Fran Lebowitz

Social media has changed the game for everyone across businesses, categories, and industries. People are seeking to use social media platforms as the primary way to advance their business and build their personal brand. Different platforms are evolving fast and the social ecosystem is constantly changing, but there are core tenets in place to help people develop the best approach to augmenting their digital presence.

Where you show up in the social landscape, as well as *how* you show up to a potential audience, is important. The following are the major landmarks of the ecosystem and each bring with them their very own POV.

FACEBOOK

> *"Facebook's mission is to give people the power to share and make the world more open and connected."*

Facebook has become a prime vehicle for business marketing, allowing photographers to connect with others easily and build audiences, with almost no friction.

For most of us, logging into Facebook to get our fix of news and updates from friends is something we do unconsciously as part of our daily routine. A key reason for a budding photographer to establish a presence on Facebook is because it provides one of the most efficient ways to reach entire networks—after all, it's the second most visited site in the world with regard to unique visits (Google being number one).

Facebook offers opportunities for photographers to market their work that are different than marketing through a website. Because websites are typically not daily destinations, photographers turn to Facebook as a space for ancillary content like updates, industry news, and "customer service" like interactions. Facebook is more oriented to storytelling, relationship building, and a focus on community. Photo image posts do the best here.

TWITTER (AS IT RELATES TO BUSINESSES)

> *"Twitter connects businesses to customers in real-time. Businesses use Twitter to quickly share information with people interested in their products and services, gather real-time market intelligence and feedback, and build relationships with customers, partners, and influential people."*

Twitter gives you 140 characters or less to say what you want to say. This means that every word counts, abbreviations are welcome, and posting frequently—a practice shunned on Facebook—is even OK. Because Twitter is all about real-time, it can be one of the most engaging and most reactive platforms. Its emphasis on immediate interaction is a key feature and an important strategy for photographers. Twitter tends to orient itself towards conversation and feedback. It's also an effective channel to refer and direct traffic to a photographer's owned properties. Always think about connecting people to great information in direct, concise ways.

LINKEDIN

> *"LinkedIn is the world's largest professional network with over 120 million members and growing rapidly. LinkedIn connects you to your trusted contacts and helps you exchange knowledge, ideas, and opportunities with a broader network of professionals."*

Unlike its social media cousins, LinkedIn is designated specifically for business professionals. Business is at the center of a LinkedIn profile—most people will consider their profile an online resume, which means that LinkedIn can be one of the best tools to build credibility. Much like Twitter, LinkedIn's Updates feature allows users to share something with their network using 140 characters or less. LinkedIn Groups can also be a useful resource to get introduced to new contacts by allowing users to discover and contribute to popular discussions and "follow" group participants, including major industry leaders.

INSTAGRAM

> *"Instagram is a fun and quirky way to share your life with friends through a series of pictures. Snap a photo with your mobile phone, then choose a filter to transform the image into a memory to keep around forever. We're building Instagram to allow you to experience moments in your friends' lives through pictures as they happen. We imagine a world more connected through photos."*

Instagram is a social media force to be reckoned with. More photographers are beginning to realize that it's more than just a mobile app: It can be a powerful showcase and one of the best ways to show their work digitally, and it can help them demonstrate a distinct POV. Think of it as a direct publishing and distribution platform. It allows you to personally curate and selectively publish work to your audience. Some more entrepreneurial photographers are even using the medium to sell prints.

Instagram can only be used on mobile devices. If you don't have a smartphone, iPad, or other mobile device you won't be able to access this app.

GOOGLE+

> *"Google+ makes connecting on the web more like connecting in the real world. Share your thoughts, links, and photos with the right circles. Use easy, spontaneous video chat to strike up conversations with as many as nine people at once."*

Google+ is probably the most similar in function to Facebook, with some lesser-known advantages, the most important of which is its effect on SEO rankings. Google+ quickly established itself as a useful marketing tool for photographers because the platform is built for photo sharing and provides a range of useful actions like viewing, managing, and editing multimedia. It's simply another way to share work—and it impacts where you show up on search, which can be a compelling enough reason to establish a presence here.

The nice thing about Google+ is its Circles feature. Circles give you a great deal more control over who sees your content. The ability to create subsets allows photographers to tailor their messages later and share them with applicable groups. For example, photos from a recent photography project can be shared directly to your circle of potential clients.

TUMBLR

"Tumblr lets you effortlessly share anything."

Tumblr, like Twitter, is considered a "micro-blogging" platform, but it allows you to post a variety of different media, such as text, photo, video, and audio. Tumblr can be useful for a photographer for a number of reasons, one of which may involve using the platform as a portfolio site or a real blog to tell stories, reveal thoughts, share advice or behind-the-scenes moments.

The site is comprised of a mix of bloggers, brands, and tastemakers in almost every area of interest. At the most basic level, there are two types of users on Tumblr: those who create original content, and those who re-blog posts. There are also a couple of notably social elements to the platform, such as the "Ask anything" function, which acts as an open Q&A between blog readers and blog owners.

Tumblr's form of social currency is the "note," which is any action involving re-blogging a post, liking a post, or responding to a post. Unlike friend-based networks, Tumblr users are connected through shared interests, rather than through their proximity or offline friendships. But like any other social platform, only great content will attract engagement, and the more a post gets re-blogged, the bigger reach it will have. The pace of Tumblr moves quickly, so always being active and engaged on this platform is key.

Which to Use for What

Some platforms may experience dominant usage more than others—it all depends on what your strategy is and knowing which channels your audience is populating. A photographer may typically have a presence across all the networks mentioned, but the content may not all exactly be the same.

For example, Facebook, Instagram, and Google+ will allow you to tell your stories in more depth, so posts that need longer copy are a better fit here. Twitter and LinkedIn, however, are better at broadcasting stories more than telling them with detail. Knowing the capabilities, limitations, and the different messaging styles can help you decide what kinds of things to post and where. A little bit of content overlap is expected, but posting identical messages to all your networks is overkill, repetitive, and may get irksome for fans who follow you on all your networks.

There are best practices for how often to post, depending on the platform. On Facebook, LinkedIn, and Google+, no more than two per day to start. Twitter, Tumblr, and Instagram operate a little differently, because these tend to be used more in real-time, but aim for no more than three posts a day to start.

LESSON PLANS

Facebook: Create an Artist Page

1. Choose a profile photo and cover photo, and create an album with ten pieces of work.
2. Add a description about yourself. Some suggestions for your profile description could be: who influences you, what camera you shoot with, where you have been published . . . etc.
3. Like three other artists' pages.
4. Invite fifteen people to Like your page.
5. Add a post to your wall. Some suggestions for the post could be: what you are currently working on, what's inspiring you, do you have an event coming up with your work featured, etc.

Twitter: Create a Twitter Account

1. Choose a profile picture.
2. Follow fifteen people.
3. Compose a minimum of two tweets per day for a week.
4. One of those tweets should be at another user. For example: "Just had an interview with @naturephoto about her trip to Spain."
5. Favorite five tweets, and repost two (the reposts do not count towards your two tweets minimum per day).
6. Use hashtag(s) in five of your tweets.

Instagram: Create an Account that Features your Work as a Photographer

If you already have an Instagram account, this should be separate from your existing account.

1. Include a link to your website or portfolio if you have one. If you don't have one, link to your Facebook or Twitter account (or both).
2. You can follow as many friends as you like, but also start following fifteen people who are not your immediate friends.
3. Post five photos. Include unique hashtags for each photo (use the # before every word you tag). You can use as many hashtags as you like, but all photos should have at least one.
4. Post a comment on a photo of another artist's work you admire.

ASSIGNMENT 41

Shameless Promoting

Contributed by Kayla Anchell

> *"Good art is good business."*
>
> —Andy Warhol

PURPOSE: TO DRAW TRAFFIC AND INTEREST TO YOUR ONLINE ACTIVITIES.

FACEBOOK: PHOTO CONTEST

Think of a photo contest to engage your followers. Include what the prize will be if they win. For example, they will get a signed copy of one of your photographs; or their winning photo will be featured on your Facebook page for a week; a gift card for Starbucks (with money on it); or they get to buy you dinner (just kidding). Kick off the contest by posting five examples of what you would enter if you were participating.

TWITTER: A DAY IN THE LIFE

Document your day by taking a photo of something you're doing or somewhere you are every hour for eight hours, and tweeting that photo. Include a short description for each photo and utilize at least two hashtags per photo. Be sure to schedule an interesting day!

INSTAGRAM: PHOTO STORY

Take three photos of things that are meaningful to you. Post the photos on Instagram and include descriptions that are at least four sentences per photo. The copy can be something creative like a poem, or in a narrative format—any words that help to get across the meaning of your photo.

Contributors

I would like to acknowledge and thank the following contributors to *Digital Photo Assignments*. Each of them has shared their experience and knowledge of the art and practice of photography and the digital world.

KAYLA ANCHELL

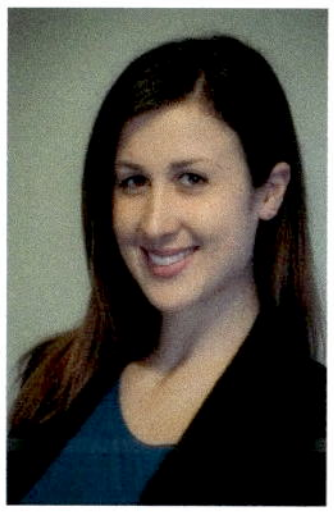

Kayla is a graduate of the University of Oregon with a degree in Journalism. She has years of experience in social media, marketing, and brand management. She currently lives in Portland, Ore. where she enjoys biking, playing piano and traveling at any opportunity. Kayla can be tweeted at @K_O_kay.

DAN BURKHOLDER

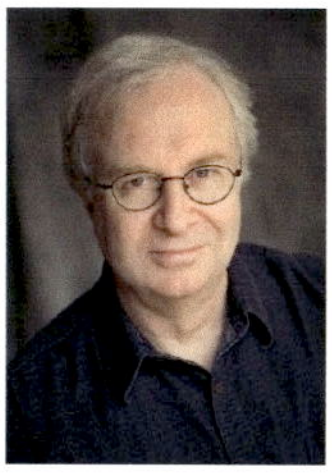

Dan Burkholder has a long history of looking beyond the photographic horizon to invent, explore, exhibit, and teach the next great thing in photography.

Dan's book, *iPhone Artistry* (Pixiq Press, 2012), is the universe's most comprehensive and fun how-to book for iPhone photographers. His poignant monograph, *The Color of Loss* (University of Texas Press, 2008), intimately documented the flooded interiors of post-Katrina New Orleans and was the first coffee-table book shot entirely using HDR (high dynamic range) methods. Dan's book, *Making Digital Negatives for Contact Printing*, lets photographers combine the charm of the handmade print with the precision of digital control and has become a standard resource in the fine-art photography community.

Dan earned his Master's degree in Photography from Brooks Institute of Photography in Santa Barbara, California. Dan's website is www.DanBurkholder.com. He can be contacted at info@DanBurkholder.com.

LINDA CONNOR

San Francisco Art Institute

Linda Connor is a fine art photographer and professor of Photography at the San Francisco Art Institute and founder and President of PhotoAlliance.

Her monograph *Odyssey* presents landscapes and culturally sacred places she has photographed during her extensive travels. She still prefers view cameras and film. Linda can be contacted by email at lindaconnor@earthlink.net.

SHAUN HUSTON

Western Oregon University

Shaun Huston is an associate professor in Geography and Film Studies at Western Oregon University where he teaches courses in cultural and political geography, including qualitative methods and film and video for the social sciences. His primary interests are in place, landscape, and popular cultures. His most recent work includes the documentary film, *Comic Book City, Portland, Oregon, USA* (2012).

His work can be seen online at www.vimeo.com/shaunhuston. To contact Shaun directly email hustons@wou.edu, or visit his faculty website, www.wou.edu/~hustons.

KAY KENNY

New York University, New York
International Center of Photography, New York

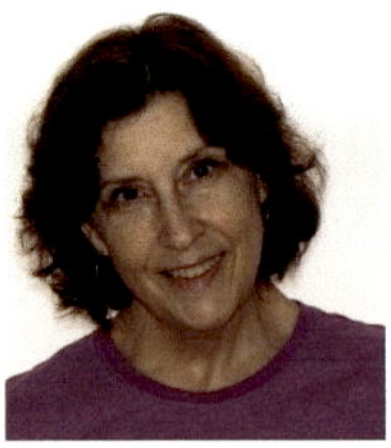

Painter, photographer, writer, educator. She has taught photography at New York University and the International Center of Photography for more than eighteen years. Kay writes art criticism and articles on the visual arts for arts magazines.

She is a three-time recipient of the NJSCA fellowship award. Recent publications about her work include *Photography's Antiquarian Avant-Garde*, by Lyle Rexer, Abrams Publishing; *Light & Lens, Photography in the Digital Age*, and *Photographic Possibilities* by Robert Hirsch, Focal Press.

Kay received her MFA in visual arts from Syracuse University. Kay's website is www.kaykenny.com.

FORD LOWCOCK

Santa Monica College, California

Ford Lowcock is the Chair of Photography and Fashion at Santa Monica College.

BRENT WOOD

Victorville College, California

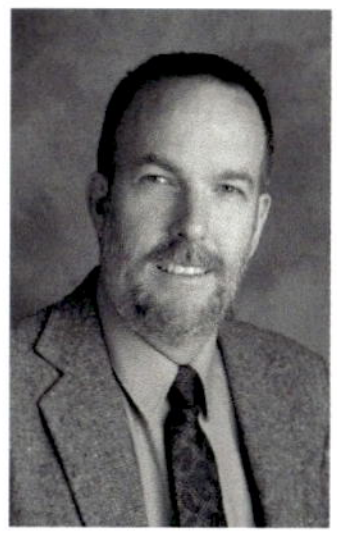

As the facilitator for art and photography, Brent Wood teaches digital and analog courses for Victorville College. He graduated from Brooks Institute of Photography in 1977, majoring in portraiture with a minor in color theory.

Upon graduation, Brent began his career as chief photographer and studio manager for O'Connor Photography located in Santa Barbara, Calif. From there he became the photo department site manager for NASA at Edwards Air Force Base. He is the Art department Chair at Victorville College. He teaches both digital and analog photography.

His personal work involves black and white large-format portraiture, large-format black and white scenic photography, and pinhole photography. He also works with alternative processes, especially the Van Dyke process. Brent can be reached by email at brent.wood@vvc.edu.

MARY ELLEN WORTHAM

Fillmore High School, California

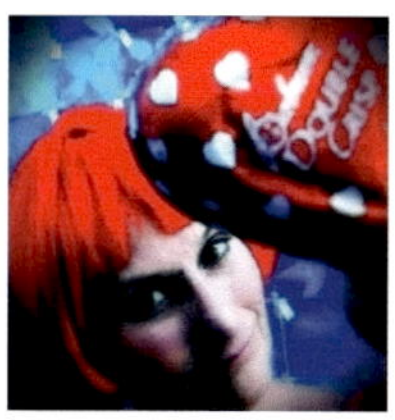

Mary Ellen is a Southern California fine art photographer whose images find liberal play across traditional, digital, alternative, mixed, experimental, emerging processes and technologies. Her photography has received the critical recognition and laudatory notice of curators from such celebrated institutions as Los Angeles County Museum of Art, San Diego Museum of Photographic Arts, Art Institute of Chicago, Museum of Fine Art—Boston, Whitney Museum, and the International Center of Photography. Select works are in the permanent collection at Ventura County Museum of History & Art. Mary Ellen's thirty-five-year freelance career is punctuated with sabbaticals into the high school classroom; she has developed university-recognized photography curricula in venues private and privileged, public and at-risk.

For creative growth, recharge and self-discovery, Mary Ellen heartedly avers: "Anyone can fall, anyone can land—no big deal. It's the challenge then thrill of the jump that brings on magic."

Mary Ellen earned her Master's degree from the University of California, Berkeley. She can be reached by email at wortham.m@aol.com.

CHARLEY ZHENG

Charley Zheng is a photographer and digital planner from Portland, Ore. As someone who spends most of her days working in the digital space, she's a big proponent of social media as a way for artists and creatives to showcase their work, connect with others, and get inspired by others.

OSU STUDENT VOLUNTEERS

OSU students provided many of the photo illustrations. Some took time out of their summer vacation to test one or more assignments; others provided images to illustrate a point made in the book. My thanks to all of them:

Martha Baker
Tiffany Cha
Thiago Moreira Da Silva
Aaron Davis
Brandi Dawson
Jacqueline Dover
Dianni Freeman
Amanda (Andie) Gildersleeve
Austin Hodaie
Megan Jaeger
Leslie Mason
Michael Paulsen

OTHER CONTRIBUTORS

Donna Conrad, writer, photographer, and my wife of thirty-six years: Her memoir, *House of the Moon: Surviving the Sixties*, is available from amazon.com and barnesandnoble.com.

I would like to especially thank Jeff Hume for his careful reading and editing of the original manuscript. Jeff is a writer, photographer, and former Peace Corp volunteer.

MOLLIE

The model who appears in many of the illustrations found in this book is Mollie. If she has a last name, I don't know it—she is silent on the issue.

Mollie is a former model for the now defunct Ohrbach's department store that once thrived in California. When Ohrbach's went belly-up in the 1980s, I offered Mollie a position in my Hollywood studio. She has been with me ever since.

Though she no longer models professionally, she does assist me on assignments, particularly when they are for educational purposes, which she fully approves of. Mollie can be reached at mollie@anchellworkshops.com.

Software

Software is an integral part of digital photography. Without software the images on your media card are of no use to anyone.

Even so, I have intentionally left software-based assignments out of *Digital Photo Assignments*, with the exception of Assignment 35-Using DSLR Video. This book is capture based, with the assumption that the course instructor will introduce you to the software they want you to use and how to import and edit your images.

If you are not currently in school, there are a number of targeted books you can use to teach yourself the important software programs. Here are some software suggestions that may save you both time and money.

SOFTWARE FOR STILL PHOTOGRAPHY

Adobe Photoshop has dominated the digital imaging software market almost since it was introduced. As a result, there is an erroneous assumption that digital imaging is not possible without at least a rudimentary knowledge of Photoshop.

In the early days of digital imaging software, Photoshop was meant to be a means for *graphic designers* to work with and insert photos into the Adobe suite of design programs. Because there was no serious competition, it was the best program for anybody, including photographers, to work with images. And while access to the powerful features included in Photoshop enables photographers to unleash their imagination, the truth is most photographers have no use for anything other than about twenty percent of the features—every one of these can be found in Adobe Lightroom.

Lightroom is an indispensible program for the photographer. It includes the all-important functions of image sorting and editing for reproduction, via the web or print media. It is easy to learn, works cross-platform with Mac and Windows, and with any camera currently made.

There are other programs beside Lightroom, such as Capture One, but nearly all of them are dedicated to a particular camera or platform: Apple

Aperture (Mac only; now discontinued), Nikon Capture NX (Nikon only), Canon Digital Photo Professional, Picture Style Editor, and Image Browser (Canon only).

There are also several photo-editing programs for under $100. These include Corel AfterShot Pro2, ACDSee, PicMonkey, ArcSoft, and a few that are free: GIMP, PhoXo, and Photo Pos Pro. Some of these, such as GIMP, are highly rated by users. If you are on a budget, you may wish to try one of these.

As for the more powerful special effects, image manipulation, and compositing features found in Photoshop, you will find that nearly everything you need or want can be found in photo collections by smaller software companies.

In my work I have found the onOne Software Perfect Photo Suite to be indispensible for compositing and retouching. The suite comes bundled with masking, portrait retouching, enhancement, resizing, black and white conversion, and other stand-alone programs. The composite image of the Jaguar car and cat that accompanies Assignment 21-Symbols was made using the Perfect Photo Suite.

For lens and image correction tools, DxO Optics has a great set that includes lens and perspective correction tools, light and contrast correction, and color correction, among others.

Specifically for HDR (high dynamic range) there are two good programs, Photomatix Pro and Nik's HDR Efex. For noise reduction you may wish to use DxO Optics, Imagenomic, or Topaz DeNoise.

What you will notice is that a version of every one of these third-party software programs can be found in Photoshop and/or Lightroom. But because plug-ins such as onOne, Nik, and DxO are targeted to specific applications, such as HDR, noise reduction, and image correction, they are almost always better at what they do.

Should you learn Photoshop in school, it will help you to work with and understand third-party programs right out of the box. If you're not in school, I recommend you skip Photoshop, start with Lightroom, and purchase plug-in applications as needed.

WEBSITES FOR EDITING SOFTWARE

ACDSee: www.acdsee.com
Adobe: www.adobe.com
Alien Skin: www.alienskin.com
ArcSoft: www.arcsoft.com
Canon Digital Photo Professional: www.usa.canon.com/cusa/support/consumer
Capture One: www.phaseone.com
Corel AfterShot Pro2: www.aftershotpro.com

DxO Optics: www.dxo.com
GIMP: www.gimp.org
Imagenomic: www.imagenomic.com
Nik: www.google.com/nikcollection
Nikon Capture NX: www.capturenx.com
onOne: www.ononesoftware.com
Photomatix Pro: www.hdrsoft.com
Photo Pos Pro: www.photopos.com
PicMonkey: www.picmonkey.com
Topaz DeNoise: www.topazlabs.com

Photo Credits

Cover photo by students of Fillmore High School in Fillmore, Calif.

Dedication: Photo of John Maul, photographer unknown.

All photographs in Assignment 24—Low-Light Photography, by Kay Kenny, are © 2015 Kay Kenny.

All photographs in Assignment 39—Camera Phones and Apps by Dan Burkholder, are © 2015 Dan Burkholder.

All photos not attributed to a photographer are by the author, Steve Anchell.

Index

Page numbers in *italics* refer to figures.